CU00646839

Anglican Papalism

Michael Yelton is the author, with Rodney Warrener, of a biography of Martin Travers, the leading twentieth-century ecclesiastical artist, *Martin Travers (1886–1948): An Appreciation* (Unicorn Press, 2003).

He is a County Court Judge and he lives in Cambridge.

ANGLICAN PAPALISM

A History: 1900–1960

MICHAEL YELTON

CANTERBURY
PRESS
Norwich

in association with
The Society of the Faith

© Michael Yelton 2005

First published in 2005 by the Canterbury Press Norwich
(a publishing imprint of Hymns Ancient & Modern Limited,
a registered charity)
9–17 St Albans Place, London N1 0NX

www.scm-canterburypress.co.uk

All rights reserved. No part of this publication may be reproduced,
stored in a retrieval system, or transmitted,
in any form or by any means, electronic, mechanical,
photocopying or otherwise, without the prior permission of
the publisher, Canterbury Press.

British Library Cataloguing in Publication data

A catalogue record for this book is available
from the British Library

ISBN 1-85311-655-6

Typeset by Regent Typesetting, London
Printed and bound in Great Britain by
William Clowes Ltd, Beccles, Suffolk

TO THE MEMORY OF WALTER GERVASE BENNETT,
PARISH PRIEST OF THE CHURCH OF THE
ANNUNCIATION, MARBLE ARCH
1947–76
RIP

CONTENTS

FOREWORD

The Society of the Faith was founded in 1905 by the Revd Charles E. Douglas and his brother, Canon John A. Douglas, Vicar of St Luke, Camberwell. Faith Press was established in the following year, ostensibly for printing Sunday School stamps, but it soon branched out into other areas of publishing, with its own printing presses at Leighton Buzzard, first in a cowshed behind the Ewe and Lamb public house and then to a permanent home, created from a derelict brewery. The Faith Press was, in its early days, unique in industrial history for every Saint's Day its employees attended Mass in the parish church, and on Ascension Day they went on an excursion into the countryside, where Mass was said in some village church before spending the rest of the day in a more leisurely way.

By 1912 it was felt able to separate Faith Press from the Society by making the factory and publishing business an incorporated limited liability company. The profits from the Faith Press enabled the Society to fulfil its primary object, namely that of helping anyone who had 'a psalm or a prophecy'. In this way Faith Press was able to assist Father Fynes-Clinton with his Anglican and Eastern Churches Association by the publication of its journal – *Eirene* – in Greek and English, and Sir Sydney Nicholson with his project of a School of Church Music by the publication of *Cathedral Quarterly*.

For some years there had been a Faith House in Manchester, with a shop and a small printing works, staffed from Leighton Buzzard, under the direction of the Revd Leigh Orton, Vicar of St James, Oldham, and by 1914 the growth of the Society's work justified opening Faith House in London. This was interrupted by the First World War, during which time a 'skeleton' staff, under the direction of Dom Anselm Hughes, kept the flag flying. In was not until 1918 that Faith Press branched out as serious publisher, especially in connection with church music, where it had not only the assistance of Sydney Nicholson, but also that of Father George Woodward and Charles Wood, whose *Mass in the Phrygian Mode* was one of the outstanding compositions of the early twentieth century.

The Society's publications between the Wars, and those of the post-Second World War period, came from some of the most well-known churchmen and women of the time. However, the late 1960s saw a decrease of public interest in the type of literature being produced by the Society and in the mid 1970s a decision was taken to dispose of the Leighton Buzzard property and henceforward produce books in association with other publishers. Not even the *Church of England Children's Newspaper*, or the earlier guidebooks printed for the Redundant Churches Fund, could stave off falling sales and creditors. By the time of its closure in the late 1970s Faith Press had been reduced to one publication a year: that of the Archbishop of Canterbury's *Lent Book*.

However, the improved financial position of the Society led to a discussion in 2003 with SCM/Canterbury Press to revive the Faith Press. This book is the first product of that association and marks the Society's return to help those who have 'a psalm or a prophecy', as it did when it was founded almost 100 years ago in 1906.

Julian W. S. Litten FSA
Principal

PREFACE

The intention behind the book is to provide information about, and to some extent to rehabilitate the memory of, those who were derided at the time for their stance but can now perhaps be seen as ahead of their age in some respects and particularly so far as Christian unity is concerned. Whether the view of some of them that a Uniate Anglican church in communion with Rome was the only logical outcome of the Oxford Movement was prophetic, only time will tell.

MICHAEL YELTON
Feast of the Immaculate Conception of Our Lady, 2004

ACKNOWLEDGEMENTS

This book has been a very long time in genesis. I carried out some research while an undergraduate (1968–71), which resulted in valuable information from those no longer with us, including Peter F. Anson, Revd G. A. C. Whatton, and L. Gray Fisher. Many years later I began to look again at that old material and to read and reread the many now forgotten books which are set out in the Bibliography, as well as more modern studies. I was very much assisted by the efficiency of the Librarians of Pusey House and the Lambeth Palace Library: in both places I was given access to material which had not been catalogued but was of importance to my enquiries. I am also most grateful to Mar Seraphim Newman-Norton of the British Orthodox Church for his hospitality and for allowing me to use some rare documents in the possession of that body, and to many others who have helped, including Robert Halliday, Paul Kitchenham, David Lindsay, and Rodney Warrener. I am very grateful to Michael Farrer and other members of the Anglo-Catholic History Society for their assistance and to Father Robert Farmer and the Catholic League for encouragement. Richard McEwan has kindly assisted with pictures from his extensive archive. I am of course most grateful to the Society of the Faith and to Canterbury Press for bringing the project of publication to fruition. My long-suffering wife Judith has again had to put up with pages of obscure documentation about the house and I am as always grateful for her indulgence.

The responsibility for errors is of course mine alone, as are the views expressed. I apologise for the poor quality of some photographs, which I hope is compensated for by their interest and rarity.

ABBREVIATIONS

APUC   Association for the Promotion of the Unity of Christendom

ARCIC   Anglican–Roman Catholic International Commission

CBS   Confraternity of the Blessed Sacrament

CHC   Community of the Holy Cross

CPCU   Council for Promoting Catholic Union

CR   Community of the Resurrection

CSI   Church of South India

CUOC   Church Unity Octave Council

ECU   English Church Union

FCP   Federation of Catholic Priests

KC   King's Counsel

OCR   Order of Corporate Reunion

OLW   Our Lady of Walsingham

OSM   Order of St Michael

PTS   Protestant Truth Society

SCK   Servants of Christ the King

SCR   Society for Catholic Reunion

SDC   Society of the Divine Compassion

SPB   Society of the Precious Blood

SPCU   Society for Promoting Catholic Union

SSC	Society of the Holy Cross
SSJE	Society of St John the Evangelist
SSM	Society of the Sacred Mission
SSPP	Society of SS Peter and Paul

1

IN TERRA ALIENA
An Introduction to the Papalist Tradition

In 1949 there appeared in the journal *Reunion*, published by an organisation called the Confraternity of Unity, an article by Revd Victor Roberts, then the warden (chaplain) of the Community of the Holy Cross, an order of Anglican nuns then in Hayward's Heath, Sussex. Father Roberts' life and work encompasses a number of the themes developed later in this book, and the central thrust of his piece, which was entitled 'In Terra Aliena', is of considerable interest. He wrote:

> There is a not inconsiderable minority of people . . . who believe ex animo the teaching of the Holy See concerning faith and morals, not on any selective principles, but upon the authority of the Holy See itself, and yet they are not in visible communion with Rome. They are designated as Anglican, although they repudiate Anglicanism. They are not Anglo-Catholics; they accept the validity of Anglican orders, but do not claim that the possession of valid orders, or their continuity, justifies the Church of England. We who belong to this minority admit that we are in schism, though not by our own fault, and we desire nothing more ardently than to be in visible communion with the Holy See.[1]

Father Roberts went on to say that the validity or otherwise of Anglican orders was the only barrier he saw to reconciliation with Rome.

In that article, Roberts was expressing a point of view incomprehensible to most Anglicans and to nearly all Roman Catholics, especially those in England. He was acting as an apologist for the Papalist Tradition in the Church of England. In fact the term Papalist itself, as used of this

---

1 *Reunion*, Vol. 5, No. 41 (1949).

group, originated as a name given in scorn to them by the well-known religious journalist Sidney Dark. The Confraternity of Unity, for whom Roberts was writing, was among the most ultramontane of a number of interlinked organisations which favoured reunion with Rome.

In 1942 Revd Donald Hole wrote a pamphlet which was actually entitled *Anglican Papalists*, for the Society for Promoting Catholic Unity, another such body. Father Hole had at one time been a follower of the Christian Socialist Guild of St Matthew founded by Revd Stewart Headlam. He was the founder of and then chaplain to the Actors' Church Union and for many years was the priest in charge of St James' House of Mercy in Fulham, which was a branch of the Wantage Sisters; he was a prolific writer on reunion and other such subjects. In the pamphlet he summarised the Anglican Papalist position in the following way:

1 Corporate Reunion presupposed complete dogmatic agreement in all matters held to be *de fide.*
2 From that it followed that the Church of England must be regarded, not as an independent and self-governing church, nor as one of the 'Three Branches' of the Church Universal, but as a 'severed limb' of the Western Church, that is to say in theological terms, as being in schism.
3 This did not involve 'the denial of everything else and the negation of a position and spiritual experiences and the whole record of a life behind them'; in other words there was no necessity for individual secession.[2]

Hole however saw that the reunion of the Church of England to that of Rome was not imminent, even when he wrote. He recognised that in order that it should happen there would have to be negotiations between the Anglican episcopate and the Pope, but that that would not occur unless the bishops were themselves converted to the Papalist point of view, were liberated from the control of Parliament, and could carry with them a sufficient proportion of the clergy and laity.

In that book, Hole had made reference to the infection of the Oxford Movement by liberal thinking, which he thought had become

---

2 Hole: *Anglican Papalists*, p. 23.

particularly apparent at the time of the centenary celebrations for that Movement in 1933.

It was in that year, perhaps the beginning of the high water mark of the Anglo-Catholic Revival, that there appeared the most complete statement of the Anglican Papalist position. The best-known proponent of that cause, although he wrote little, was Revd H. J. Fynes-Clinton, rector of St Magnus the Martyr in the City of London from 1921 to his death in 1959. In 1933 the leaders of the Papalists produced a series of tractates entitled *The Church of England and the Holy See*. The majority were historical in content, and were designed to show that throughout history England had been strongly dependent on Rome. However, the last tractate in the series, number 8, was entitled *What Are We to Say?* and dealt with the situation at the time it was written. Part I came from the pen of Father Fynes-Clinton, Part II from another equally consistent advocate of reunion with Rome, Revd W. Robert Corbould, for many years parish priest of All Saints, Carshalton, Surrey.

Father Fynes-Clinton was scathing about the attitude of the bishops of the Church of England. He said that although they were

> Armed with the weapon of spiritual authority restored to it by the Catholic Movement, the Episcopal Bench as a whole has used it not as a crook to guide the sheep into true pastures, but to restrain or turn aside those who would follow in the ancient use and teaching of Christ's fold.[3]

This was a fairly typical attitude to bishops by those who on the other hand sought to uphold church order, displaying one of the ambiguities which has plagued the Catholic Revival throughout its existence. Fynes-Clinton was however nothing but optimistic. He noted:

> In spite of all, Divine Providence saved the English Church from ever formally repudiating the Pope as Successor of St. Peter and Primate of Christendom.[4]

His final plea was unequivocal:

---

3 Fynes-Clinton and Corbould: *What Are We to Say?*, p. 9.
4 Ibid., p. 11.

The supreme need of the Church of England today is Corporate Return to the Holy See, and this is but a return to her natural and original life.[5]

Father Corbould was equally clear, declaring:

We seek unity, not mere friendly relationship and co-operation.[6]

It is, however, interesting to recall the context in which those words were written. It is easy to forget that at that time there was effectively a system of ecclesiastical apartheid in England, in which there were few if any contacts between the Church of England and that of Rome, and certainly no jointly attended services or initiatives. The authors of that tractate saw clearly that if Christian unity were to mean anything, it would involve the actual reunion of churches rather than mere mutual assistance. It would also involve the Church of England accepting the primacy of the Bishop of Rome. As will be shown in more detail in Chapter 2, it was from the Anglican Papalist Movement that there sprang the modern-day Week of Prayer for Christian Unity.

Writers on the Church of England during the period in question have generally treated the streams within it as High, Moderate or Broad, and Low. That generalisation, however, conceals as much as it shows. One of the few Roman Catholics during this era who understood the movements towards unity in the Church of England was the French priest Abbé Couturier (1881–1953), who had close contact with Father Fynes-Clinton and his associates, particularly in the period just before the Second World War. He was able to bring a more objective eye to bear on the situation than some of those who were engaged in the party politics of Anglicanism. His biographer, Father Geoffrey Curtis CR, in *Paul Couturier and Unity in Christ* (1964) refers to his prefatory note to a record of conversations between Fynes-Clinton, Father Gregory Dix, then an internal oblate of the Benedictines at Nashdom, and French priests, which was published in *Revue Apologetique* in January 1937. In it Couturier, writing in French for a predominantly French-speaking audience, divided the Church of England into five separate categories, namely:

5 Ibid., p. 16.
6 Ibid., p. 21.

4

1 Evangelical or Low Church;
2 Central or Moderate Church, 'conformist' to the Book of Common Prayer;
3 High Church and ritualistic although still following the Book of Common Prayer;
4 Anglo-Catholic as a continuation of Tractarian;
5 Romanised, being those who accept integrally or all but entirely Roman Catholic life.[7]

A similar analysis was made by another Frenchman, Maurice Villain, in his book *Unity: A History and Some Reflections*, published the year before Father Curtis' biography. He started with Anglo-Papalism, of which he said its members' 'disagreement with Rome is confined to the validity of ordinations and certain papal prerogatives'. He then moved to Anglo-Catholicism, then to the Moderate High Church party, who desired continuity but called themselves both Catholic and Reformed and whose views were best represented by Archbishop Garbett's book *The Claims of the Church of England.* His fourth category was the Low Church party, and his fifth the Broad Church party, which contained within it all the modernist traditions.[8]

Even the most superficial study of the ecclesiastical history of the period shows that there were overlaps, particularly between categories 3 and 4 in Couturier's scheme, and even his category 5 merged into mainstream Anglo-Catholicism in some ways.

Perhaps the most distinctive position taken by the Papalists, which clearly differentiated themselves from other Anglo-Catholics, was in relation to the nature of the Church of England. A great deal of learning was devoted by disciples of the Oxford Movement to the retrospective writing of history, particularly so far as the Reformation is concerned. Many of those in category 4 of Couturier's scheme, and nearly all those in category 3, took the view that the Anglican Communion was one of the three major branches of the Church Universal, the other two being the Roman Catholic and Eastern Orthodox Churches. Seen from that perspective, the Church of England was entitled to develop liturgical practices of its own and these need not follow the traditions of any other branch. Some, particularly those in category 4, developed this thesis

---

7 Curtis: *Paul Couturier and Unity in Christ*, pp. 169–70.
8 Villain: *Unity: A History and Some Reflections*, p. 145.

further in holding that the Church of England was not only part of the Universal Church, but was the *only* true part of the Church in England. This was well expressed by Revd J. Embry, in his book *The Catholic Movement and the Society of the Holy Cross* (1931), in which he presumably expressed the views of a majority of the members of the Society at that time in what was an official history. The Society had been founded as means of raising the standards of holiness among priests by Revd C. F. Lowder in 1855 and was and remains influential. Embry set out that the Church of England should follow the custom of the wider Western Church (that is Rome) but then said:

> [the Society] has never wavered from the strictest allegiance to the English hierarchy. [It] has been bound to see that the attempt to establish a hierarchy in opposition to the lawful occupants of the ancient sees must be a schismatic one, and that the Roman Catholic bishops in England and the priests under them must be in the position of schismatics.[9]

The problem with such a position, which was widely held, was not only that it contributed to an almost complete disregard of English Roman Catholicism by Anglicans, who tended to look for inspiration to the Continent, but also that it failed to take account of the position of the recusants, many of whom had been tortured or killed by Anglicans, and also of the chaplaincies of the Church of England in Europe and the missionary dioceses in countries which were predominantly Roman Catholic. A similar argument was advanced by some Episcopalians in Scotland, to the effect that their small church was the only legitimate part of the Catholic Church north of the border.

The Papalists on the other hand held the conviction set out in Father Hole's pamphlet above. This was well summarized by Father Curtis in his book on Couturier, in which he noted that the Papalists faced up honestly to the relationship between the Church of England and the Roman Catholic Church in England. He set out the position of the group thus:

> It holds strongly that the Catholic Church in England bifurcated in the sixteenth century; that the true Church of England in our times is not merely the Church of England by law established, but is the

---

9 Embry: *The Catholic Movement and the Society of the Holy Cross*, p. 309.

Catholic Church in our land *as a whole*, albeit at present outwardly divided; that the Roman Church in England is not an intruded schismatic body, but the other section, so to speak, of the pre-Reformation English Church.[10]

This argument can be seen developed in a number of writings of the time, such as a learned article by Revd Thomas Parker, librarian of Pusey House and a well-known scholar, in *Reunion* in 1939, in which he expressly refers to the schism in Elizabethan times as being *within* the Church of England, thus indicating that Roman Catholics were not schismatics.[11] In 1935 a book was published entitled *Catholic Reunion: An Anglican Plea for a Uniate Patriarchate and for an Anglican Ultramontanism*. The author was Father Clement, the nom de plume of Revd J. T. Plowden-Wardlaw, a well-known controversialist of the time and then vicar of St Clement, Cambridge. He regarded this as a most important principle for Anglicans to face, writing:

> But before all things we must abandon wholly and utterly the High Church denial of the continuity of the present Latin Church in England with the pre-Reformation Church of England. With the facts of history before us it is astounding impertinence to look upon the Roman Church in England as schismatic.[12]

Plowden-Wardlaw had qualified as a barrister before being ordained and his book is well and closely argued. He had been a curate at St George, Beckenham (1910–13), before moving as chaplain to the church of St Edward, Cambridge (1913–17), returning to Beckenham as rector (1919–25), and then acting as chaplain of St Paul, Cannes (1928–9) before returning to Cambridge in 1931. It may be that his views had developed during his sojourn abroad, because while he was at Beckenham he was not regarded as a reunionist.[13]

It was a logical development from this train of thought that the Papalists should strongly oppose any attempt by the Church of England to enter into closer relations with any Protestant church, or otherwise to compromise its orders. It was that which led to the vehement opposition

---

10 Curtis: *Paul Couturier and Unity in Christ*, p. 192.
11 *Reunion*, Vol. 3, No. 21 (1939).
12 Plowden-Wardlaw: *Catholic Reunion*, p. 44.
13 Clutterbuck: *Marginal Catholics*, ch. 8.

to the establishment of the Church of South India prior to its inauguration in 1947.

More interesting, and in some ways less predictable, was the attitude of Anglo-Catholics to the Old Catholic Church. Following the proclamation of Papal Infallibility in 1870, some congregations in Germany and Switzerland joined those congregations in the Netherlands which had already been separated from Rome for many years, to form the Old Catholic Church. For many Anglo-Catholics the Old Catholic Church, although quite small, provided a model of that to which they aspired. It was undeniably Catholic in its orders and teaching, but was free from Roman control. On the other hand, it was not under state direction, and had not adopted what were regarded as recent accretions to the Roman faith. It had moved to a vernacular liturgy, and clerical celibacy was abandoned by its priests in Switzerland in 1875, in Germany in 1877, and even in Holland in 1922.

In the post-First World War period there had been a move, particularly supported by moderate Anglo-Catholics and influenced by the Society of St Willibrord, which sought closer links between the two churches and for inter-communion between the Church of England and the Old Catholics. These culminated in an agreement to that effect signed at Bonn in 1932.[14]

Fynes-Clinton was scathing about that move. He wrote in his tractate the following year:

> The recent sanction of quasi-official inter-communion with the Old Catholic Churches of the Continent has for the first time established such relations with a body schismatic from the historic hierarchy of a European country. This has seriously injured our position in the eyes of Latin Catholics.[15]

In his part of the tractate Corbould wrote, 'we see even Anglo-Catholicism going down into a cul-de-sac in its pursuit of the chimaera [*sic*] of a non-papal Catholicism...'[16] It is true to say, however, that there were others who believed that the participation after the Bonn Agreement by Old Catholics in the consecration of Anglican bishops would strengthen the case for the recognition of Anglican orders.

---

14 Moss: *The Old Catholic Movement, passim.*
15 Fynes-Clinton and Corbould: *What Are We to Say?*, p. 5.
16 Ibid., p. 23.

It would be a mistake to think that it was only the form of liturgy which divided the Papalists from other groups in the Church of England, although they certainly were the strongest supporters of the adoption of the Roman Missal. It was only in Papalist churches that Latin was used publicly, and then only rarely, although it appears to have been used quite frequently in private, and even the Society of the Holy Cross usually used Latin at that time for masses at their meetings. One or two churches, such as St Saviour, Hoxton, and St Alban, Fulham, did adopt Latin as their normal liturgical language for periods of time, and in many more places the English liturgy was supplemented silently by the use of parts of the mass in Latin. It was within the religious communities that English was more frequently displaced in favour of a full replica of Roman services.

Many Anglo-Catholics within Couturier's category 4 used the English Missal, which had been translated by Father Kenrick of Holy Trinity, Hoxton, and was available from about 1910 onwards. Others disguised the Book of Common Prayer by elaborate Roman ceremonial, but in fact used Cranmer's words, sometimes rearranged. The great master of this technique was Revd E. O. Humphrey Whitby, vicar of St Mary, Bourne Street, 1916–48, where the masses were in conformity with the letter but certainly not the spirit of the Book of Common Prayer. However, by the outbreak of the First World War most of those within that grouping were using Western, as opposed to English, ceremonial.

In the last twenty years of the nineteenth century there had been a fierce conflict within the Anglo-Catholic Movement between the adherents of the two uses. There had before then been a certain amount of liturgical anarchy, with the incumbent adopting such practices as he thought fit. However, more conformity arose on the Western side with the spread of what was termed the Plymouth School, following the system introduced by Revd Charles Rose Chase after his appointment at All Saints, Plymouth, in 1878. By 1882 at the latest he had introduced perpetual reservation of the Blessed Sacrament, and services were generally in accordance with Roman precedents, but in English. Father Chase resigned the benefice in 1898 as a result of ill health, and then in 1900 seceded to Rome.[17] This was a great blow at the time, particularly to the Society of the Holy Cross, of which he had been Master from 1889 to

---

17 Russell: *From Hussar to Priest, passim.*

1891 and again from 1895 to 1897, but it did not check the onward flow of the Western Use among Anglo-Catholics.

It follows from what has earlier been said that the Anglican Papalists were strongly opposed to those who advocated the Sarum or English Use, derided as 'British Museum Religion' because the scholarly work which produced the books propounding its ceremonies was largely based on research there. The Alcuin Club, founded in 1897 to promote the study of the history and use of the Book of Common Prayer, was an organisation which was particularly influential in these researches, and they published a number of learned books on the subject, although they turned down the best-selling *Parson's Handbook* by Percy Dearmer, which attempted to show that worship in the Church of England not only could be carried out in accordance with the rites used in 1549, but must be so carried out. In the post-First World War period the Club published a two-part *Directory of Ceremonial*, which expressly stated that 'Directions and ceremonial are based upon the practice of some English cathedrals during the Middle Ages.'

All this was anathema to the Papalists. They saw in it an attempt to beautify services, to import high standards of music and decoration, but an attempt also to promote a purely nationalistic and backward-looking view of the Church which ignored the Counter-Reformation and all that had succeeded it. Dearmer was the subject of a savage caricature in Compton Mackenzie's *The Parson's Progress*, in which a thinly-disguised Revd J. Q. B. Moxon-Hughes 'claimed for his pastiche fearless logic, historical accuracy, liturgical infallibility, artistic form, romantic association, loyalty to the Book of Common Prayer, practical utility, and the certainty of its overawing bishops'.[18]

Ironically, although the English Use was succeeded by the Western in all but a very few centres of Anglo-Catholicism, it had a wide long-term effect on the Church of England as a whole. An important indirect effect of the Oxford Movement and its successors was the raising of the standards of furnishings in churches, especially cathedrals, and of the decorum with which services were conducted. It was thought that by adopting English altars, as popularised by Ninian Comper, and aesthetically pleasing fittings, these objectives were attained without the taint of Romanism being attached. There is a wonderful passage in a

18 Mackenzie: *The Parson's Progress*, p. 135.

sermon entitled 'Elijah's Mantle' delivered by Ronald Knox and published in his collection *The Church in Bondage* in 1914, in which he makes that point with some force in these words:

> I should imagine that most Bishops of our Church would, if they had to foreshadow a utopia for it, allow for a Choral Eucharist, celebrated in balloon like chasubles, and guarded prayers intimating that the faithful departed are not quite so well off, at present, as they hope to be some day, and processions of interminable length, provided that they are going nowhere in particular and carrying nothing with them; and reservation of the Most Holy Sacrament, provided it is reserved in a disused coal-hole under the infants' Sunday School.[19]

Knox of course could not foresee the immense liturgical changes which were to come about later in the century, but his words, even if strongly stated, foreshadow much of Anglican cathedral worship in the second half of the twentieth century.

Apart from the differences in relation to liturgy, there was another important fault line among Anglo-Catholics. That was between those who looked upon the Church as an hierarchical body and those who regarded it as an expression of social democracy. During the first half of the twentieth century, almost all the Socialists in the Church of England were Anglo-Catholics, but there were far more Anglo-Catholics who were not Socialists. In general terms, the Anglican Papalists were strongly of the view that the Church was hierarchical, and were opposed to lay involvement in its affairs, whether by the establishment of Parochial Church Councils or otherwise. They tended to follow the lead of Rome politically as well as ecclesiastically, which at the time meant that they were well to the right of the political centre, particularly over issues such as the Spanish Civil War. Some were less than critical of the dictatorships established in Italy, Spain and Portugal during the inter-war period, and even praised the Vichy regime in France.

There were of course exceptions to those generalisations: Raymond Raynes, who turned the Community of the Resurrection in a definite Romeward direction, was also a committed Socialist.

Many Anglo-Catholic Socialists were anti-Roman; the best known of these was Revd Conrad Noel, vicar of Thaxted, Essex, who combined

---

19 Knox: *The Church in Bondage*, p. 12.

mediaevalism in liturgy with violently anti-colonial and left-wing views which eventually led him through his own foundation, the Catholic Crusade of the Servants of the Precious Blood, to transform the Kingdom of this World into the Commonwealth of God, to neo-Trotskyism in the Order of the Church Militant. In 1918 Noel placed an advertisement for a curate in the *Church Times* which made his position clear:

> Missionary work in England. Priest wanted for some months or permanent. In general sympathy with Manifesto of Catholic Crusade and with decisions of Catholic Reforming Councils versus Papal Autocracy of all kinds . . . Piety preferred to Pietism . . . Healthy active revolutionary, good singing voice.[20]

Although some Papalists supported Noel's defiance when faced with a ban on Benediction by the Bishop of Chelmsford (his reply was to put up a card in the church asking his parishioners to pray for the conversion of their diocesan to the Catholic Faith), in fact the two groups were mutually incompatible, and that soon became clear. Further, although Noel had outdoor processions of the Host followed by Benediction, he had been a curate to Dearmer and was in general a convinced follower of the English Use, and the liturgy at Thaxted was based on the Book of 1549. Noel wrote to his fellow Christian Socialist P. E. T. Widdrington when the latter was appointed incumbent of the neighbouring parish of Great Easton: 'Do get a square cap, made up the Warham Guild . . . I think it important not to wear a headdress of the damned swanking, aristocratic-loving, rich-pleasing Romans with their shallowness and insufferable airs . . . They are not on the side of the revolution, these papist creatures.'[21] In his book *Jesus the Heretic* Noel wrote, 'The papacy always prefers the ruthless aggressions of the ruling class to revolutions of the workers.'[22] Those were not attitudes which were acceptable to Anglican Papalists, and they regarded the Morris Dancing which was promoted at Thaxted and at some churches with similar teaching as an irrelevance. Almost the only church in the East End of London where the English Use persisted was Christ Church, Stepney, where the

---

20 Groves: *Conrad Noel and the Thaxted Movement*, p. 219.
21 Ibid., p. 193.
22 Noel: *Jesus the Heretic*, p. 144.

charismatic Father St John Groser promoted mediaeval ceremonial, plainsong, and street dancing, whereas there were many surrounding parishes where neo-Romanism in different degrees was promoted. The only Papalist priest for whom Noel had much regard was Revd Alban Baverstock, who supported the local farmworkers, writing a treatise in 1912 entitled *The English Agricultural Labourer*, and who also set up a children's home in his Dorset parish.

The Papalists saw it as their mission to make the Church of England as much like the Roman Catholic Church on the Continent as was possible. That required parish-by-parish changes, as they were not in a position to impose change from above. They therefore promoted devotional societies both in the parish and in the wider Church, although almost all of these were narrow in their appeal and did not attract other groupings.

Another very important aspect of Anglican Papalist thinking was the belief that in order to show that the Church of England was in fact part of the Catholic Church, it had to produce the religious communities, shrines, pilgrimages, and popular piety which they saw abroad. They believed that Roman Catholics would be able to see that the internal life of the Church of England was vital enough to produce these external manifestations, and would thus become convinced of the common heritage of the two churches. The re-establishment of the shrine of Our Lady of Walsingham by Father Hope Patten was one of the most public examples of this tendency; for many years the shrine was visited almost exclusively by those from a discrete and limited section of the Church of England, and it was only after the death of the founder that it began to widen its appeal. An attempt by another Papalist, Revd Silas Harris, to develop the shrine of Our Lady at Egmanton, Nottinghamshire, was much less successful.

It is important to bear in mind that throughout the period described in this book the Papalists were a derided minority, assailed for their dis-loyalty and deprived of virtually all preferment within the Church of England. Father Fynes-Clinton himself said that 'Romanophiles . . . have to face much opposition and rejoice to do so . . . they are exposed to the disapproval of the authorities, and as far as possible, they are refused posts of responsibility.'[23] Thus they were normally restricted to posts in

---

23 Curtis: *Paul Couturier and Unity in Christ*, p. 172.

a relatively small number of parishes, although occasionally a priest was appointed to a country parish with no tradition of Catholic worship: sometimes the result was that the congregation disappeared, in other places force of personality inspired great devotion among the people. The chaplaincies to various religious orders were also places where priests whose views were regarded as unacceptable for parish life found sanctuary: within that context they were then free to teach with little external supervision, which in some cases resulted in such communities moving well outside the mainstream of Anglicanism.

It may be instructive to look at a couple of examples of the careers of men firmly committed to the cause of reunion with Rome.

Revd Clive Beresford was attracted to Anglican Papalism by his attendance at St Alban, Fulham. On ordination, he served curacies in London, at St Barnabas, Kentish Town, 1922–7 and then for seven years at St Thomas, Shepherd's Bush. He then had two short spells at St Swithun, Worcester, from where the vicar, W. B. Monahan, issued pro-reunion letters under the style 'The Voice from Worcester', interspersed with a period at St Luke, Swindon. From 1939 to 1947 he was vicar of St Michael, Edinburgh, the most ultramontane church in the Scottish Episcopal Church, and then moved to the country, becoming parish priest of Tickencote, Rutland, for two years, and finally of Newborough in the then Soke of Peterborough. He refurnished the interior of the small church with a variety of shrines and remained there until his death on 30 July 1967.

Revd Basil Joblin began as curate at St Alphege, Southwark, and then after a short spell in Lancashire returned to London for further curacies at St Augustine, Victoria Park, and then from 1928 to 1932 at St Saviour, Hoxton. He then became vicar of St Michael, Edinburgh, for seven years, moving in 1939 to become chaplain to the women's Community of St Peter at Laleham, Surrey, and being succeeded in Edinburgh by Beresford. He remained there until 1956 and then spent two years as curate to Father Corbould and in charge of the mission church of the Good Shepherd, Carshalton Beeches, before assisting elsewhere. He died in 1971. Both these men were at one stage in their lives Priest Directors of the Catholic League, the most important Papalist organisation, which is dealt with further in Chapters 2 and 3. The narrowness of the opportunities available is apparent from those two curricula vitae. No member of the Catholic League has ever been consecrated as a bishop, although

14

one (G. H. Bown) died in 1919 after being chosen for an episcopate in the Bahamas.

An even more illuminating example than the two quoted is perhaps provided by Father Alban Baverstock (1871–1950). He came from a home where both parents were deeply influenced by the Catholic Revival and worshipped at St Alban, Holborn. He and his brother Francis both became priests, and after two curacies Alban was appointed to the living of Hinton Martel, Dorset, in 1899. He remained there until 1930, by which time the church was thoroughly Roman in its teaching and appearance. Baverstock was an attractive character who found it easy to relate to his rural parishioners, and won them over by his personality. By 1911 he had set up a shrine of Our Lady of Lourdes in the church, but Protestant objections to his ministry were muted, perhaps because he was genuinely popular with his flock.[24] By the 1920s there were processions around the village on the Feasts of the Assumption and of St Joseph, and an outdoor procession on Corpus Christi Day. In 1903 he established St Joseph's Home in the village to care for boys with various problems, and in due course a network of such centres, known as the Holy Family Homes, was established in a number of places across the South of England. Alban Baverstock was also a writer of some accomplishment, and he produced a number of works of lasting value, such as *The Priest as Confessor* (1914) and *Priesthood in Liturgy and Life* (1917). He was Master of the SSC from 1921 to 1924 and again from 1927 to 1929.

In 1930, however, Baverstock resigned the living of Hinton Martel for health reasons. Initially his intention was to devote himself to the Holy Family Homes, and he moved to be Priest Director at their premises at Duxhurst, near Reigate in Surrey. However, in 1932 the Homes suffered a financial collapse and the parent company went into liquidation, although some continued in existence after that date. He then moved to Basingstoke to spend two years as chaplain to the Sisters of the Transfiguration, an order he had himself founded: see Chapter 5. In 1933 he managed to return to parish life, as non-stipendiary curate at Holy Trinity, Reading, and the next year he was given an income. However, he fell out with the vicar, Revd Francis Judd, who was

---

24 The statue of Our Lady brought back by Baverstock from France in 1911 remains in the church, as do a number of his embellishments, although the sanctuary has been much simplified in recent years.

notoriously difficult, and in 1938 was forced out of the parish. By then he had taken on the position as Chaplain General of the Society of Mary, a post which reflected his long-standing devotion to Our Lady. At that point, however, this talented man was unable to find another post within the Church of England, and supported himself for three years by working as a civil servant, although still licensed to officiate. Finally, in 1942, at the age of 71, he was offered the Chaplaincy of the Radcliffe Infirmary, Oxford, which he held until he retired in 1946.[25]

The Papalists have been almost completely ignored in the history of the Church of England in the twentieth century, partly because little sympathy has been exhibited towards their views and also because the revolutionary changes which swept over the Roman Catholic Church in the 40 years after 1960 made the views which they had been expressing before that date unfashionable. Although the Papalist position in many ways savoured of illogicality, it was prophetic in the sense that its adherents saw the reality of unity at a time when others did not.

However, as Roberts said in his article, the minority whose view was expressed by the Papalists was not inconsiderable in size, which makes the neglect by historians the more reprehensible. A manifesto dated October 1932 and issued to the clergy, which asserted that the inevitable end of the Catholic Revival was the corporate return of the English Church to the Holy See, and that was the aim for which all Catholics should strive, was signed by 350 of the 15,000-odd Anglican clergy at that time. Perhaps the increased publicity provided the following year by the centenary celebrations ensured that the appeal of the Committee for Promoting the Church Unity Octave, stating the same position even more definitively, received 760 signatures. Even in 1953 it was said that over 1,000 clergy agreed with the aims of the Octave, and in 1959 almost 1,500. These are not insignificant figures.

The real undermining of the Papalist tradition came in the period after 1960, which is not dealt with in detail in this study. The most important development without doubt was the revolution which encompassed the Roman Catholic Church after Vatican II. There had

---

25 See Farmer: *Father Alban Baverstock, passim.* Baverstock died in 1950 and is buried in Hinton Martel churchyard.

been a universal assumption during the inter-war period that the liturgy and teaching of the Roman church was constant and that it was those who wished to join it who had to modify their practices. This view prevailed until after the proclamation of the Assumption of Our Lady as an article of faith in 1950.

That proclamation can now be seen, with the benefit of hindsight, as the apex of the centralising, inward-looking view which then prevailed in Rome. The wind began to blow in the opposite direction almost immediately. Some conservative Anglo-Catholics thought that the relaxation by the Vatican of the regulations on fasting before communion, which began to take effect after about 1953, were a change too far, and when the tempest of change began to envelop Rome, it found many in the Anglican Communion unready.

On the face of it, the changes within the Roman Communion removed many of the barriers to unity. A vernacular liturgy, a new openness, and a move away from excessive pietism were exactly the changes for which moderate Anglo-Catholics had been asking for so many years. There was a window of opportunity between the Council and the more conservative regime of Pope John Paul II, but although much more friendly relations were established and the decades of non-cooperation soon melted away, the chance was not decisively seized. By that time too Anglo-Catholicism was a diffused force.

Although there were some who still regarded themselves as Papalists, the face of Anglican worship had been changed beyond measure by the influence of the Liturgical Movement, and by the acceptance even of the Evangelical wing of the Church, after the Keele Conference in 1967, that the Eucharist should be the centre of the Church's worship. All were able to come together in the Parish Communion, and in many cases there was no choice because the shortage of priests and of money with which to pay them led to the amalgamation of many livings, especially in rural areas. The situation where a devoted priest was able to spend 40 years building up his own style of worship in a village disappeared. His successor had to cater for the various traditions which had grown up over the years, and the Parish Communion was a service acceptable to most people.

The Oxford Movement has taken over great areas of the Church of England in the diluted form of the Family Communion, but the dogmatic base upon which the need for more frequent eucharistic worship was built has all but disappeared as it has been absorbed into the all-embracing centre of the National Church; the spiritual discipline which underlay Anglo-Catholicism has been weakened by compromise and introspection. Unity with Rome was far away even before the Church of England decided to ordain women, a step which resulted in the most significant series of defections to Rome since the Reformation and materially weakened what was left of the Papalist Tradition within the Church of England.

It is salutary to recall that the issue of the ordination of women was raised as early as the inter-war period. In Father Clement's book referred to above he wrote in 1935 that the Catholic Church 'has its own use for devout women in religious communities' and went on, prophetically, to say, 'the erection of a female priesthood is an actual project in neo-Evangelical circles . . . Any successful attempt to establish the official ministry of women in the Church of England would for ever debar her claim to be a potential part of the Catholic Church.'[26] In 1945 L. E. Jack, the then secretary of the Confraternity of Unity and the last churchwarden of St Saviour, Hoxton, commented on the then recent irregular ordination of a woman in Hong Kong by the laconic comment: 'It is no more possible validly to ordain a woman than to baptise a cow.'[27]

The essence of the Papalist position is perhaps contained in the purple prose of Ronald Knox before he himself succumbed to the temptation to climb aboard the barque of St Peter. In his sermon 'Windows in Heaven', also from *The Church in Bondage* he looked round to his fellow travellers in the Church of England and lamented:

It is not for us, the glamour of the Seven Hills, and the confidence of membership, living and actual, in the Church of the Ages; we cannot set our feet upon the rock of Peter, but only watch the shadow of Peter passing by, and hope that it may fall on us and heal us. We shall bear the reproach of the Catholic name, without enjoying the full privileges of the Catholic heritage. And yet, even now, we are not left without hope. Our needs have still a place in the compassionate heart of Mary, where she sits by her Father's side; she has not forgotten her children, just because they have run away from their schoolmaster

26 Plowden-Wardlaw: *Catholic Reunion*, pp. 28–9.
27 *Reunion*, Vol. 5, No. 34 (1945).

and unlearnt their lessons, and are trying to find their way home again, humbled and terrified in the darkness.[28]

In 'The Thirtieth of January', in the same collection, he was moved to declaim:

> And surely we dare not doubt that Jesus will be our Shepherd, till the time when he gathers his fold together; and that, although we do not live to see it, England will once again become the dowry of Mary, and the Church of England will once again be builded on the Rock she was hewn from, and find a place, although it be a place of penitence and tears, in the eternal purposes of God.[29]

Anglican Papalists were indeed wont to say, perhaps more prosaically, that Rome was the rock from which the Church of England was hewn and the Mother to whom she would return.

---

28 Knox: *The Church in Bondage*, p. 24.
29 Ibid., p. 33.

2

THE HISTORICAL DEVELOPMENT OF THE PAPALIST TRADITION
Part 1 1900–1930

The development of the Papalist Tradition in the Church of England during the period covered in this book is largely attributable to three men, namely Lord Halifax, Revd S. J. Jones, and Revd H. J. Fynes-Clinton. At one important moment at the beginning of that period, it happened that they came together, with far-reaching consequences.

In addition to their personal contributions, it is also necessary to consider the influence of the various organisations within the Church with which they were connected. The Church of England has always had within it many societies, guilds, and pressure groups and the ultramontane wing was no exception. Father Fynes-Clinton in particular was an inveterate founder of organisations of various sorts, some of which have endured and others of which were merely ephemeral. It perhaps almost comes as a surprise to discover that the Guild of St Zenas and St Zita, founded in 1922 to strengthen Anglo-Catholicism among domestic servants, was not one of his progeny, but rather was centred around St Alban, Holborn.

Although throughout the nineteenth century there were a number of converts to Rome, of whom of course the most famous were Newman and Manning, there was little pressure within the Church of England for corporate reunion. The only body of substance which advocated such a course was the Association for the Promotion of the Unity of Christendom, which was established in 1857 largely due to the efforts of Ambrose Phillipps de Lisle, a wealthy Roman Catholic landowner. The importance of this organisation was that it was open to membership from both churches, and provided a forum for discussion which was sadly lacking elsewhere. The *Union Newspaper*, which was founded by Revd F. G. Lee in late 1856 and allied itself to the APUC, had an uncompromising pro-Roman approach with which many of the older generation of Tractarians felt uncomfortable. It ceased publication in 1862, and in 1864, as a result of representations by Manning and other English Romans who were strongly opposed to any reunion save that based on individual submission, Roman Catholics were forbidden to associate with the Association. It therefore continued as an Anglican pressure group only, with a small membership, and was tainted by the disloyalty charged against one of its most prominent adherents, Dr Lee, after the latter was ordained bishop in the Order of Corporate Reunion in 1877: see Chapter 10. By the turn of the century the Master of the Association was the well-known lay Anglo-Catholic Athelstan Riley. The APUC did, however, celebrate a Novena of Prayer for Unity in the period immediately before Whitsunday each year, a practice which had been commended by Pope Leo XIII.

The most significant organisation numerically on the Anglo-Catholic side in the late nineteenth and early twentieth centuries was the English Church Union. It was well organised, particularly in the first decade of the twentieth century while under the secretaryship of H. W. Hill. However, the majority of its members were conservative in relation to matters of liturgy and of reunion and were anxious not to be seen as moving forward too aggressively, although they were prepared to defend with vigour any attack on established practices, and it took up support for the Novena of Prayer for Unity.

The most important priests' body in the last quarter of the nineteenth century was the Society of the Holy Cross, usually known by the initials SSC for its Latin name of Societas Sanctae Crucis. Father Lowder of St Peter, London Docks, had founded the Society with a view to increasing the personal devotion of the priesthood: it was one of many attempts made by Anglo-Catholics to distinguish themselves from the 'parson' image and to demonstrate the professionalism and self-sacrifice needed from the clergy. Although the SSC was not strictly Papalist in that, as already discussed, it was not committed to the theory that the Church in England bifurcated at the Reformation, many of its members lay firmly within the Western Use party and advocated the introduction of many Roman devotions. It again is a Society which continues in existence today.

The other main organisation for priests, the Federation of Catholic Priests or FCP, was not formed until the First World War. It arose from one of a number of attempts by the episcopal bench to control Reservation of the Blessed Sacrament. In 1916 a memorial was sent to all the bishops indicating that a restriction on the right of access to the Blessed Sacrament 'cannot rightly be demanded and will not be given'. It was then published signed by about 1,000 clergy. When the bishops reaffirmed their position, the FCP was formed with Revd Darwell Stone (1859–1941), the learned and wise principal of Pusey House, Oxford, as the Chairman. By 1929 the Federation had 1,530 members: there was nothing in its constitution relating specifically to reunion, and it is difficult to see why a new body was required when the SSC already existed. However, it was a characteristic of Anglo-Catholicism that fissiparous groups came into being.

Charles Lindley Wood, Viscount Halifax (1839–1934) at first sight appears an unlikely subject for discussion in the context of Anglican Papalism. He was in many ways very moderate in his ecclesiastical views, and his very long presidency of the English Church Union (1868–1919 and again 1931–4) reflected that moderation. Throughout his life, he remained perfectly content with the First Prayer Book of Edward VI (1549), which was a rite usually advocated by those who supported a non-Papal Anglo-Catholicism; it was used from as early as 1894 in Hickleton church, on his Yorkshire estates, with the permission of the Archbishop of York. He was discontented while churchwarden at St Mary, Bourne Street, with passages of the mass being said silently in the Roman fashion, but in due course his increasing deafness made it impossible for him to discern whether or not the words were being spoken aloud.

On the other hand, as Father Corbould, who had at one time been his chaplain, wrote in his obituary: 'Above all causes the life of Lord Halifax was devoted to the supreme cause of the reunion of Christendom.'[1] Halifax had a vision which minimised the differences between Rome and Canterbury and made little of the opinion of the vast majority of members of the Church of England who were steadfastly opposed to reunion.

There is no doubt about Halifax's sincerity and personal piety, which made him respected by all, even if they did not agree with him. When Father Tooth was prosecuted and imprisoned under the Public Worship

---

1 *Reunion*, Vol. 1, No. 1 (1934).

Regulation Act, Halifax thought it appropriate to resign his position as Groom of the Bedchamber to the Prince of Wales because his conscience was in conflict with the law of the land. In 1919 he wrote a long letter to a friend in which he set out the basis of his faith in these terms:

> What I want to emphasize is that as I look back I see that it is the Blessed Sacrament to which I owe everything. I cannot imagine my life without it. It has helped me in all my temptations, it has kept me, so far as I have been kept, straight, as nothing else could ... Teach our people what the Blessed Sacrament is, and the battle of the Faith is largely won ...[2]

Corbould records that even in old age Halifax frequently stayed for several hours in silent prayer before the Sacrament after early mass.

Halifax was very generous with his money as well as his time, supporting many organisations and financing on his account the building of one of the early ferro-concrete churches, at Goldthorpe in Yorkshire, in 1917, the first incumbent of which was Father C. P. Shaw, who was later the leader of the rebellion against episcopal control of Benediction in the Diocese of London after the rejection of the Revised Prayer Books. Halifax was also President of the League of Our Lady (founded about 1902) which in 1931 merged with the Confraternity of Our Lady (founded 1880 under the name Confraternity of the Children of Mary and itself merged in 1920 with the Union of the Holy Rosary, founded 1886) to form the present-day Society of Mary.[3]

In 1890 Halifax was on holiday in Madeira when he met the French Lazarist Abbé Portal, and found that he too had a mind which made light of the historic differences between the two churches. Portal began a campaign within the Roman Church for the recognition of Anglican orders and in 1894 came to England, but like other continental visitors over the years, he was shown a somewhat narrow section of the Church of England. He then went to see Pope Leo XIII in order to press the cause; in February 1896 Halifax went to France and stayed at the Lazarist headquarters in Paris, where he found more enthusiasm for reunion than would have been the case in England. Halifax displayed a lack of

---

2 Lockhart: *Charles Lindley Viscount Halifax, Part One*, p. 82.
3 See W. Davage: 'Our Lady and the Catholic Revival', *Pusey House Annual Report and Journal 2003–4* (Pusey House, 2004), pp. 20–30. Some of the dates are not clear from the extant papers.

understanding of the position of English Roman Catholics, which was characteristic of the position he held. Manning and his ultramontane supporters were totally opposed to the recognition of Anglican orders, and their pressure was in the opposite direction.

The publication of the Papal Bull *Apostolicae Curae* in September 1896 temporarily dashed the hopes of Halifax and Portal, while the flood of converts to Rome which Manning expected did not materialise.

Halifax then turned his attention back to the fostering of groups within the Church of England which favoured reunion.

On the feast of St Peter, 1900, a sermon was delivered at St Matthew, Westminster, as part of a series organised by the Association for the Promotion of the Unity of Christendom. This was the occasion mentioned above which brought together the three men of influence in Anglican Papalism: the preacher was Father Jones, and among the congregation were Lord Halifax and Fynes-Clinton, then still a layman.

Spencer John Jones was ordained deacon in 1880 and priest in 1882. He was a relative of John Keble, and like Halifax, his life spanned the period from Tractarianism into the twentieth century. He has been described as a scholar athlete, who was content to live the life of a country priest: he was vicar of Moreton-in-Marsh with Batsford from 1887 to 1932 and then had a further 11 years of retirement in Taunton until his death on 28 January 1943. He is credited with introducing to the Church of England the catechist method of teaching. Unlike many Anglican Papalists, he was married, and indeed his requiem was celebrated by his son, Revd E. Spencer Jones, then vicar of Richard's Castle, Shropshire.

Jones was, however, throughout his long life a consistent propagandist for the reunion of the Church of England with Rome. It appears from the surviving correspondence that Halifax was in close touch with him even before the delivery of the sermon,[4] and after he had given it both Halifax and Fynes-Clinton urged him to publish it: in 1902 it appeared as *England and the Holy See*. The book created a minor sensation, particularly on the Continent of Europe, and was widely reviewed in a variety of publications. In his introduction, Lord Halifax said, 'I cannot believe that [reunion with Rome] is as difficult as it is thought', which provides a fair résumé of his thought throughout his life.[5]

4 See the uncatalogued Rea papers in Pusey House.
5 Jones: *England and the Holy See*, p. xv.

Despite his mild and scholarly approach, Jones could be quite forthright when he wished. His aim was made quite clear: 'When I speak of "Reunion" the specific aim I am contemplating throughout . . . is the reunion of England with the Holy See.'[6] He also referred to the problem of discipline among Anglo-Catholics in the following terms:

> We have said to the Civil courts – we will not obey you; and on certain specific questions we have said also to the bishops – we will not obey you. The bishops in their turn now ask us . . . whom, then, will you obey? And to this we return the answer – we will obey the Holy Church throughout all the world.[7]

Following the extensive publicity given to *England and the Holy See*, 40 clergy decided at a meeting in London to form the Western Church Association, which was placed under the patronage of St Thomas Becket and was generally known as the Association of St Thomas of Canterbury. It was to have one meeting a year addressed alternately by an Anglican and a Roman, and the first was given by Jones, who was also elected as president of the Association. His inaugural lecture was delivered on 17 February 1904 and was published later that year under the title *Rome and Reunion*.

The tone of that lecture was equally uncompromising. Jones was sure that the new century revealed promise for the future, and said 'a Roman school may also be necessary if the road is to be kept clear and the way made plain for the due consideration of the Holy See . . . we are entering upon a new phase . . .'[8] Later he said with some optimism: 'We recognize, or think we recognize, in the Oxford Revival a movement which manifests a definite drift in the direction of the Holy See.'[9] In 1909 the Society sent its congratulations to Pope Pius X on his Jubilee.[10]

Following the publication of his earlier book, Father Jones received a flood of correspondence from all over the world. One person who wrote to him was Revd Lewis Thomas Wattson, an Episcopalian priest who had taken the name in religion of Paul James Francis and had founded the Order of the Atonement at Graymoor, New York. The two men

6 Ibid., p. 11.
7 Ibid., p. 2.
8 Jones: *Rome and Reunion*, p. 5.
9 Ibid., p. 78.
10 Rea papers, Pusey House.

quickly became friends, and together they wrote *The Prince of the Apostles* (published 1904). Father Paul's community produced from 1903 a magazine, *The Lamp*, to which Father Jones contributed, and which strongly advocated Roman doctrines. From 1904 the community contributed to Peter's Pence, which gives some indication of the way in which their mind was set.

In November 1907, in the course of the correspondence between them, Jones suggested 29 June (St Peter's Day) as the appropriate day for preaching sermons on the prerogatives of St Peter and on the Holy See as the centre of unity. Father Paul, however, suggested January and it was agreed that an Octave of Prayer for Christian Unity be established, running from the Feast of St Peter's Chair in Rome (18 January) to the Feast of the Conversion of St Paul (25 January).

The Octave was celebrated for the first time in January 1908, and the following month Father Paul started the Anglo-Roman Union. However, on 30 October 1909 the Community at Graymoor was received into the Roman Church, and thereafter experienced very considerable growth. The secession did not mean an end to the friendship between the two men, although they did not meet face to face until 1936 when Wattson came to England and met Jones at Exeter. The friendship indeed continued until Wattson's death on 8 February 1940, and Jones wrote an obituary of him with some personal memories.

It also happened that as a result of the conversion of the Graymoor community, the Octave became far better known in the Roman Church. As early as 1909 Pope Pius X approved its observance, and in 1916 Pope Benedict XV extended its observance to the whole Church.

It can thus be seen that the tradition of January Prayers for Christian Unity was established originally as an Anglican Papalist initiative, and was supported almost entirely by churches within that tradition. Thereafter the Octave was superceded by the Week of Prayer for Christian Unity, founded on more central Anglican thinking, and its message was very strongly diluted, as with so many other such innovations.

In the period leading up to the First World War, Lord Halifax was preoccupied with the growth and subsequent collapse of the Caldey Community and with the early moves towards the Revision of the Book of Common Prayer. In any event, his position with the English Church Union meant that he was unwilling to become involved in any new

Papalist organisation. The foundation of that group was left to Fynes-Clinton.

Henry Joy Fynes-Clinton (1876–1959) came from a clerical family, albeit the Clinton name spoke of connections with the Dukes of Newcastle, and although in general admired for his courtesy, he could also be autocratic in manner. He was born at Cromwell, Nottinghamshire, a small village just off the A1 where there are many tablets to members of the family (sometimes spelled Fiennes-Clinton), and where a relative was the parish priest: his own father however spent his entire ministry as curate and then rector of Blandford Forum, Dorset. Cromwell is one of those village churches over which the Oxford Movement has washed, leaving behind it furnishings which are now little used, as without a resident priest services are few and far between.

The young Fynes-Clinton went to King's School, Canterbury (where he and some other ritual-minded boys used to attend Sung Eucharist at St Peter in that city), then Trinity College, Oxford, followed by Ely Theological College, although he spent some considerable time in Russia in the later years of the century. He was ordained deacon in 1901, and priest in 1902. His first position was as curate at St John, Upper Norwood (1901–4), and he then moved to St Martin, Brighton (1904–6), St Michael, Shoreditch (1906–14), and St Stephen, Lewisham (1914–21) before taking on the living of the Wren church of St Magnus the Martyr in the City in 1921, which he was to hold until his death. Throughout his life he urged the promotion of Roman doctrinal and liturgical standards among separated Christians, but he was not narrowly devoted to Rome: as early as 1906 he was instrumental in the foundation of the Anglican and Eastern Orthodox Churches Union, later known as the Anglican and Eastern Churches Association, and later received decorations from both the Russian and Serbian Orthodox Churches for his interest in and work for them. He was a man who was entirely forthright in what he believed, but respected for his sincerity and lack of underhand dealing, even by those who became exasperated by his erudite references. There is a well-known passage in a letter by Ronald Knox dated 29 April 1915 in which he describes a meeting he had just attended with other clergy of like mind. He says, 'Then Fynes-Clinton arose, and we thought we were to have nothing but accounts of the antics of Hippopotamus Copronymous and the Liturgy of Prmysl for the rest of the evening.'[11] In later years Fynes-Clinton showed much more readiness to adapt than did many of his contemporaries, and after the relaxation of the fasting rules by the Vatican he held lunchtime masses in the City well before they became commonplace. He was also involved in the wider City in various ways.

Father Fynes-Clinton and others saw the need for a new organisation which would reflect more fully the Papalist position in the Church of England. In 1912 he and various other members sought to press the leadership of the Guild of the Love of God, a body founded by Revd A. V. Magee, for more definite proposals in relation to reunion. They were not forthcoming, and there was a secession from the Guild, which itself continued in existence for many years thereafter.

At a meeting in London on 2 July 1913 Father Fynes-Clinton and Revd R. L. Langford-James, then vicar of St Mark, Bush Hill Park, Enfield, and later for many years parish priest of St James, Edgbaston, Birmingham, founded the Catholic League, in many ways the most important Papalist body in the Church of England, and one which, unlike many of Fynes-Clinton's creations, remains in being today. Langford-James was appointed Superior with Fynes-Clinton as his assistant.

On 5 July 1913, only three days after that meeting, a formal inauguration of the League took place at St Mary, Corringham, Essex, which was then a somewhat remote place. The invitation to join the people there at their own patronal festival came from Clifton Kelway, a founder member of the League who was a lay reader in the parish and also a well-known journalist and an author on church affairs. The 97 foundation members of the League therefore joined the parish and sang the Litany of Our Lady and the *Salve Regina* in Latin. The League was solemnly inaugurated and the foundation deed was signed by those present, following which Solemn Vespers of Our Lady were sung.

However, the Bishop of St Albans (in whose diocese Corringham then was) came across a copy of the service and immediately took drastic action. Langford-James and Fynes-Clinton were required to stand down, although Fynes-Clinton regarded himself as no longer bound by this after he moved to a new curacy in 1914. Kelway's licence as a lay reader was withdrawn. Father Greatheed, the parish priest of

---

11 Waugh: *The Life of Ronald Knox*, p. 119.

Corringham, was made to remove the statue of Our Lady from the church; it was later replaced by an image made by the well-known artist Martin Travers. All other members of the League were inhibited from any activity in the Diocese of St Albans.

The League took this early setback in their stride. The duumvirate was replaced by Father E. S. Maltby, another well-known figure in Anglican Papalist circles. Edward Secker Maltby ran St Mary's Mission, Erlam Road, South Bermondsey, and we have a description of him by Father Bruno Scott James, who was a member of the Nashdom Benedictines until he went over to Rome and became the first Roman parish priest in Walsingham. He said of Maltby:

> He served a church in the slums of London which, it was said, he had built himself, and at the back of which he kept a huge picture of the Pope, which he never passed without saluting by taking off his biretta. He preached quite openly and very well, on the Infallibility of the Pope, to which, with a solidarity worthy of a better cause, he adjusted his position in the Church of England, apparently without any misgivings or qualms ... He approached more closely than any of the clergy of the extreme right wing of the Anglo-Catholic party the ideal of the Catholic priest, and more clearly than any of the others he bore the mark of holiness. Not only was he a scholar and something of a theologian, but he was much more, he was a man of profound interior life.[12]

However, the work of running his mission single-handed caused Maltby to resign after a short time, and in 1914 Revd W. J. Scott, an older priest who had by then retired from his ministry at St Saviour, Sunbury Common, took over. He had been ordained deacon in 1876, priest in 1878, and had been perpetual curate at Sunbury from 1889 to 1908. Scott was an authority on railways, especially the Great Western, as well as being described by Ronald Knox in the same letter which mentions Fynes-Clinton, as being 'wonderfully sound'.[13] Knox was himself a member of the League, and as a result of the disciplinary action taken after the Corringham service he was prevented from assisting at a college mission in West Ham, then in the Diocese of St Albans. However, he did

---

12 Scott James: *Asking for Trouble*, p. 34.
13 Waugh, *The Life of Ronald Knox*, p. 119.

preach at the first annual festa, which was held at St Michael, Bingfield Street, Islington, on 25 October 1913. The parish priest of that small back-street church, Revd J. H. Boudier, was another strong supporter of Papalism. The tradition he established there, very different from that in most Islington churches, was continued by Revd C. E. Simes during his long incumbency from 1924 to 1969.

On 17 February 1914 Father Maltby and Father Fynes-Clinton set up as an adjunct to the League the Sodality of the Precious Blood, membership of which was restricted to celibate priests. Members were bound also to the full recitation of the Latin breviary, and to eschew any connection with Freemasonry. The requirement for Latin excluded from the Sodality some, such as Father Hope Patten, who might have been expected to join: Hope Patten's lack of formal education was such that he was unable properly to understand the language. Father Hole too was excluded because he was married, as were a minority of other Papalist priests.

Father Maltby was the first Director of the Sodality and Father Fynes-Clinton the first secretary. The new organisation held retreats, initially monthly but later annually. It remained a small core body, never exceeding 50 members at any one time and usually having 30 to 40 adherents.

In 1914 the League began publishing its journal *The Catholic* but the following year its name was changed to *The Messenger*. In 1915 Fynes-Clinton professed the first member of the women's Community of Our Lady of Victory, which again was an adjunct to the League, but which was not to prove as long lasting: see Chapter 5. Also, on 12 June that year the League inaugurated the Apostleship of Prayer, linked to the Community and dedicated to the Sacred Heart of Jesus, with a votive mass on the First Friday of each month offered by the Priest Director. That too survives.

In addition to these groups, the structure of the League was complicated by smaller organisations, most of which were the product of Fynes-Clinton's fertile brain. There was, for instance, a Tabernacle Treasury, which provided funds for monstrances for churches: particular appeals were made for certain churches, such as St Alban, Fulham, when it fell under episcopal ban even from the lax Bishop Winnington-Ingram for its refusal to abandon Benediction of the Blessed Sacrament. There was also a Spiritual Treasury, the Women's and Men's respective Retreat Organisations, the Living Crown of Our Lady of Victory, the

Guard of Honour of the Sacred Heart of Jesus, the Chantry Fund, and probably others. Some were short-lived, whereas others, such as the Tabernacle Treasury, lasted for many years.

The First World War was a period of growth for many Anglo-Catholic organisations, partly because of the popularity of requiem masses for the dead and of increased devotion to the Blessed Sacrament as the losses mounted, but also because the gaze of the episcopate was elsewhere.

In 1916 Father Scott resigned, and was replaced by an anonymous group, which was headed by Fynes-Clinton: he later emerged as the Priest Director, and of course had been the moving spirit throughout.

In 1920 the League for the first time held its festa at the Convent of the Paraclete at Woodside, Croydon, which had been founded by the imprisoned ritualist, Father Tooth, who after his release was unable to find a living. During the day, Father Fynes-Clinton received the profession of a brother of the Society of St Augustine (later the Servitors of Mary and St Austin), another of his less successful enterprises, which is further discussed in Chapter 5. In 1925 the function moved to Otford School, which was also a foundation associated with Father Tooth, and there they continued for many years. The association with Tooth also provided links with the earlier history of the Oxford Movement: it was a constant theme in Papalist literature that they were the true successors of the pioneers of the Revival.

On 23 October 1920 another sub-group of the League was founded, when at Holy Trinity, Hoxton, the Rosary Confraternity was dedicated to the Sacred Heart of Jesus and the Immaculate Heart of Mary: the sisters of the Community of Our Lady of Victory were living in the parish at that time.

Two other significant developments in the progress of the Catholic League took place in the same year. The first was the adoption by it of the Profession of Faith of the Council of Trent. In its explanatory booklet the League said:

Our present circumstances, then, in these two provinces of Canterbury and York, are very similar to those of the Western Church as a whole before the Council of Trent, only that it is with a very much more advanced and virulent form of the disease that we are beset . . .

So the Catholic League adopts as its profession of faith THE CREED OF THE COUNCIL OF TRENT.[14]

The second such development was the formation of the Church Unity Octave Committee, which was at that stage a sub-committee of the League. The League had first mentioned the Octave in its literature as early as 16 January 1914, but the first formal call to prayer for it was made in *Messenger* 17 (January–March 1918). Following that, in the inter-war period observance of the Octave became of very great importance to Anglican Papalists. The Committee was chaired by Fynes-Clinton and included representatives from the Society of SS Peter and Paul (as to which see Chapter 11) and an organisation entitled the Federation of Catholic Laity. It then absorbed the pioneering Association for the Promotion of the Reunion of Christendom, which was apparently wound up by Athelstan Riley at a meeting on 27 January 1921, on the grounds of the absence of Roman Catholic involvement, but without, apparently, any consultation with the wider membership.[15] Father Tooth preached at the 1921 observance of the Octave, which was centred upon the now demolished church of St Mary, Charing Cross Road. On the feast of St Matthew, 1925, the Council for Observance of the Church Unity Octave was formed, with Spencer Jones as its President, and on 14 June 1926 this seems from the contemporary evidence to have become transformed into the Executive Committee of the Church Unity Octave,[16] although confusingly the literature thereafter refers to the Church Unity Octave Council. The secretary was initially Revd William Kewley, who was then a curate at St Alban, Fulham. Kewley's career followed a similar path to that of Beresford, although he was ordained in the Scottish Episcopal Church and served his title in Kirkcaldy (1914–16). He then moved to All Saints, Middlesbrough, a famous centre in the North-East (1916–19), St Andrew, Plaistow (1919–22), St Alban, Fulham (1922–6), and then St Peter, Folkestone, another well-known Anglo-Catholic church (1926–9). He was then appointed to the rural living of Skirwith in the Diocese of Carlisle before moving in 1946 to Shouldham in Norfolk.

---

14 Catholic League: *An Explanation of the Profession of Faith of the Council of Trent*, unnumbered pages.
15 Chapman: *The Fantasy of Reunion*, p. 25.
16 Rea papers, Pusey House.

As these developments were occurring, Fynes-Clinton finally acquired a living of his own, and after his institution in 1921 St Magnus the Martyr, Lower Thames Street, became the centre of the League's spiritual activities: from 1923 until the Second World War it also had an administrative centre in Finsbury from which correspondence came. In 1922 Fynes-Clinton revived the Fraternity of Our Lady de Salve Regina, which dated originally from 1343, and which held devotions at midday every day, and in 1924 he aggregated it to the League, thus providing yet another associated and interlocked group.

The League achieved a degree of notoriety in 1924 when there was a long correspondence in the *Church Times* over the question of whether there could be a non-Papal Catholicism: the League was attacked for disloyalty, but defended by two well-known priests, Prebendary H. P. Denison and Revd Roger Wodehouse. Spencer Jones also defended the Papalist position strongly, citing Pusey's view that the Tridentine Creed was compatible with membership of the Anglican Communion.

On All Saints' Day 1926 a completely new body, the Confraternity of Unity, was founded by four priests at St Mary the Virgin, New York. Its aims were similar to the Catholic League, although the emphasis was almost exclusively on reunion. The constitution contained the following declaration, which was required of all members: 'I believe in the Primacy, not only of honour but of jurisdiction, of the Bishop of Rome, successor of St Peter, Prince of the Apostles, Vicar of Jesus Christ.' The Councils of Trent and the Vatican were also accepted, together with everything defined in them 'especially concerning the Primacy of the Roman Pontiff, and his infallible authority'.

Three of the four Americans, Fathers Campbell, Pierce, and Walker, came to Oxford in 1928 and met various like-minded priests in England. On 5 November 1928 Father T. Bowyer Campbell, who was later to become Professor of History at the University of Notre Dame, Indiana, addressed the Sodality of the Precious Blood at St Magnus, and it was agreed that a secretariat should be opened in England to promote the Confraternity. On 3 February 1929 this opened at the presbytery of the church of St Saviour, Hoxton, with Father Joblin, then curate at the church, as its representative in England. Mass was thereafter said for the Confraternity at St Saviour every Thursday. The Confraternity was correlated with the Catholic League, and from 1934 onwards published regularly its journal *Reunion*, which replaced earlier occasional papers and is a valuable record of thinking among the ultramontane wing. The journal was published until 1965, but with a gap from 1952 to 1957, and in latter years was very lacklustre in content. In the pre-war and wartime issues however there was a considerable amount of scholarly writing in its pages.

Fynes-Clinton joined the new body, but was never very enthusiastic about organisations which he was not himself running. Joblin wrote in a letter of 5 May 1929 to Campbell that Fynes-Clinton was 'scarcely an enthusiastic member' of the Confraternity.[17] Equally, there were some who thought that the Confraternity was less partisan and narrow than the Fynes-Clinton groupings: in 1930 Kewley and Revd Donald Rea resigned from the Church Unity Octave Council as they felt themselves out of accord with its approach, which they thought ignored all but the Romans. Rea (born 1894) had assisted Maltby at his mission and also helped at St Saviour, Hoxton, before acting as chaplain at the Holy Cross Sisters' branch house at Limpsfield for a number of years. In 1934 he became the incumbent of Eye, Suffolk, where he remained until his death in 1967. He was editor of *Reunion* for many years and Chairman of the Council of the Confraternity of Unity from 1943 until 1965, although that organisation of course was almost entirely Western in out-look, which seems at odds with his earlier resignation from the CUOC. It may be that there was a personality clash and certainly in Rea's papers there are records of the Suffolk Freemasons having their annual service at Eye, which Fynes-Clinton would never have countenanced.

The Confraternity continued also in the United States, although the Papalist wing of the Episcopal Church was very small, and by the end of the Second World War the organisation in that country was described as almost defunct. There was a later attempt at revival. Father H. K. Pierce stayed in Oxford for a number of years, until in due course he went over to Rome and indeed lived there for some years, even into the War, although continuing his friendly correspondence with the leaders of the Confraternity in England. In 1932, while still within the Anglican Communion, he made a pilgrimage to Rome and presented the Pope with details of the Confraternity.

In 1929 yet another reunion society was started. This was the Society of Catholic Reunion (more formally constituted in 1931), which was

---

17 Ibid.

based among priests in the Southwell diocese and was guided by Father Silas Harris, parish priest of Egmanton, although in post-war years the moving force was Revd Frank Harwood, then of Radwinter, Essex. Despite its separate existence, its members appear to have collaborated with those of the other bodies in propaganda, although they issued their own quarterly leaflet, *The Bond of Peace*, which appeared from 1936 to 1949.

During the 1920s Halifax, then nearing the end of his very long life, was again involved in an initiative to bridge the gap between Rome and Canterbury, which, as always, he regarded as narrower than did most observers. Once more the introduction was provided by his friend Portal, who, encouraged by the apparent openness shown by the Church of England in setting out the Lambeth Quadrilateral at the Conference of 1920, suggested that Halifax contact Archbishop Mercier of Malines. The Cardinal Archbishop had unique status in Belgium because of his dignified and principled behaviour during the War, but he knew little of the inner workings of the Church of England. Although the series of Malines Conversations which followed was aimed at discovering a way in which the Church of England could be reconciled with Rome, the Anglican side was not composed of Papalists: the first members were Halifax himself, Frere, who was deeply anti-Roman in many respects, and the moderate Armitage Robinson, Dean of Wells, who was a friend of the Archbishop of Canterbury, Randall Davidson. Later Gore participated: Halifax had originally been very opposed to his presence as despite his intellectual prestige he regarded him as a modernist. Armitage Robinson found it necessary to write to Mercier on 17 December 1921 because Father Boudier of Islington had apparently had an audience with the Pope and had left the impression that the whole Church of England was ready to submit, which was of course far from the truth.

The Malines Conversations were remarkable in the sense that the discussions anticipated by about 50 years the agenda of the modern-day ARCIC: the sacraments, the nature and meaning of dogma, and the history, nature, and exercise of papal authority were all discussed. As a modern writer has it, they concentrated on practical steps towards reunion, presupposing previously agreed doctrinal agreement.[18] However, perhaps the most remarkable feature was that the Conversations

---

18 Barlow: *A Brother Knocking at the Door*, p. 5.

occurred at all, at a time when it was almost unheard of for Roman Catholics to talk to members of any other church.

There were serious flaws in the arrangements for the Conversations. Neither side wished to make them official, and that allowed the Romans in due course to question the authority of Mercier and his associates. Most importantly, but characteristically, they did not involve English Roman Catholics, who by nature and history were most opposed to any accommodation with Canterbury. Further, the sudden death of Mercier, on 23 January 1926, took away the momentum of the meetings.

Halifax was an enthusiastic writer at the time, and indeed it is clear that he broke the promise which all participants had given to keep the discussions secret when, after they had ended, he published his account of what had occurred. He justified this to himself by the belief that he had been released from the promise of secrecy by the rejection by the House of Commons of the Revised Prayer Books, which seems an odd train of thought.

From a Papalist viewpoint, the most important feature of the Conversations was the contribution of the Belgian monk, Dom Lambert Beauduin: his Benedictines of the Order of Unity had been established at Amay-sur-Meuse in 1925 and again were before their time. He contributed a confidential paper, *The Church of England United not Absorbed*, which suggested a Uniate Church in England along the lines of those found in the East. The main proposals of this paper were that the Church of England would continue with its own liturgy and without the imposition of Latin canon law, and that the Archbishop of Canterbury would be re-established as Patriarch after receiving the pallium from the Pope, and would therefore retain power over the internal organisation of the Church of England. However, in addition, not only would the traditional sees of the Church of England be preserved, but the new Roman sees established after 1851 would be suppressed.

There is no doubt that that proposal was extremely attractive to many Anglo-Catholics. On the other hand, it was several steps too far for many in the Church of England and complete anathema to the Roman hierarchy in England. It must also be remembered that while these Conversations were being pursued, with at least covert approval from the Vatican, at the same time the Roman Church was canonising St Theresa of Lisieux and instituting the devotion to Christ the King (both in 1925), both of which events indicated a continued movement away from any accommodation with any other body.

Halifax published a pamphlet entitled *A Call to Reunion* in 1922, followed closely by *Further Considerations on Behalf of Reunion* in 1923, *Reunion and the Roman Primacy*, 1925, and *Catholic Reunion* in 1926. Then he published *Notes on the Conversations at Malines* in 1928 and finally *The Conversations at Malines: Original Documents* in 1930. These last two writings are often said not only to have been a major error of judgement, but also as leading to the exile of Dom Lambert from his monastery from 1931 to 1952, although it has equally been said that the real reason for his expulsion was his proposal that the Conversations continue. Beauduin was perhaps vindicated when, in 1959, the Benedictine abbots suggested that there should be one abbey in each country devoted to the cause of unity.

It is clear that the conservative faction in the Vatican won the day, and the publication of the encyclical *Mortalium Animos* in 1928 brought to an end any such initiatives for many years.

The paper of Beauduin thus became public, and an English translation was made available for many years from 1936 onwards by the Anglican reunion societies. It was echoed later from the Anglican side in the elegantly written *Catholic Reunion: An Anglican Plea for a Uniate Patriarchate and for an Anglican Ultramontanism* written by Father Clement (J. T. Plowden-Wardlaw) in 1935, which has already been quoted. He argued for the recognition by Rome of an English Uniate Patriarchate, probably with a celibate priesthood, and probably also leaving behind 'modernists, irreconcilable protestants, and those obsessed by the state connection'.[19] The book is interesting in that the author, who was a prolific pamphleteer for Father Silas Harris' SCR (calling his letters *Clementine Tracts*), envisaged that reunion with Rome might envisage a split in the Church of England, a prospect many did not feel able to contemplate.

As the Malines Conversations were continuing, so was the Church of England reaching the conclusion of the long process of revision of its form of worship, a conclusion which inflicted severe damage on its leaders when the House of Commons twice rejected the proposals. That

---

19 Plowden-Wardlaw: *Catholic Reunion*, p. 10.

episode is important enough in the history of Anglican Papalism to require extended treatment, which is given in Chapter 4.

However, the development of the reunion societies and in particular the events in Belgium must also be seen against a period lasting about 15 years, from the end of the First World War to the Oxford Movement Centenary celebrations in 1933, during which almost all the energy in the Church of England was Catholic in inspiration. Evangelicalism appeared moribund, and although there was strong anti-Roman feeling, much of it was visceral and outside the established church. Anglo-Catholicism appeared to be an irresistible force within the Anglican Communion, and nowhere was this better demonstrated than in the Congresses, which were held in London in 1920, 1923, 1927, 1930, and, most notably, in 1933 for the Centenary itself.

It has become fashionable in later years to decry the Congresses as triumphalist. That they were, but it is perfectly clear looking back at contemporary accounts that they were remarkably successful in exciting the interest of many, especially the young. Attention is also directed almost exclusively at the London events, whereas in fact there were many well-supported meetings outside the capital. A vivid account of the Newcastle Congress of 1921 is given by Revd W. Rowland Jones, whose autobiography describes his conversion from Methodism to Anglo-Catholicism, an interval following his reordination by Bishop Vernon Herford, an eccentric irregular, and his eventual return to the Wesleyan fold. He described the Congress as 'The greatest thrill of my life, before or since . . . Every time a cassocked priest on the platform spoke of "the conversion of England to the Catholic Faith" a terrific roar went up from that vast crowd.'[20] In London, Revd H. A. Wilson, the Secretary of the 1920 Congress, describes queues for the best seats at the Albert Hall forming at 7.30 a.m., and at the closing service a file of worshippers waiting to get into Southwark Cathedral spanning the Thames as they sang the Hail Mary.[21]

The reports of the Congresses give testimony to the quality of the contributions and also witness that on the whole they were ignored by a narrow-minded episcopate in England, although patronised by some colonial bishops, most notably Frank Weston of Zanzibar, who

20 Jones: *Diary of a Misfit Priest*, p. 65.
21 Wilson: *Received with Thanks*, in his chapter on Revd M. E. Atlay.

galvanised the 1923 Congress. Weston is nowadays an almost-forgotten figure, regarded as an eccentric because of his protest at the 1913 Kikuyu meeting at which intercommunion had taken place between Anglicans and Nonconformists. However, he was a theologian of considerable weight, and a talented organiser who used his gifts to full effect in the side-show war fought in East Africa against the Germans. More notably, he was far ahead of his time in appreciating the importance of an African church with African priests. He rejected racialism when it was instinctive to most English people abroad.

Weston was willing to face problems which others swept aside. In his Kikuyu protest (which was ultimately, and after a decent interval, upheld) he asked the Church of England to cease to be 'a society for shirking issues'.[22] His participation in the 1920 Lambeth Conference was widely regarded as a personal triumph, and he contributed to the appeal for reunion which followed it. However, it was for his speech at the 1923 Anglo-Catholic Congress, calling for devotion to Christ in the poor as well as to Christ in the tabernacle, that many remember him, and it does appear even from the flat words of the printed record to have been an electrifying piece of oratory. Revd Desmond Morse-Boycott, a journalist and priest with a somewhat hyperbolic style, described him in 1932 as 'the hero of the movement . . . a man in a million, nay more, of a century, even of an aeon'.[23] His early death shortly after the 1923 Congress may have deprived Anglo-Catholicism of the charismatic leader which it always lacked.

On the whole the leaders of the Papalist party stood back from the Congresses, although there were occasional calls for reunion from some speakers. The guiding light behind the Congress movement was Revd Maurice Child, another underrated figure, who was admired for his wit, zest, and enthusiasm almost as much as some disliked him for his love of intrigue. Child, however, although he loved the exuberances of the Baroque, was an Anglican by temperament in a way that set him aside from many calling for immediate reunion.

Weston had a narrow but powerful focus which gave little thought to those who held differing opinions. It appears to have been a spontaneous gesture on his part while chairing the 1923 Congress to suggest sending

---

22 Smith: *Frank Bishop of Zanzibar*, p. 157.
23 Morse-Boycott: *Lead Kindly Light*, p. 17.

a telegram to Rome thus: 'Sixteen thousand Anglo-Catholics, in Congress assembled, offer respectful greetings to the Holy Father, humbly praying that the day of peace may quickly break.' The immediate reaction to the proposal was enthusiastic, but thereafter the residual anti-Romanism of many in the High Church group began to assert itself. That response was, however, regarded as of great importance among the Papalists: Fynes-Clinton saw it as the beginning of a move towards a non-Papal Catholicism, and L. E. Jack, looking back from the perspective of 1959, said that after the drawing back from the greeting, 'So began the gradual decline of a movement of great promise and vigour though which, had it remained true to the ideals of its originators, the conversion of England and her reunion with the Holy See might be reasonably near fulfilment'; he then referred to 'the negative policy of organized Anglo-Catholicism', or in other words the lack of emphasis on reunion.[24]

The English Church Union had lost a considerable amount of influence during the years after the First World War, with the Congress Movement gaining at its expense. Child was an extraordinarily able propagandist and organiser, and his flair for publicity encouraged recruits to his body rather than to the older and more staid English Church Union. Halifax himself rather liked Child, and had in fact given to his Society of SS Peter and Paul one of its earliest commissions, namely the printing for him of the Prayer Book of 1549. Halifax was by the end of the 1920s a very old man: he published his last book, *The Good Estate of the Catholic Church*, in 1930 and by the time of the Centenary celebrations three years later he was too infirm to travel to London. Characteristically, he set up at his own expense a large altar and held his own local celebration at Hickleton: the altar was later taken to Walsingham, where it stood for many years.

Halifax's last contribution to the causes he held so dear was to engineer the union of the English Church Union with the Anglo-Catholic Congress, which was not accomplished without some considerable resistance on the part of the Council of the ECU. Halifax, however, appealed over their head to the ordinary members, and succeeded: the Church Union, as the new body was called, came into existence on 1 January 1934, the drafting being carried out by H. H.

---

24 *Reunion*, Vol. 6, No. 52 (1959).

Slesser, a distinguished lawyer and sometime Lord Justice of Appeal, who in due course went over to Rome. It had already been agreed that, notwithstanding (or perhaps because of) the great success of the Centenary Congress no further such event would be held until 1940. Indeed, a Seven Year Association was launched which had as its aim the education and conversion particularly of the youth of the country in the intervening period: the secretary was H. R. T. Brandreth, who was later ordained and was a distinguished writer on Reunion and on Episcopi Vagantes, among other subjects. The 1940 Congress of course never took place because of the onset of the War. It is noteworthy that some Anglican Papalists thought that the new Church Union would only encourage compromises on the Anglo-Catholic side: it was strongly attacked by Revd R. E. Young of St Thomas, Shepherd's Bush, for that reason at the time.[25]

In order to bring together the various groups, in 1930 Father Fynes-Clinton formed the Council for Promoting Catholic Unity, on which were represented the Catholic League, the Sodality of the Precious Blood, the Confraternity of Unity, the Association of St Thomas of Canterbury and the Catholic Propaganda Society, which had been run by Father Alban Baverstock. Baverstock had earlier run the Catholic Literature Association, of which the secretary was Langford-James, but this had been associated with the Anglo-Catholic Congress in 1924 and continued as the Church Literature Association under the auspices of the Church Union. The St Thomas Association ceased functioning altogether at this time: the President of that Association at the time that the Council was formed was Father Maltby, who had succeeded Spencer Jones, but the latter then became the President of the new Council.

The new decade of the 1930s therefore began with some confidence among the Papalists that their voice was at last beginning to be heard.

---

25 In *The Pilot*, No. 2 (1934).

3

THE HISTORICAL DEVELOPMENT OF THE PAPALIST TRADITION
Part 2 1930–1960

Although the increasing popularity of Anglo-Catholicism, as demonstrated at the time of the centenary celebrations in 1933, was an encouragement to many, the perceived dilution of its teachings as it reached out to touch more churches was a source of considerable discomfort to those whose object was reunion with Rome. It was to counter what were seen as these liberal tendencies within the wider Anglo-Catholic movement that the leaders of the Papalist Movement issued their Centenary Manifesto (dated 1 October 1932) and then wrote the Oxford Movement Centenary Tractates (published in 1933) entitled *The Church of England and the Holy See*, to both of which reference has already been made.

The manifesto, calling for reunion with Rome as the natural aim of the Oxford Movement, and also attacking liberalism among Anglo-Catholics, was signed by all the leaders of the Papalist party, and by some others less well known, such as Revd W. Dolman, the vicar of Fynes-Clinton's birthplace, Cromwell, Nottinghamshire, and Revd H. C. Butler, who had in 1930 begun a long incumbency in the tiny Suffolk village of Kettlebaston. Its publication led to a bitter internal dispute within the Anglican and Eastern Churches Association which led to Father Fynes-Clinton having to leave the organisation: his views were thought by other members to be too pro-Western for them.

It was decided to publish the Tractates at a meeting of the Church Unity Octave Council on 10 March 1932, and they were written with remarkable speed thereafter, although not appearing quite as originally planned. The first, *What Do the Celtic Churches Say?*, was written by Father Silas Harris. The second, *What Does the Anglo-Saxon Church*

Say?, and the fourth, *What Did the Church of England Say?*, were both the work of Revd J. G. Morton Howard, whose work had been entirely in the north of England: he had two spells as curate at Holy Trinity, Gains-borough, Lincolnshire, and one at St Mary, Sculcoates, Hull, before becoming successively parish priest of Huttoft, East Lincolnshire (1916–18), South Elmsall, South Yorkshire, (1918–26), the small and remote village of Wetwang in the East Riding (1926–35), SS Mary and Peter, Dairycoates, Hull (1936–9), and St Margaret, York (1939–41). He was eventually appointed to the important parish of Worksop, where he was vicar from 1941 to his retirement in 1955. He too was a prolific writer on reunion matters. The third Tractate, *What Do the General Councils Say?*, came from the pen of Revd S. Herbert Scott (sometimes known as Drane-Scott), a distinguished scholar whose work *Eastern Churches and the Papacy* was widely consulted in specialist circles, and who also wrote *Anglo-Catholicism and Reunion* (1923). He was for many years after 1915 parish priest of Oddington, Oxfordshire, and appears to have been somewhat disputatious: he certainly quarrelled bitterly with the mild-mannered American Father Pierce, whom he ignored when they met in the street, leading to long correspondence with others.[1] When he died, his old friend Father Morton Howard, after commending him and remarking upon his great love of all canines, remarked that he had 'a bitter tongue and a vitriolic pen' when roused.[2]

Spencer Jones himself wrote the fifth Tractate, *What Does the XVIth Century Say?*, and the seventh, *What Do the Tractarians Say?*, in which he argued there was no real distinction between Catholicism and Roman Catholicism. The sixth, *What Do the English Divines Say?*, was by Revd L. F. Simmons, who was a curate to Father Corbould in Carshalton. The eighth, which has already been quoted, was the work of Father Fynes-Clinton (Part I) and Father Corbould (Part II). Entitled *What Are We to Say?* it gave an unequivocal answer, namely that the Church of England should accept the claims of Rome and move towards union as soon as possible. Father Fynes-Clinton declared confidently:

We have to insist, against all the insular prejudices carefully fostered by an interested officialdom, that the Church of England has no

---

1 In the uncatalogued Rea papers in Pusey House.
2 *The Pilot*, Vol. 3, No. 1 (1949).

legitimate existence except as part of the Catholic world and therefore dependant on the Holy See.[3]

It is not clear how many copies of the Tractates were sold, although it does appear from the figures already quoted that support for the Church Unity Octave was growing. A ninth, *Modernism in Anglo-Catholicism*, also by Scott, followed soon afterwards, although not always referred to as a part of the series, but a projected second set of Tractates got no further than the first, *The First Ten Years: The Witness of the Early Tractarians*, by Silas Harris. Although historical in title, the book looks forward with considerable confidence:

In whatever direction we look the Romeward tendency predominates. The whole devotional life of those influenced by the Revival has been nurtured on Roman books and manuals from Pusey's day to our own. The devotional practices of its followers have been borrowed from the same source. The existence of retreats and missions, the revival of the religious life, all show their Roman inspiration. The ritualism which followed upon the spread of the early Tractarian message meant in effect nothing but the adoption of the ceremonial practices of the Roman Church, extending often to the minutest details of the decoration of churches and the cut of vestments. In the realm of liturgy the 'enrichment' of the jejune State rites has meant increasingly the borrowing of Roman liturgical features, until in our own day the logical end of the process has been reached by their adoption *in toto* in many places and the complete displacement on principle of the compromised Erastian forms . . . Across the whole movement stands written *Tendimus in Latium*; its followers move along a path foreordained, as though the secret counsel sounded ceaselessly in their ears *Antiquam exquirite matrem*.[4]

It was perhaps more than symbolic that although the Catholic League joined in some of the Centenary celebrations in 1933, their own major event that year was a pilgrimage to Rome in September, led by Father Fynes-Clinton, and commencing with Solemn Exposition of the Holy Shroud in Turin. They carried out the appointed exercises for the Holy

---

3 Fynes-Clinton and Corbould: *What Are We to Say?*, p. 12.
4 Harris: *The First Ten Years*, pp. 21 and 24.

Year and the leaders then met the Pope in special audience, during which they presented him with a hand-bound copy of the Tractates. On 22 January 1934 there was a meeting at the Caxton Hall under the slogan: 'Modernism the Enemy: Rome the Remedy'.

The Society for Catholic Reunion stood rather apart from the other groups at this time, although some, such as Baverstock, were members of it as well as of the Catholic League and other societies. The SCR prided itself in pressing for reunion with more urgency than the other bodies: in 1933 Revd T. Whitton, parish priest of Langenhoe, Essex, wrote to Harris of conversations he had had with the Roman Bishop of Brentwood, who had in turn spoken to the Pope himself about the aspirations of the Anglican reunionists.[5]

In 1934 the SCR itself sent a direct address to the Pope indicating how much they sought reunion, and this led to a two-day meeting between its leaders and Father Woodlock SJ of Farm Street, in which the Anglicans suggested that they be allowed to proceed to union on the basis that at any rate for public services the vernacular could be used, and communion given in both kinds, with married priests allowed as a temporary measure. Nothing came of this conference, and on the Feast of St Thomas Aquinas (7 March) 1939 the SCR sent another address to the Holy Father.

A considerable body of Papalist literature was produced during the inter-war years, especially around 1933, although the number of writers was relatively restricted. Alban Baverstock had produced *Benediction and the Bishops* in 1919, which dealt with the constant dilemma between obedience to episcopal directions and the practice of the wider Church. His conclusion was, 'We have to choose, as Pusey and our fathers in the Catholic Movement chose, between the Church and the bishops. We dare not conform to the wishes of the latter at the expense of the ends of the former.'[6]

Donald Hole wrote *The Church and 'The Church of England'* (undated, but about 1929: the quotation marks are illuminating) in which he took up the familiar theme of authority, remarking:

Today, we have to contend against the attempt to make the Church of England an independent, self-contained body, with a distinctive

---

5 In the uncatalogued Harris papers in Pusey House.
6 Baverstock: *Benediction and the Bishops*, p. 8.

teaching and worship of its own, regulated by bishops who regard themselves as absolutely independent of the rest of the Catholic movement.[7]

Baverstock and Hole then collaborated in *The Truth about the Prayer Book* (1935), asserting that the only solution to liturgical chaos was the adoption of the Roman Missal and making the relevant point in the light of the rejection of the Revised Prayer Books by Parliament that:

> The first step towards the full exercise of spiritual authority consists in severing the bonds which bind the Church of England to the State; the second lies in pressing towards the goal of the Oxford Movement – the attainment of Catholic reunion under the Primacy of the Holy See.[8]

In the meantime, Spencer Jones himself wrote *Catholic Reunion* for the Confraternity of Unity, in 1930. The familiar arguments were deployed in the work, but it included the memorable phrase: 'our differences (with Rome) are due to our separation, and not our separa-tion to our differences'.[9] The author echoed the words of Pusey, whom he had known when young, in declaring: 'Those of us who believe we are right in contemplating corporate re-union, as distinguished from indi-vidual submission, take our stand upon the principles of Tract XC.'[10] This book was sent by the Confraternity to all the bishops in the Church of England save one, it being decided that the modernist Barnes of Birmingham was beyond persuasion.[11]

That last proposition was further taken up by Father H. E. Symonds CR in his work *The Council of Trent and Anglican Formularies*, published in 1933 and written at the request of Bishop Frere: the question of whether or not the 39 Articles were capable of an interpreta-tion which accorded with the decisions on dogma made at the Council of Trent had been raised at the Malines Conversations, at which Frere had of course been present. Symonds tended to take a similar view to

---

7 Hole: *The Church and 'The Church of England'*, p. 76.
8 Baverstock and Hole: *The Truth about the Prayer Book*, p. 81.
9 Jones: *Catholic Reunion*, p. 108.
10 Ibid., p. 109.
11 Rea papers, Pusey House.

Halifax, in that he minimised the differences between Rome and Canterbury, saying that many matters of controversy:

> are largely, if not entirely, matters of discipline, rather than of doctrine. Such are the Marriage of the Clergy, the use of the Vernacular, and, as we have seen, Communion in both kinds, on all of which different usages prevail within the present Roman Catholic Communion, all three being permitted to Catholics of the oriental rites in communion with the Holy See.[12]

Symonds later wrote *The Church Universal and the See of Rome* (1939), in which he argued that to be cut off from Rome was not to be cut off from the Church: however, the papacy could again be a focus for unity.

Spencer Jones had earlier produced *The Counter-Reformation in the Church of England*, which is not dated but was written about 1920 in reply to a pamphlet from Bishop Knox of Manchester, and apart from his own writings he also wrote the foreword to *The Necessity for Catholic Reunion* by Father Whitton, published in 1933. According to Brandreth's bibliography of work on reunion, the author wrote the book to justify remaining in the Anglican Communion, but then found himself convinced to the contrary and went over to Rome. The book is interesting however as a further reflection of the view that the Anglo-Catholic Movement as a whole was riddled with liberal thought, particularly because of the influence of Gore. Whitton specifically attacked the Congress Committee in the year of the Centenary, saying that the 52 pamphlets or 'Green Books' which they had issued 'abound in heresies which would have to be renounced before their authors could be received into communion with Rome'.[13] He also took up the argument which Father Plowden-Wardlaw had propounded, namely that it might be necessary for some members only of the Church of England to leave and reunite with Rome, but thought that that might form the best platform for the conversion of England.[14] In 1933 Plowden-Wardlaw published the *Oxford Movement Centenary (Supplemental) Missal*, which provided for the commemoration of a large number of 'Beati' of the Revival from Keble to Weston, with a Unity Day in memory of Cardinal Mercier.

---

12 Symonds: *The Council of Trent and Anglican Formularies*, p. 218.
13 Whitton: *The Necessity for Catholic Reunion*, p. 106.
14 Ibid., p. 134.

Other like-minded books were: *The Bridge Church* (1930) and *The Peril of Isolation* (1937) by Father Langford-James, who was also concerned with the locally based Birmingham Reunion Society; *Loyalty to the Church of England* and *Rome the Goal of the Oxford Movement* by the 'Voice from Worcester' (W. B. Monahan, a scholar of St Thomas Aquinas who was vicar of St Swithun in that city for many years from 1902 onwards) (both undated); and *Aspects of Catholic Unity* by 'Isidor' (1938). The only reply from Rome which carried any hope for the Anglicans was the idiosyncratic *A Catholic Plea for Reunion* (1934) by 'Father Jerome' (in fact a Belgian Jesuit, Father A. J. A. Gille), which did not meet with any great support on his side of the divide, and indeed resulted in his own expulsion from the Society of Jesus.

In September 1933 the CPCU began the publication of the monthly magazine *The Pilot*, originally edited by Father Simmonds. The first issue contained the rousing cry: 'The Church of England is committed to the whole Catholic Faith. That that faith is obscured or denied or apologised for by many of her perverse or ignorant children is a commonplace.' The new magazine was in fact initially much less substantial and less scholarly than was *Reunion*.

On 17 September 1934 Father Maltby died; he was commemorated by a plaque in the porch of the church he had built, but subsequently the mission has been closed and demolished, and indeed even the street where it once stood has vanished. He was replaced as Director of the Sodality of the Precious Blood by Father Wilmot Phillips of Plaxtol, Kent. The latter is well described in the autobiography of the writer and critic Rupert Croft-Cooke, *The Altar in the Loft*, in which he says of him that he was a man 'whose strong benign character and quietly devout life influenced me greatly at this time . . . he really was a father to his little congregation, interpreting his duty as rector as that of a parish priest before the Reformation, and giving a decent working imitation of it . . . When I think of him now . . . I get a glimpse of what England might have been if she had never changed her faith, and every village parson was a Catholic priest.'[15] Father Phillips had earlier been priest of St Ethelburga, Bishopsgate in the City of London, from which he had been forced to resign in 1928 after refusing to give communion to the Protestant agitator Kensit, who had

---

15 Croft-Cooke: *The Altar in the Loft*, pp. 73 and 152.

established himself as a parishioner purely in order to create a scene in the church.

In 1936 there was a further reorganisation among the reunion Societies. The Council for Promoting Catholic Unity set up the Society for Promoting Catholic Unity (motto *Ut omnes unum sint*) which thereafter published *The Pilot*. The SPCU was responsible also for the Council of the Church Unity Octave, which was particularly appropriate since the new Society had been set up during the Octave of 1936. As has been seen, the membership of these societies is very difficult to enumerate, as they all interlinked and on occasion membership of one automatically brought with it membership of another. There is however a reference in the minutes of the Executive of the SPCU that in 1938 the circulation of *The Pilot* was about 1,000.[16] Corbould became the President of the SPCU, Fynes-Clinton the Treasurer. The Confraternity of Unity agreed to co-operate provided that it retained its own independent existence. The Society for Catholic Reunion continued outside of this structure.

In 1939 the SPCU organised a High Mass at St Augustine, Queen's Gate, to commemorate the centenary of the birth of Lord Halifax, showing that they respected his contribution to the cause of reunion. Spencer Jones preached on this occasion and his sermon was reprinted in *The Pilot* for July 1939.

There had always been contacts between these organisations and those on the Continent who were well-disposed towards them. In 1929 Harris had contributed an article in French for the Belgian *Bulletin des Missions* setting out the position of Catholics in the Church of England, and in the early 1930s there was considerable correspondence between the Confraternity of Unity and Italian, French, and Belgian priests.[17] In the mid-1930s the leaders of the Papalist party began to correspond with Abbé Paul Couturier in France: he was in touch with Jones, Fynes-Clinton, and Abbot Martin Collett of Nashdom. In 1936 Dom Benedict Ley, the novice master of Nashdom, visited Abbé Couturier in Lyons and then went to Ars and to Paray-le-Monial, the scene of the apparitions to St Margaret Marie Alacoque; four months later Fynes-Clinton himself went over to France together with Dom Gregory Dix of

---

16 These are in Lambeth Palace Library.
17 Rea papers, Pusey House.

Nashdom, and they were able to speak in French at various meetings they attended. These addresses were reported in *Revue Apologetique*. The following year Couturier returned the visit, and was met in London by Fynes-Clinton, who acted as his host throughout, with Ley, and Revd A. T. Phyall, then curate of St Andrew, Willesden Green. Fynes-Clinton asked the elderly and infirm Spencer Jones to lunch at St Ermin's, Westminster, where he lived in a service flat, and the Abbé was delighted to meet him. As a result of that meeting, Jones began writing articles in French, which were eventually gathered into a new book, *L'Eglise d'Angleterre et la Sainte-Siege: Propos sur la Reunion* (introduction in some editions by Maurice Villain), which is an entirely different work from his earlier book, although on the same lines: it was never translated into English. In addition Fynes-Clinton introduced Couturier to various other leaders of the ultramontane wing of the Church of England, including Corbould, Plowden-Wardlaw, Silas Harris, and Revd Ivan Young, parish priest of Kensworth, near Dunstable, who co-edited *The Pilot* with Dix for a time. He also went to Nashdom, and the nearby enclosed women's community of the Servants of Christ at Burnham. Couturier came again to England in 1938, and on this occasion broadened his contacts to those who were not wholly committed to the Roman cause: he visited Nashdom again, and also the Benedictine nuns at West Malling, but he also went to Mirfield, Kelham, Cowley, and Wantage, to see more moderate communities. Father Curtis CR, when he later wrote Couturier's biography, attributed to his visit an awakening of the need for Christian unity among the Community of the Resurrection. Curtis also took Couturier to York, where he met Archbishop Temple.

These contacts appear retrospectively to be tentative and marginal to the life of both churches, but the situation at the time was such that they were very significant. Couturier thereafter understood the inner workings of the Anglican Communion more than almost any other continental Roman Catholic, although he appears to have over-emphasised the importance of Fynes-Clinton's associates. The effect internally was that, under Couturier's influence, on 3 November 1939 the superiors of the seven largest religious communities for men launched an attempt to broaden the appeal of the call to Christian unity, by moving to January the prayers which had been held in the Novena before Whitsunday, and renaming that devotion as the Week of Universal Prayer: Brandreth became the secretary of the committee promoting the Week. This development was not welcomed by Fynes-Clinton and his group, and Dix resigned from the Council of the Church Unity Octave when it refused to back the new initiative. In due course he and Young were in any event replaced as editors of *The Pilot* by Hole. This resentment did not end at that time, and in December 1945 Fynes-Clinton wrote an open letter to Father Biggart CR complaining that the Octave was being superseded by the Week.

The political divide among Anglo-Catholics has already been remarked upon. The outbreak of the Spanish Civil War in 1936 excited much feeling on all sides, but particularly among Roman Catholics in England, who observed that the Republicans were strongly and often brutally anti-clerical. Adrian Hastings, in his magisterial *A History of English Christianity 1920–1990*, says: 'Probably at no other moment in twentieth century history has the English Catholic Community taken up so strongly a political position and to such effect.'[18]

It was perhaps inevitable that the Anglican Papalists should follow the same course. On 17 November 1936 Fynes-Clinton, Corbould, Collett, and the Duke of Argyll jointly signed a letter sent to the Roman Catholic newspapers which expressed views contrary to those which had recently appeared in the *Church Times*. The letter was in unequivocal terms:

> We believe that we represent the feelings of countless English Church people, especially the Catholic-minded clergy and laity, of shame for the sympathy being shown with the Red enemies of the Church, for the suppression of facts and of admiration for the faithful and splendid stand that is being taken by His Holiness the Pope and the Roman Catholic Church against the common enemy of civilisation and Christendom.[19]

Those opinions were mirrored by a number of articles which appeared in *Reunion* at this time: in March 1938 the reviewer of a new book on Spain asserted that it demonstrated that the burning of the Basque town of Guernica was the work of retreating members of the Republican forces, and commented, 'The truth about Spain has been determinedly hindered from reaching public opinion in Great Britain.'[20]

---

18 Hastings: *A History of English Christianity 1920–1990*, p. 325.
19 Quoted in Doolan: *The First Fifty Years*, pp. 22–3.
20 *Reunion*, Vol. 3, No. 16 (1938).

It is perhaps understandable that doubt was thrown on what had occurred at Guernica, because at that time the full facts were obfuscated by propaganda on both sides. However, by the time that the Second World War broke out there was little sympathy in England for Franco, because his pro-German feelings were by then well known. However, in June 1940 Spencer Jones wrote an article entitled 'General Franco and what brought him to the front'; this was continued in December of that year by further praise of Franco and laudatory remarks about Salazar in Portugal. Jones referred to Franco as 'the Saviour of his country'.[21]

It must be remembered that by this time Father Jones was a very old man, although in 1928 he had written a laudatory book on Mussolini and the Fascist Movement in Italy, referring to Il Duce's 'powerful intellect' (not observed by many other commentators) and also to his convictions which stamped 'his enterprise with a unity of direction which render[ed] it well nigh irresistible'.[22] Jones' attitude and that of some of his associates to the collaborationist regime in France was also somewhat ambivalent, and it is remarkable not only that his book in French had run into its third edition by 1941, but that it should be republished that year in Paris.

This tendency is even more apparent in the thought of Hugh Ross Williamson (1901–78). He was a well-known historian and writer, whose father was a Nonconformist minister. Although he first attended High Mass as early as 1918 (at St Michael, Brighton) it was a very long time before he decided to be ordained: indeed he was not confirmed until 1940 and then went straight on to ordination in 1943. He had at one stage attended both Roman and Anglican churches while formally a member of neither body, but his marriage precluded any question of ordination in the Roman priesthood. In any event, he had decided that 'England would only return to the Faith through the instrumentality of the Church of England. The Catholicization of it from the inside was the first step towards the reunion of Christendom. And that reunion, after all, was the only world issue of the slightest importance . . . I decided to become, not, indeed an Anglican parson but a Catholic priest in the Church of England . . . it should be possible to preach the Faith within [that Church] and ultimately win from the Erastian element and the

---

21 Ibid., Vol. 3, No. 24 (1940).
22 Jones: *Benito Mussolini*, p. 117.

pseudo-Nonconformists sufficient Catholic converts to make the Establishment itself seek reconciliation with the Holy See.'[23]

At the outbreak of the Second World War Ross Williamson was of course still a layman. He refused to be conscripted on the grounds that it was not a just war, and succeeded in that contention on appeal, an appeal which was academic in any event since he was medically unfit for service. His views on the conflict were, however, unusual, to say the least, particularly from a man who until shortly before that time had been a parliamentary candidate for the Labour party. It appears that he simply ignored the Nazi atrocities, an extreme example of the lack of perspective which was quite frequently found among the ultra-montanes.

In his autobiography, *The Walled Garden*, written in 1956 when the truth about the nature of the wartime French regime was well known, Ross Williamson was unrepentant. He thought that atheism, as represented by the Revolution in France, was a direct consequence of the work of the Protestant reformers, and was clear in his approbation of the reaction to it:

> The French repudiation of the Revolution was to be Petain and Vichy – a regime inaugurated by a performance of the greatest Christian play of the century, Claudel's *L'Annonce faite à Marie*, with a new prologue written by the author for the occasion. On the other hand, the mainspring of the 'Resistance', once the convenient coating of 'patriotism' had worn off, was in the very spirit of Carrier and Marat. This antithesis was to lead me to question, when the term 'Crusade' became applied to the struggle of atheist Russia, Protestant England, Mammon-worshipping America and Jewish capital against what was left of Catholic Christendom, which side represented the Crusaders.[24]

It is perhaps not surprising that the expression of views of that nature did nothing to enhance the standing of the Papalist group within the Church of England. Further, support for the right in Spain alienated completely that considerable body of Anglo-Catholics who were Socialist in out-

---

23 Ross Williamson: *The Walled Garden*, pp. 109 and 112.
24 Ibid., p. 111.

look.[25] It is only fair, however, to point out that at a Caxton Hall meeting in 1942 Revd J. H. C. Twisaday, another well-known Papalist, called not only for reunion but also for decent wages for the working man in accordance with Papal social teaching, which he coupled with a relatively unusual plea to support 'the fight against birth control'.

Following Spencer Jones' death, the Presidency of the Church Unity Octave Council was taken over by Bishop Vibert Jackson, a veteran Anglo-Catholic who had originally run a mission in a tough area of Newcastle: later he became Bishop of the Windward Islands, and on his return to England was parish priest of All Souls, South Ascot, for many years. In 1942 he wrote *Christian Unity*, which was a further defence of the Papalist position. It was at this time too that Donald Hole published his pamphlet *Anglican Papalists*, to which reference has already been made. It was one of a series of tractates published by the CPCU or the SPCU, of which others included *Epistola ad Romanos* by Morton Howard, and a reissue of *Modernism in Anglo-Catholicism* by Scott. Hole was also writing much of *The Pilot* at this time. In 1940 also Catholic Reunion Photographs were advertised, showing the Pope and the Archbishop of Canterbury on the same card.

During the Second World War a new crisis occurred for Anglican Papalists, which would no doubt have created even more of a furore had it not been for the overwhelming impact of external events. Indeed, some thought it unseemly that so much opposition was put up to the plans for a united Church of South India, published in 1943, when there were so many more pressing concerns.

The religious communities for men, who were not usually overactive in ecclesiastical politics, were at the forefront of the opposition to the South India proposals. They perceived that the CSI was a stalking horse for a pan-Protestant Federation in England, with the Church of England turning away from Rome. They were of course much criticised for this, but on the other hand time was to tell that they were absolutely correct: the CSI was indeed the prototype for the later Anglican–Methodist unity scheme. It was only because the scheme related to far-off provinces of

25 Those on the left were equally blinkered. In his autobiography, written as late as 1977, Revd Jack Putterill, Father Noel's son-in-law and successor at Thaxted, wrote that some in Czechoslovakia had required the 'help of the USSR' to overcome the dangers of 'a return to the old ways', a commentary on the Prague Spring of almost unequalled crassness: see Putterill: *Thaxted Quest for Social Justice*, p. 97.

the Anglican Communion that the opposition was not more wide-spread.

The superiors of the main communities (not the Society of the Sacred Mission at Kelham) issued an *Open Letter* to the Archbishop of Canterbury in which the threat of secession was more than implicit. They were instrumental in 1942 in the formation of yet another new group, the Council for the Defence of Church Principles, under the chairmanship of Father W. J. O'Brien SSJE, which began a campaign of propaganda and meetings. It would be wrong, however, to say that this was an abstract issue devoid of meaning for all but a few fanatics. The later Archbishop Trevor Huddleston CR had serious doubts about the Church of England over the South India issue, and no less a luminary than T. S. Eliot wrote a forceful attack on the proposals, published as *Reunion by Destruction* in 1943. Eliot's considerable influence in Anglo-Catholic thinking has been understated by his biographers, who do not appear fully to understand the various groupings in the Church of England. He was followed by Revd T. G. Jalland, later a professor at Exeter University, who published *The Bible, The Church and South India* in 1944.

When Geoffrey Fisher was appointed as Archbishop of Canterbury in 1945 following the unexpected death of Temple, he was faced with the real possibility of a schism over South India. Fisher had no sympathy with or real understanding of the Catholic Movement, and even less with those who sought a closer accommodation with Rome. His experience in teaching had left him with no experience of or feel for parish life, and his strong interest in Freemasonry made him even less acceptable to Anglican Papalists.

Fisher had come to the conclusion immediately upon arriving at Lambeth that his first priority was to restore liturgical order and discipline to the life of the Church. His own words were revealing: he said, 'Because I had been a headmaster I knew that [coping with this] was absolutely essential for the well-ordering of the Church of England. The lack of order had been quite dreadful.'[26] It was this emphasis on order which led him to regard the prolonged revision of canon law as the supreme achievement of his archiepiscopate. He was in fact too narrow-minded and too arrogant to be a success at Canterbury.

---

26 Carpenter: *Archbishop Fisher*, p. 205.

Despite these serious temperamental deficiencies however, Fisher handled the South India issue with considerable diplomatic skill. In May 1945 he said that the new church would not be in communion with the Church of England, and this defused the opposition. In effect, Fisher was proposing a trial period, during which episcopal ordination would become the norm in South India, and that enabled both sides to consider that they had been at least partly satisfied by what occurred. On 27 September 1947 the Church of South India was formally inaugurated, and although there were formal protests from the Catholic League and other such bodies there were no mass defections to Rome. In 1943 Hole had seriously foreseen a substantial secession to form a Uniate Church if the CSI came into being.[27]

It is often said that the 1933 Centenary celebrations marked the high-water mark of the Anglo-Catholic Movement in England. However, it may be more appropriate to consider that the movement traversed a plateau between then and 1939, which was followed after the war by rapid decline at a parochial level, although conversely the episcopate, which represented in the 1950s those ordained in the 1930s, became more Catholic in outlook. The war destroyed many strongholds of the Catholic Movement in cities, and afterwards there was a dispersal of population from the inner cities where those churches had stood. Although the Church of England enjoyed a modest but real revival in numbers from 1945 to about 1960, that revival was not reflected in a growth in Couturier's groups 4 and 5. The new source of energy in the Church was a watered-down version of Catholicism centred upon the Parish Communion, the Church of England's own liturgical movement, which enabled those of all persuasions within the Church save at either extremity to accept a common form of worship. This occurred particularly in the country, where livings were amalgamated and the separate tradition which had grown up over the previous half-century or so was abandoned. There are many country churches which bear the signs of an Anglo-Catholic incumbent in the 1930s in the form of some shrines and sometimes six candlesticks on the altar, but where the liturgy has levelled down to that of the next village, where in turn Matins has been abandoned in favour of Parish Communion.

The only post-war Anglo-Catholic Congress, in 1948, was reasonably

27 *The Pilot*, August 1943.

successful but although the churches were full for the celebrations it appears not to have created the enthusiasm which had characterised the earlier meetings. No more were held, although the Church Union held some Eucharistic Congresses from 1958 onwards, and much later attempts to revive the spirit of the Congresses in more modern form for the 150th Anniversary of Keble's 1833 sermon met with very limited response.

There was still a market for publications of a Papalist nature, although they were fewer in number than before, and paper was of course scarce for some time. The Dacre Press in Westminster was prominent in the immediate post-war period (see Chapter 6) as was the Coelian Press in Hove. The latter was run by Revd H. Hamilton Maughan, who was the author in earlier years of an extraordinarily partisan book entitled *Some Brighton Churches* (1922), which describes the English Use as having 'grotesque eccentricities'.[28] He has been aptly described as 'a caricature of extreme Anglo-Catholicism in the first three decades of the century'.[29] Other pamphlets published by the Press at this time were a series by an anonymous author calling himself 'Vindex': these included *General Disorder or the Establishment at the Cross Roads, Stunt Religion, An Open Letter to a Bishop* (protesting at a proposed Chapel of Unity), and *Why the Movement Does Not Move*. A savage attack on the Life and Liberty Movement and the apparatus of representative church government it had promoted was entitled *Death and Bondage, or the Liberty of Bureaucracy*. However, established authors also wrote for the Press, and they produced *The Conspiracy to Unchurch the Church of England*, by Alban Baverstock, and *Reverence*, by Joblin. The Press also sent out *The Ordination of Women* by Canon C. E. Whiting and *The Nonconformist Witness* by Revd Gilbert Pawson, both of which took a predictable line upon their subject matter.

Maughan moved from England and in 1947 established himself in the unlikely surroundings of Loughlinstown, County Dublin, from where he attempted to raise money to decorate a chapel in a Counter-Reformation style which was, as he accepted, alien to the staunchly anti-ritualistic Church of Ireland.[30] He continued to publish however, in

28 Maughan: *Some Brighton Churches*, p. v.
29 By J. Pinnington, in Leech and Williams: *Essays Catholic and Radical*, p. 112.
30 Rea papers, Pusey House.

1948 producing his own work *Seven Churches* followed the next year by *Wagner of Brighton* and in 1953 by *Anglican Circus*. The chapel was in due course decorated and was dedicated to St Gregory: in 1958 Maughan celebrated his sacerdotal Jubilee there.

The Catholic League and its associated organisations continued after the war in much the same way as before, and in 1950 they celebrated the Holy Year with a pilgrimage to Rome by Fathers Fynes-Clinton and Ivan Young, accompanied by Mr L. G. Fisher, the long-serving Secretary of the League. The two priests were received in private audience by Pope Pius XII, who blessed the work of the Council for the Church Unity Octave. It is not clear how influential visits such as this were in Rome: it is however apparent that in that year, when the summit of the ecclesiastical illiberalism which Fynes-Clinton so admired was attained in Rome, there were few other contacts with the Church of England. In 1954 Fynes-Clinton was given a primary relic of St Theresa of Lisieux by the Mother Prioress of the Carmelites in the town, who kept the Octave every year and with whom he had been in correspondence for many years.

However, death had begun to remove from the scene many of the prominent members of the Papalist party, and they were not adequately replaced. Jones had of course died in 1943, and he was followed by others. Hole died in 1947; he had married, and his daughter reported that he had received the last sacraments 'in Latin as he would have wished'.[31] Revd G. S. Dunbar, another supporter, also died in 1947: like Hole, he was married and also like him was Chaplain to a Home (in his case St Mary's, Chiswick) for many years. Langford-James died in 1948, and Alban Baverstock in 1950. The latter had been acting as editor of *The Pilot* since 1947, taking over when Hole became ill, and had also become President of the SPCU.

It seems clear that there was a lack of impetus behind the movement for union with Rome in the 1950–60 period. After the South India controversy, Anglo-Catholicism was constantly on the back foot, responding to initiatives from others with which its adherents disagreed, but not setting forward a programme which looked ahead. As has been mentioned, *Reunion* actually ceased publication for a number of years until revived for a time in 1957, still under the editorship of Rea. *The*

---

31 *The Pilot*, September 1947.

Pilot was reduced to a quarterly in June 1947, although more substantial in form than previously, and from 1949 it incorporated *The Bond of Peace*, which had been the journal of the SCR. The latter group finally became a constituent society of the CPCU in 1948.

At the beginning of the decade, yet another new organisation arose. The Annunciation Group was formed in 1951, originally to protest at joint services with Nonconformists being held by Fisher and Wand (the then Bishop of London) as part of the Festival of Britain, but later to uphold more generally Catholic teaching in the Church of England. It took its name from the Church of the Annunciation, Bryanston Street, near Marble Arch, and was the creation of the vicar, Revd W. G. Bennett. Father Bennett was a good and pious man who generally kept himself out of church politics, although his church was a stronghold of the most ultramontane teaching and practice. Father Ross Williamson was the preacher at the inaugural meeting to a church crammed with people: almost immediately 2,000 signed the manifesto pledging not to take part in united services, and the Group thereafter settled down to a membership of about 1,500.

Fynes-Clinton himself was on the Committee of the Group, as was Ivan Young. It may be that the former was by that time less concerned to keep control of organisations, and as he grew older he began to relinquish some positions. He resigned as director of the Sodality in 1953 in favour of Joblin, as director of the Apostleship of Prayer in 1955 in favour of Revd Peter Sanderson of Poundstock, Cornwall, and as chairman of the Church Unity Octave Council in January 1958 in favour of Revd Mervyn Pendleton of Wollaston, Northamptonshire.

The Annunciation Group returned to prominence in 1955 when the probationary period provided for the Church of South India came to an end. By this time, a combination of the lapse of time and of the existence of an episcopate within the new church had taken the sting out of the opposition to it. In July 1955 the Church of England officially recognised the Church of South India. Many Anglo-Catholics refused to accept that the CSI was indeed in communion with the Church of England, and placed on the doors of their churches notices to the effect that it was not possible to admit to communion any member of the Church of South India. The practical consequences of that action were of course limited and it made the protesters look petty-minded: Father Bennett, who put up such a notice on the door of his church, at least looked back on it in later years with a certain amusement. In due course the Group was absorbed into the Church Union.

However, there was a small minority who thought that the recognition of the CSI was a step too far. These included Ross Williamson and Revd W. W. T. Hannah, the secretary of the Annunciation Group and at that time an honorary assistant priest at St Augustine, Queen's Gate, who had written to *The Tablet* under the pseudonym Pastor Anglicanus criticising his own church. That small minority went over to Rome, but the vast majority stayed within the Anglican Communion. On 5 February 1956 Father Pierce, by then a convert for many years, wrote to Silas Harris that Father Walton Hannah himself had told him that only seven priests seceded at that time.[32] Shortly before these events Ross Williamson had written *The Great Prayer*, a book on the Roman canon, which he then saw as a focus for union: he dedicated it to Father Bennett. In their aftermath he wrote his autobiography, which has already been quoted, and which is full of rancour against the Church of England. He referred with approval to his own statement made on 6 July 1955 that:

> The body which still calls itself the Church of England is, in fact, only the English branch of the undenominational Church of South India.[33]

Ross Williamson was initially happy in the Roman Church in which, of course, being married he could function only as a layman. However, he was one of those most disturbed by the earthquake which was soon to convulse the whole life of the Church, and he was later to be found doubting whether the new liturgy was properly called a mass at all.

Rea on the other hand had by this time become a canon of the cathedral at Bury St Edmunds. He had come to the conclusion that the arrangements for the Church of South India were by then reasonably satisfactory, and wrote a tract, *The Church of South India and the Church*, to demonstrate this. That led to a furious protest from Silas Harris, who in consequence of the line Rea had taken resigned from the Confraternity of Unity.[34] In 1957 Rea sent to Pope Pius XII a copy of his book, and in the following year he became the first Anglican priest to

---

32 Harris papers, Pusey House.
33 Ross Williamson: *The Walled Garden*, p. 227.
34 Rea papers, Pusey House.

visit the newly enthroned Pope John XXIII. He assured the Pope of the desire of the various societies with which he was concerned for reunion, and was given for his own use the personal breviary which John XXIII had been using: this is now in the Library of Lambeth Palace.

In 1958 an effort was made to establish a new newspaper to represent the Anglo-Catholic point of view. *The Dome* first appeared in January of that year, but ceased publication in July 1959: the editor, Father Davis of St Francis, Oxhey, Hertfordshire, went over to Rome at about the same time. In 1960 the Catholic League began a monthly newsletter entitled *Crux*, but that too ceased in due course. A later publication, *The Catholic Standard*, produced in the 1960s and 1970s under the auspices of the SSC, was more successful, but ultimately it too failed.

On 12 February 1958 there was a meeting of all the reunion organisations except the SCR, under the chairmanship of Revd N. P. Sturt of Holy Cross, Cromer Street, St Pancras, another long-time supporter and an exemplar of the emotionally restrained style of some priests, which invited respect rather than affection, but repelled some. It was decided that the Council for the Promotion of Catholic Unity should be dissolved but that both the SPCU and the Confraternity of Unity should continue in being as separate organisations, and should co-operate as much as possible. However, that decision was rescinded the following year and the Council was reconstituted in 1959 with two members each from the Catholic League, the Confraternity of Unity, and the Church Unity Octave Committee, and one from the Society for Catholic Reunion, although Father Harwood, who was then running the SCR, himself accepted it was effectively moribund and had not met for some years. By this time the Church Unity Octave, with its uncompromisingly Papalist position, was being overtaken by the much more widely based Week of Prayer for Christian Unity. The annual Call to Prayer for Unity, which was issued to coincide with the Octave, was made for the last time in 1964. *The Pilot*, which had been edited for most of the post-Second World War period by Revd James Hutton of English Bicknor, Herefordshire, ceased publication in 1962. It had become duller as the years went by, and was enlivened only by oddities such as contributions from Revd Ronald Baron, who was a mission priest in Argentina and later Professor of English at the University of Tucuman in that country. The last few editions were enlivened by the outpourings of Father Hamilton Maughan, entitled 'Rites and Usages', in which he fulminated against the practice of not wearing a biretta and regretted the decline of lace on albs and cottas.

By the end of the 1950s most of the remaining leaders of the Papalists had died: Corbould in 1957, Hope Patten in 1958 and Fynes-Clinton himself on 4 December 1959. His requiem was, appropriately, on the Feast of the Immaculate Conception of Our Lady, four days after his decease.

Father Corbould had been vicar of All Saints, Carshalton, since 1919. In later years his congregation had sadly diminished and the Bishop of Southwark, Mervyn Stockwood, was anxious to rid his diocese of the enclave of pro-Roman teaching which was represented by that church and its daughter churches of the Good Shepherd and of St Andrew. A new vicar was appointed (who as it happened remained there for over 40 years), and the Good Shepherd, Carshalton Beeches, became in due course a separate parish. The priest in charge of the small mission church of St Andrew, Wrythe Lane, was Revd R. A. E. Harris, an elderly Papalist whose views were so uncompromising that he had never held a living of his own. He took up his first curacy, at Castleford in Yorkshire, in 1914, but was sacked in 1916 for his expressions of devotion to Our Lady. He then assisted at Holy Trinity, Reading, and followed Revd Elton Lury from that church to St Peter, Limehouse, before moving to Liverpool, where he worked for some years without stipend assisting the veteran Revd Ernest Underhill without pay in the parish of St Thomas, Toxteth, which was under episcopal discipline. He then spent many years at Carshalton. In August 1959 Father Harris refused to obey the request of his new rector to abandon using the Roman liturgy, and told the Bishop that he would have to suffer the fate of a martyr for what he believed to be the Catholic Church. He eventually tendered his resignation, but then attempted to withdraw the resignation: Stockwood refused to allow him to do so and there was a bitter public slanging match which ended with the closure of the church. Stockwood said that he was placed in an impossible position because he was 'dealing with an inflexible bigot'.[35] Father Harris was indeed treated as a martyr by some and appeared in extreme old age at Anglo-Catholic functions as a sort of successor to Father Tooth. He died on 12 October 1972, an unrepentant survivor of an earlier age.

---

35 Stockwood: *Chanctonbury Ring*, pp. 103–4.

It is ironic that in 1960, the year after Fynes-Clinton's death, Pope John and Archbishop Fisher finally met face to face. The propaganda of the reunion societies had probably had more effect on the former than the latter, as it was reported that he knew all about the revival of the Walsingham pilgrimage, an interest which Fisher did not share.

Events beyond 1960 are strictly outside the scope of this book, but must be reviewed shortly in order to place in perspective what had gone before.

Fisher's successor Michael Ramsey met the Pope in 1966, and was received more warmly still. In 1970 Pope Paul VI said at the canonisation of the Forty Martyrs of England and Wales: 'There will be no seeking to lessen the legitimate prestige and usage proper to the Anglican church when the Roman church . . . is able to embrace firmly her ever-loved sister in the authentic communion of the family of Christ.'[36] Then in 1982 Pope John Paul II came to England and was received by Archbishop Runcie at Canterbury.

Those events would have seemed inconceivable to those who had laboured so long and in such a barren field for reunion between Rome and Canterbury. The two churches have never appeared closer than at the time of the Papal visit in 1982, but the leadership on the Anglican side made no use of the opportunities which were available in that twenty-year period after Vatican II. There was a lack of vision and of willingness to take bold steps and a constant retreat into the ingrained committee structure of the Church of England.

It was also the case that by the time these doors appeared to be opening, Anglo-Catholicism was a very much weakened force in the Church. The changes in outlook in Rome had left it drifting rudderless: some adopted the new ways enthusiastically, although they ran contrary in many respects to that which they had been teaching for many years. Others, fearful of change, clung to traditional teaching which now resembled only obsolete Roman models. Still more were drawn along by the advance of the Parish Communion movement, which frequently combined some externals of Catholic worship with a wishy-washy theology overlain with glutinous sentimentality.

It is far too early to tell what effect the decision to ordain women will have on the future of ecumenical relations with Rome. The decision to

---

36 As quoted in Welsby: *A History of the Church of England 1945–1980*, p. 181.

go ahead was made either in ignorance of the effect that it might have, or with a view that the unity of the Church was unimportant. Ironically, the decision not only precipitated the most substantial body of secessions to Rome since the Reformation, including of course many of those who had previously been involved in the reunion societies, but also appears to have galvanised Anglo-Catholics by providing a focal point upon which they can all agree. Forward in Faith seems at the time of writing to have been the most successful of many attempts to bring together the successors of the Oxford Movement.

4

THE REVISION OF THE PRAYER BOOK AND THE UNPOPULARITY OF ANGLICAN PAPALISM

The Revision of the Book of Common Prayer of 1662 was a prolonged process, and one which ended in utter humiliation for the episcopate of the Church of England.

The events which led to the House of Commons rejecting the proposed revisions in 1927 and the re-revisions in 1928 are normally portrayed as resulting from the inherent Protestant feeling of the wider population, and to some extent they were. On the other hand, the role of the Anglo-Catholic opposition to the book, and particularly the opposition of the Papalist wing, has been largely neglected and misunderstood. In fact, the two furthest wings of the Church of England had a common cause in opposing the attempts to revise the Book.

It is important to appreciate the conditions in which Anglo-Catholicism had grown. There was in the nineteenth century widespread opposition to even the most minor of changes in ritual and there is no doubt that outside of those who were attracted to the cause, the Oxford Movement and its successors were deeply unpopular. The Public Worship Regulation Act of 1874 was an extremely well-received piece of legislation when it was placed on the statute book, because the vast majority of the people thought that it would halt the drift to Rome within the Established Church. However, like many ill-thought-out statutes, its effect in practice was the opposite of that intended. It resulted in the locking up of devoted priests who might be thought wrong-headed but were certainly not criminals. By the end of the century it was clear that the Act was a dead letter.

On the other hand, it was equally clear that although there had been considerable advances in ceremonial by 1900, these remained controversial and unattractive to many and there was strong pressure for 'discipline' within the Church from many quarters.

It was against this background that the Royal Commission on Ecclesiastical Discipline reported in 1906. The major conclusion of the Commission was that 'the law of public worship in the Church of England is too narrow for the religious life of the present generation'. They meant by that that the Book of Common Prayer should be revised so as to give effect to the acceptable face of Anglo-Catholicism, particularly the higher standards of decorum which had gradually come about in the latter half of the nineteenth century, but should not countenance the use of Roman practices. In other words, it was sought to redefine what was acceptable in the light of what was then liturgical practice, but, crucially, then to enforce strictly the new limits. Gregory Dix wrote later, but with his usual insight, that the new Book 'was intended as a *ne plus ultra*, the extreme limit of innovation, the Prayer Book of King Canute'.[1]

There were serious inherent problems with the whole process of Revision. The first and most obvious was the length of time that it took. The matter was put in train after the report of the Commission in 1906, but it was 1927 before the Book was put before the House of Commons. In the interim, the Anglo-Catholic Movement had moved forward very considerably, and, for example, by the latter date there were many churches with Reservation of the Blessed Sacrament, whereas in 1906 there were few. Fowler, the Secretary of the Protestant Alliance, claimed in early 1927 that there was Perpetual Reservation in 144 London churches and 410 provincial.[2] The Royal Commission had said that in 1906 there were only two churches in London where the Sacrament was openly reserved (as opposed to being in a chapel to which public access was restricted), these being St Cuthbert, Philbeach Gardens, and St Columba, Haggerston.

The second inherent problem was the fact that nothing of any consequence was done in order to reform the antiquated disciplinary machinery of the Church: if therefore the new Book had in fact been approved by the House of Commons the bishops would still have had to consider how to enforce its use. One of the most potent arguments used

---

1 Dix: *The Shape of the Liturgy*, pp. 707–8.
2 *Daily Sketch*, 11 February 1927, quoted in *The Month*, Vol. 149, p. 344.

by the Protestant side was that the bishops would not properly discipline those who broke any new liturgical regime.

The third serious deficiency in the case for revision was that those who thought there should be change could not agree on what change was desirable, and perhaps more importantly, whether or not the changes should provide for a permissive alternative to the 1662 Book, or a mandatory replacement. There were many Anglo-Catholics who, like Lord Halifax, would have been happy with the permissive use of the Book of 1549, an easy and convenient solution which would on the other hand not have satisfied those who wanted nothing more than to stifle the apparently irresistible growth of Anglo-Catholicism by closer policing of the form of services.

The consequence of the use of a Prayer Book which was widely seen as in need of revision, while at the same time there was an obsolete and discredited system of regulation of liturgical life, was that there was a vacuum into which the Anglo-Catholic party was able to advance. This process was particularly marked in the Diocese of London, under the long and in many ways benign episcopate of A. F. Winnington-Ingram (1901–39). He was a moderate Anglo-Catholic by inclination, but primarily a benevolent man who usually thought the best of those with whom he had dealings, a trait which the unscrupulous were able to exploit to their own considerable advantage. He allowed many to hold office in his diocese who should never have been permitted so to do: some examples are shown in Chapter 10.

The rejection of the Prayer Book Revisions made the position of those Anglo-Catholics who refused to use the Book of 1662, or refused to use it unaltered, much stronger. Since the bishops accepted that the 1662 book was inadequate and for that reason had attempted to revise it, they could hardly complain if others sought to supplement it. Use of the Roman Missal on the other hand was never officially condoned, and no bishop would authorise the rite of Benediction of the Blessed Sacrament. It was this last devotion more than any other which caused conflict between Anglican Papalists and the episcopate in the inter-war period: it is a devotion now rarely practised, but more frequently found at that time partly because of the intensity of focus of eucharistic worship but also for the practical reason that the fasting regulations meant that there could not be masses in the evenings. It also divided Anglo-Catholics: those who favoured the English Use did not on the whole adopt the practice, which they regarded as redolent of the Counter-Reformation. D. L. Murray, writing a pamphlet for the Alcuin Club on Prayer Book Revision in 1923 entitled *Reservation: Its Purpose and Method*, wrote: 'For the altar tabernacle there is nothing to be said, except by those who promote the cult we deprecate. It is not sanctioned by our traditions or by our existing rubrics, and is fitted to no style but the baroque.'[3] Conrad Noel was as usual an exception to this generalisation and held outdoor processions of the Host on Corpus Christi Day.

Those offering sage counsel saw from the very start the dangers which were inherent in the whole process of Revision. The Royal Commission had condemned ten practices, namely:

1 The interpolation of the prayers and ceremonies of the Roman Canon;
2 The use of the words 'Behold the Lamb of God' with the exhibition of the consecrated wafer;
3 Reservation of the Blessed Sacrament leading to adoration;
4 The mass of the presanctified on Good Friday;
5 Corpus Christi processions with the sacrament;
6 Benediction;
7 Celebrations of the eucharist with a view to only the celebrant communicating;
8 Hymns, and prayers involving invocations to the saints;
9 The observances of festivals of the Assumption and of the Sacred Heart;
10 The veneration of images.

As early as 21 November 1906 Father Darwell Stone, the librarian of Pusey House, said to a meeting of the Church Union that 'to revise the Book of Common Prayer along the principles that are involved in ... the Report of the Commission would be to court the gravest disaster that could befall the English Church'.[4]

In August 1911 Lord Halifax called a conference at Hickleton of many prominent Anglo-Catholics including Stone, Father Howell of St Mary, Bourne Street, H. W. Hill, and Athelstan Riley. The object of the meeting was to consider the whole question of Revision, but in fact the

---

3 Murray: *Reservation: Its Purpose and Method*, p. 33.
4 Cross: *Darwell Stone*, p. 84.

primary purpose of the conference was overtaken by the ultimately vain attempt to keep the Caldey Benedictines within the Church of England. However, a report edited by Riley was produced by the Alcuin Club and set out what was said to be the 'irreducible minimum' in relation to Revision. Those present at the Hickleton Conference pledged themselves to resist, and to refuse to employ, any revised form of the Book of Common Prayer which:

1 Relaxed the existing directions of the Ornaments Rubric;
2 Altered the substance or use of the Athanasian Creed;
3 Sanctioned the giving of Communion to those not confirmed;
4 Failed to restore a 'better and more primitive' order for the administration of Communion, including (a) the linking together of the Preface and Sanctus, the existing Prayer of Consecration and Prayer of Oblation and the Lord's Prayer and (b) the placing of the Exhortation, Confession, Absolution and Comfortable Words 'in their proper place' after the Communion of the Priest;
5 Sanctioned the postponement of Baptism beyond the time appointed in the existing Book;
6 Failed to provide for unction of the sick;
7 Interfered with or failed to recognise continuous Reservation;
8 Failed to direct prayers for the dead.[5]

It is clear that even at that early stage in the process the Catholic wing of the Church of England was unhappy both about matters contained in the 1662 Book which might be removed and also about matters not contained in that Book which might become the subject of regulation. The crucial point was actually that of Reservation of the Blessed Sacrament, which one wing of the Church sought to defend at all costs, and another to prevent in any circumstances. Between those two extremes the bishops wanted to regulate Reservation so that the Sacrament was available for the sick but was not used for extra-liturgical adoration. Since the 1662 Book did not directly refer to the practice at all, it afforded more freedom to those who wished to encourage Benediction and other such devotions than would have done new regulations which purported to lay down the conditions under which the Sacrament could be kept in

5 Riley: *Prayer Book Revision.*

churches. It was not an issue which could readily be avoided if there was to be a revision of the liturgy, since as time passed after the initial decision to proceed with the process it became the most pressing debating point of the time, and excited the most extreme emotions on both sides. Raymond Raynes, later to be Superior of the Community of the Resurrection, said, while still a secular priest in Bury, Lancashire, that if the Blessed Sacrament were exposed on every altar then England would be converted.[6]

As already noted, it was the threat to the practice of Reservation which brought about the formation of the Federation of Catholic Priests in 1917. The Papalist party went even further in their opposition. Alban Baverstock in his book *Benediction and the Bishops* written in 1919 wrote:

> If we are told that it is contrary to all Catholic practice for a priest to refuse obedience to his Bishop in a matter which throughout the church admittedly rests with the Bishop, namely the regulation of services and ceremonies, we can only retort that for the bishops of two provinces of the Church to set themselves for successive generations in opposition to the piety which seeks the honour of our Lord in the Blessed Sacrament is unprecedented in the history of Catholic Christendom, and that where bishops set themselves to defeat objects the importance of which has been recognized from the earliest days of the Church, unquestioning obedience becomes a disaster and disobedience often a duty.[7]

In the same book he set out the positive position as he saw it, namely:

> The Canon Law of Western Christendom, promulgated in these provinces, never repealed and therefore still binding, not only requires the Blessed Sacrament to be reserved in every parish church, but requires it to be reserved under one kind only.[8]

A similar position was taken by Father Silas Harris in 1936, when he said in a pamphlet issued by the Society for Catholic Reunion:

---

6 Mosley: *The Life of Raymond Raynes*, p. 43.
7 Baverstock: *Benediction and the Bishops*, p. 8.
8 Ibid., p. 50.

The authority for Reservation in a parish church is the common law of the whole church. It is not within the competence of any lesser or local authority to interfere with the requirement of this universal canon law, which applies to all parishes alike.[9]

The Catholic League issued a pamphlet in about 1927 entitled *Adoration of the Blessed Sacrament Reserved* in which they took the argument yet one stage further. It was asserted that:

Reservation is already not only lawful but ordered by English Canon Law in every parish church; and our complaint is that the Bishops and Clergy who do not obey this Canon are themselves lawbreakers.

It continued:

We would urge that all priests should immediately start public service of Adoration of the Blessed Sacrament and that all should earnestly pray . . . for the Divine Guidance in the crisis, for the conversion to the Faith of all Bishops and those in authority and for the increase in adoration of the august Mystery of the Altar.[10]

Baverstock's book was written in the immediate aftermath of a purported ban on Exposition and Benediction by Bishop Winnington-Ingram in January 1919: characteristically, he did not enforce his own directive with any great vigour. It also followed the ejection from their livings of Father Reginald Wynter in Taunton and Father Sandys Wason in Cornwall: the latter is dealt with in more detail in Chapter 9.

Winnington-Ingram's main complaints were against the two back-street churches of St Alban, Fulham, and particularly St Saviour, Hoxton, which are discussed in Chapter 8.

The assertion made by Baverstock that there was authority higher than the bishops of the Church of England was not of course an original one. When Fynes-Clinton looked back at 1927/8 he commented that in the Anglican Communion 'There is . . . an almost total lack of consciousness that obedience is due to superior authority . . . This was

---

9 Harris: *Reservation of the Blessed Sacrament*, p. 5.
10 Catholic League: *Adoration of the Blessed Sacrament Reserved*, unnumbered pages.

patent even to absurdity in the debates concerning the new Prayer Book, in the assumption that provincial regulations could override universal law.'[11] Hope Patten was wont to speak of 'two potty little provinces of no importance compared with the whole of Western Christendom'.[12]

By the early 1920s there was a variety of liturgical use even within those who considered themselves followers of the Western Tradition and even apart from those few parishes where the entire Roman liturgy was used. In the early decades of the twentieth century many priests altered the order of the mass by transposing the Gloria to its historically correct position at the beginning of the liturgy and adding portions of the Roman canon, often silently. The main purpose could be said to have been to get in as much as possible of the Roman mass, without making the changes too obvious. However, from 1911 onwards the influence of the Society of SS Peter and Paul began to spread. Although this organisation (which is dealt with in more detail in Chapter 11) is often thought of as thoroughly Romanising, in fact the true picture is more subtle. Although the SSPP promoted and popularised continental baroque fittings and vestments, often of a most elaborate type, the words of the liturgy were usually Cranmerian. The 1662 Book was disguised, or perhaps overlaid, with an elaborate ceremonial which misled most observers into believing that what they were observing was the Roman mass in English. It is not without importance that on 13 February 1930 Father Humphrey Whitby, the leading exponent of this style of liturgy, wrote refusing to join the Confraternity of Unity on the grounds that he had undertaken at ordination to use the Book of Common Prayer, of which he was throughout his life a great defender.[13]

By about 1920 it had been accepted that the 1662 Book should remain, but with permissive alternatives, and thereafter three separate serious independent proposals emerged, which were known by the colour of the covers of the respective written versions. The Green Book (October 1922) was the proposal of the English Church Union, and reflected a moderate Anglo-Catholic response along Western lines and in accordance with the Hickleton Conference proposals. The Grey Book (mid 1923) was the work of the Life and Liberty Movement, representing central but forward-looking thinking in the Church of England. The

11 Fynes-Clinton and Corbould: *What Are We to Say?*, p. 13.
12 Stephenson: *Walsingham Way*, p. 103.
13 Uncatalogued Rea papers, Pusey House.

Orange Book (the Alcuin Club's Survey of the Proposals for an Alternative Prayer Book) (1923–4) was largely written by Bishop W. H. Frere to reflect the views of the English Use school, and therefore represented a non-papal, nationalist and somewhat antiquarian approach to the problem. None of these proposals in any way foreshadowed the Liturgical Movement in providing for increased congregational participation.

The final form of the 1927 Book was undoubtedly designed to provide a settled form of worship which could then be rigorously enforced, and, more importantly, it was perceived as such at the time. A writer to the *Church Times* at the beginning of 1927, about ten months before the Book came before Parliament, summarised the position as many saw it:

> Prayer Book Revision may, incidentally, have other aims; but its raison d'être is to give effect to the recommendations of the Report on Ecclesiastical Discipline.[14]

Archbishop Randall Davidson himself was less than enthusiastic about the whole process, but he told the Church Assembly in June 1927, 'You may take it from me that the bishops will require obedience to the new rules and will do their utmost to secure it.'[15]

Dean W. R. Matthews, admittedly looking back at the episode from many years later, was both clear and precise:

> the chaos in episcopal regulation would, it was hoped, be halted and excuses for 'supplementing' or 'supplanting' the Holy Communion by the Roman liturgy would be abolished.[16]

When Matthews referred to the end of supplementation he was aware that the Book had been drafted with a view to preventing it being disguised as the Roman mass, particularly by the insertion of the Epiklesis or invocation of the Holy Spirit. Bishop A. C. Headlam of Gloucester was a prominent supporter of the new form, and in the *Church Quarterly Review* shortly before the Parliamentary debates he wrote:

---

14 Letter from L. W. Hodson to *Church Times*, 11 February 1927.
15 Bell: *Randall Davidson*, p. 1340.
16 Matthews: *Memories and Meanings*, p. 149.

It is possible to fit the service of the Mass into the Communion Office as we have it at present . . . It is equally possible to harmonize the Communion Office published in the Green Book with the Roman ceremonial. It was constructed to make that possible. What is not possible is to do it with regard to the present Book.[17]

Some 15 years after the controversy, W. K. Lowther Clarke wrote a retrospective critique of the book, in which he trenchantly criticised what he regarded as its amateur draughtsmanship, and he made the same point as Headlam rather more directly: 'When highly-placed advocates of the new Prayer Book declared that the Canon would stop the sounding of bells and gongs at the words "This is My Body" etc., all chances of its acceptance by Anglo-Catholics as a whole vanished.'[18] Ross Williamson made a similar accusation, saying later that the Book's 'only objective was to make the use of the Canon of the Mass impossible within the terms of canonical obedience'.[19]

Not only were Anglo-Catholics under-represented in the House of Commons, but they took the view that it was wrong that the civil authority should regulate worship, and therefore would not lobby as a matter of principle. Darwell Stone, writing to Hope Patten, made the position quite clear, saying: 'I do not think it would be wise or politic to take any public steps in the way of opposing the Measure in Parliament because any such step could be misunderstood as a recognition of the authority of Parliament.'[20]

There were many who called themselves Anglo-Catholics who supported the new Book, because it appeared to make legal the practices which had become widespread since the Oxford Movement had reached out into the parishes. Neither the English Church Union nor the *Church Times* gave a very definite lead. An editorial in the latter in early 1927 commented: 'What an abundant cause of thanksgiving we have in all that has been gained by this Revision!'[21] There were letters to that paper in the summer of 1927 from supporters of the Book who complained

---

17 Headlam: 'A Defence of the New Prayer Book', *Church Quarterly Review*, Vol. 208, No. 7 (1927), p. 205.
18 Clarke: *The Prayer Book of 1928 Reconsidered*, p. 46.
19 Ross Williamson: *The Walled Garden*, p. 202.
20 Cross: *Darwell Stone*, p. 191.
21 *Church Times*, 11 February 1927.

that many Anglo-Catholics agreed with them, but that their voice was not being heard because of the extremists. Father Edwards of St Faith, Stepney, asserted specifically that the lay majority in the ECU was in favour of the Book.[22]

There is, however, no doubt at all that what was then called 'advanced' opinion in the Anglo-Catholic movement, going beyond those who would describe themselves as Papalists, was adamantly opposed to the new Book. It became clear that even if the new Book were placed on the statute book, there would be many who would refuse to obey it and in particular would refuse to comply with what was in effect a licensing system for Reservation of the Sacrament. Whitby wrote that: 'All that will really have happened, then, if the Prayer Book Measure passes Parliament, is that the Bishops will have gained permission from the State to allow priests to communicate the sick from the Reserved Sacrament should they wish to grant a licence, and it is difficult to see how any priest will be able to apply for such a licence without admitting the rights of Parliament to regulate the administration of Sacraments.'[23]

The 1927 proposals included in the draft Prayer Book itself provision for Reservation for the sick only, and even then at the discretion of the local bishop, and the Book had appended to it regulations in which it was specifically provided that the door of the receptacle in which the Sacrament was kept was only to be opened when necessary to move or replace the Consecrated elements for the purpose of Communion or renewal.

On 4 May 1927 a synod of the SSC carried unanimously the following resolution:

That this Society of the Holy Cross . . . expresses its unqualified condemnation of the Book as heretical in tendency, subversive of Catholic constitutional principles and liturgical proprieties and mischievous in the highest degree, and advises priests without hesitation or qualification to refuse acceptance of it.[24]

In June 1927 the Confraternity of the Blessed Sacrament, a generally moderate devotional group, came out against the Revision because of

22 Ibid., 12 August 1927.
23 Ibid., 22 April 1927.
24 Ibid., 13 May 1927.

the attitude expressed towards Reservation. Its Superior General, Father C. P. Shaw, was to play an important part in events after the rejection of the proposals.

The Catholic League was vigorous in its condemnation also. At its General Meeting on 23 June 1927 it was resolved that:

> No assent can be given to the Deposited Book by loyal churchmen inasmuch as by its provisions the Faith is gravely compromised, the mind of the Catholic Church flouted in such matters as the regulations concerning Reservation, veneration of the Saints, and the complete ignoring of one of the Holy Sacraments [unction], and inasmuch as by the prohibition of corporate adoration of the Holy Sacrament Reserved grave insult is offered to the Divine Majesty of Christ therein present.[25]

It is of some importance that at the same time that a measure was being promoted which was criticised for its laxity towards Anglo-Catholics, many of the latter grouping were so bitterly opposed to it. The League issued another pamphlet at about the same time, written by 'A Committee of Anglican Priests'. Entitled *The Calamity of the New Prayer Book* it can hardly have been more vehement in its opposition or less trusting of the bishops. The use of expressions such as 'Reservation, the duty of every parish priest, is now to be subject to the whim of disbelieving Bishops' were not calculated to ease the dispute, and it concluded: 'As always it is the truth of the Real Change effected by the Consecration of the Blessed Sacrament and its consequence of adoration against which the attack is directed. This is the body of Christ. Worshippers will be prosecuted. By Order of the Bishops.'[26]

As the time for the debate in Parliament approached, it was apparent that the new Book was opposed by Protestants on the grounds that it gave too many concessions to Anglo-Catholics, and was opposed by many Anglo-Catholics on the basis that it provided regulation of them rather than allowing them the benefit of the uncertainty which they had enjoyed before. In those circumstances, it is perhaps easy to see why the Book was rejected at its hearing on 15 December 1927, although it is absolutely clear from reading the contemporary accounts that the defeat in the House of Commons was completely unexpected.

25 Doolan: *The First Fifty Years*, p. 19.
26 Catholic League: *The Calamity of the New Prayer Book*, unnumbered pages.

There can be no escape from the conclusion, however, that the single most important reason for the rejection was antipathy to Anglo-Catholicism. Hensley Henson, Bishop of Durham, wrote two days later: 'The real causes of the vote on Thursday night . . . were certainly not the defects of the Revised Book, nor the arguments advanced against it, but mainly the volume of exasperation against the excesses of the law-breaking clergy.'[27] The Archbishop of York, Cosmo Lang, was soon to succeed Davidson at Canterbury. He was more sympathetic than many bishops to Anglo-Catholicism and had been a personal friend of Halifax for many years. Lang's patrician manner and lack of any common touch concealed an acute intelligence. He wrote: 'It is no use denying that one cause of the temper of the House, at least certainly among a large number of quiet English members – especially from the country – was the long-accumulating resentment against too many Anglo-Catholics who had thrust their ways upon quiet country folk entirely unprepared for them.'[28]

Perhaps more pertinently, Dean Carpenter records an eye witness who was with Winnington-Ingram immediately after the vote. He indicated that the Bishop of London 'was quiet for a minute, and then said in a low voice "It was my fault." ' Carpenter added his own comment: 'He must have meant that his own lack of success in controlling difficult elements had given to members of Parliament a false impression of what the Church of England really was.'[29]

The bishops appear to have attributed the defeat not to the real problems described above, but rather to bad management. With that in mind, they reintroduced the Book in a re-revised form in 1928. It is customary to link the two debates together as if there were no real difference of substance between them, but in fact the new proposals resulted in a very significant strengthening of opposition from the Anglo-Catholic side. A number of changes of detail were introduced in order to strengthen the Protestant nature of the new Book, but one important alteration was that the restrictions on Reservation, which had previously been in the regulations, were printed in the rubrics and therefore became part of the Book itself. Tabernacles on the altar as well as the

---

27 Henson: *Retrospect of an Unimportant Life*, Vol. 2, p. 167.
28 Lockhart: *Cosmo Gordon Lang*, p. 308.
29 Carpenter: *Winnington-Ingram*, p. 204.

hanging pyx, which a few of the more antiquarian-minded supported, were specifically excluded.

On the appearance of the 1928 version of the Book, a joint committee of the English Church Union, Anglo-Catholic Congress, Federation of Catholic Priests and Confraternity of the Blessed Sacrament issued a statement affirming 'belief in the Real Presence and the Eucharistic sacrifice and rightness of adoration of the Christ present in the Reserved Sacrament'. More than 2,000 priests in England signed.

On 19 March 1928 Bishop Frere of Truro, the most distinguished liturgist of his generation, a champion of Anglo-Catholic moderation and the draughtsman of parts of the 1927 Book, repudiated the re-revised form. In a contemporary letter he wrote: 'In this new form I cannot now support it, for it seems to offer now no sufficient hope of settlement, but on the contrary to lead up to acute trouble.'[30] He was followed by the *Church Times*, which declared on 5 April 1928: 'If the measure now receives the sanction of the Church assembly and Parliament, its administration will be made impossible by the resistance of practically the whole Anglo-Catholic party.'[31] This further opposition was reflected in the vote in the Church Assembly, in which the percentage of those dissenting increased from 25 per cent to 38 per cent compared with the previous year when the first proposal was discussed.

On 13 June 1928 the latest version of the Book was introduced to the House of Commons and again was rejected. It may be that this time there were far fewer who were surprised by what had occurred. One of the enclosed communities for women had held an all-night vigil praying for its rejection, and on this occasion the prayers were answered.

The entire episode was on the face of it a disaster for the episcopate, whose prolonged consideration had given birth to a Book that satisfied very few. It was subsequently said that the new form for the communion service was by 1940 in use in only about 100 churches. The bishops had authorised its use 'during the present emergency'.[32]

On the other hand, the penetrating mind of Dean W. R. Inge recorded in his diary: 'The rejection of the Book really saves them [the bishops]

30 Jasper: *Walter Howard Frere: His Correspondence on Liturgical Revision and Construction*, p. 155, the letter being dated 10 March 1928 to Chancellor Cooper.
31 *Church Times*, 5 April 1928.
32 Dix, *The Shape of the Liturgy*, p. 710.

from a humiliating position; for they would not have been obeyed.'[33] It also however made it far more difficult for the bishops to attempt to enforce discipline along the lines of regulations or rubrics which had been rejected by Parliament.

The Anglican Papalists were of course delighted by the rejection. Not only were they afforded greater freedom to continue with services in the way they preferred, but the authority of the episcopate had been damaged and the dependence of the Church of England on the will of a Parliament which was no longer made up of members of that Church was manifest. Raymond Raynes was clear that a church which was subject to the civil authorities was not worthy of respect and declared the same with some force:

> She [the Church of England] has submitted to the State in the matter of the Prayer Book. Christ never submitted on a principle. The Church, anxious to please Parliament, has given way. The system which looks to the world for support is bound to fail. The Official Church of England will go under. The true Anglican Church – the Church of this land since the days of Augustine – will prevail if it maintains unflinching the Catholic Faith and practice, because it rests upon the promise of Christ that the powers of hell shall not prevail against it.[34]

Some priests were even more adamant that they would have nothing to do with any authority which was compromised by state control. Father Butler, in his tiny Suffolk village, refused even to co-operate with the annual archdeacon's visitation: the only record he kept of the services held in the church over his long ministry was a note that in 1933 the archdeacon had appeared and, finding no churchwardens present, had departed 'on his high horse'.

However, the bishops remained under some pressure to take action, particularly in the Diocese of London where there were so many churches which were not complying with the proposed regulations or rubrics on Reservation. Bishop C. F. Garbett, then of Southwark, later of Winchester, and eventually Archbishop of York, had been waiting for some years even by 1928 in the expectation of replacing Winnington-

---

33 Fox: *Dean Inge*, p. 216.
34 Mosley: *The Life of Raymond Raynes*, p. 31.

Ingram. He had drafted the rubrics for the Revised Book in an attempt to control Reservation in the same way as he did in his own diocese, although it is fair to say that only a few streets from his cathedral was to be found the ultra-Roman stronghold of St Alphege, Southwark, with its attendant convent of the Community of Reparation to Jesus in the Blessed Sacrament, which continued in existence throughout this period, and not far away was Father Maltby's mission church of St Mary, South Bermondsey. Garbett's biographer tells us that he positively relished the prospect of cleaning the 'Augean stable' of the Diocese of London, but in the event he never had the opportunity.[35] It is also only fair to him to say that looking back on the episode he came to the conclusion that 'the Bishops made a serious mistake in treating the new Book as a disciplinary measure rather than an enrichment of the worship of Almighty God . . .', a statement which of course admits a substantial part of the case for the Anglo-Catholic party.[36]

Garbett saw Winnington-Ingram after the latter finally retired in 1939, and wrote in his diary, 'He [i.e. the Bishop of London] always told us . . . that there was no disobedience, but that was only because there were no rules to obey. He has left the diocese in a condition of ecclesiastical chaos.'[37]

It was, however, Winnington-Ingram who decided after the failure of attempts to control Reservation by rubric, that he would attempt to do so by regulation imposed locally by himself: it is a reasonable inference that pressure was put on him to make that initiative, on the basis that if he succeeded in London then other bishops elsewhere were unlikely to have any real problems.

On 7 November 1928 Winnington-Ingram sent out a letter to all the incumbents within his diocese where continuous Reservation of the Sacrament was the practice in their churches. At that time there were some 170 such churches, and the Bishop required them to reserve for the Communion of the sick only, to reserve the Consecrated Elements in a place approved by him, provided that it was not immediately behind or above the altar, and as from Advent Sunday to cease services directly connected with the Reserved Sacrament. Winnington-Ingram then held a meeting at which, characteristically, he was much less firm than he had

35 Smyth: *Cyril Foster Garbett, Archbishop of York*, p. 183.
36 Ibid., p. 184.
37 Ibid., p. 405 n.

been on paper. Many thought they could live with the regulations provided that they were interpreted with his usual generosity of spirit.
However, a stand as a matter of principle was made by a group under the
chairmanship of Father Shaw of the CBS, who was then vicar of St Mary
Magdalene, Paddington. They became known as 'The Twenty One'
since that was their number, and they subsequently published details of
the affair under the title *The Transactions of the 21.*

It is interesting to look at the group, as they represented a nucleus of
hard-line Anglo-Catholicism and Anglican Papalism within the diocese.
Strangely enough, there were some, such as Father Fynes-Clinton and
Father Ross of St Saviour, Hoxton, whose names were not to be found
on the list, perhaps because they simply continued as before and disregarded these instructions from the bishop as they had become
accustomed to disregard earlier such edicts. Fynes-Clinton is reported to
have said that the term Deposited Book was a mot juste for the 1928
version, as it should properly be deposited in the rubbish bin.[38]

The majority of the group of 21 came from churches in poor and run-
down areas in the East End, such as W. A. Aglionby (St Frideswide,
Poplar), A. F. Asher (St Augustine, Poplar), P. M. Bartlett (St Saviour,
Poplar), J. H. Hardy (Christ Church, Isle of Dogs), R. A. Kingdon
(St John, Isle of Dogs), H. E. Lury (St Peter, Limehouse), F. C. S. Nicolle
(St Thomas, Bethnal Green), F. C. Pond (St Peter, London Docks), C. E.
Story (St Augustine, Victoria Park), W. A. F. Waters (St Luke, Millwall),
and H. A. Wilson (St Augustine, Haggerston). Others from less affluent
areas included A. E. Cornibeer (St Matthew, Westminster), which was
then in a very heavily populated area, C. P. Shaw himself, and the well-
known Papalists J. E. Watson (St Alban, Fulham) and R. E. Young (St
Thomas, Shepherd's Bush). There were only four of the more fashion-
able West End churches, represented by C. R. Deakin (St Augustine,
Queen's Gate), J. L. B. Pinchard (St John the Baptist, Holland Road),
Lord Victor Seymour (St Stephen, Gloucester Road), and E. O. H.
Whitby (St Mary, Bourne Street) and two from the suburbs, R. B. Abell
(SS Peter and Paul, Teddington) and T. C. Calvert (St Peter, Acton
Green). The Bishop was therefore being asked to discipline clergy who in
the main worked hard in difficult parishes which were not attractive to
many save of their own cast of mind.

---

38 Information from the late L. G. Fisher.

The first response of the 21 was an open letter entitled *Obedience: A Plea for Catholic Order* in which they put forward the familiar argument that the Church of England was not autonomous but rather part of the wider Church. They asserted:

We are aware that practical appeal to the whole Church of Christ carries little weight with those who assume the title Catholic for themselves and the National Church simply on the ground that they think that Anglican Sacraments are as valid as any others. In effect they seem to think that having valid Sacraments, the Church of England can claim an independent endowment of the Spirit, and is thus justified in acting without regard to the rest of historic Christianity.[39]

On 14 May 1929 the Bishop replied, saying, 'the greatest fallacy of all in your argument is the belief that because things have been obtained by disobedience in the past, therefore they will be in the future'.[40] However, he also said that he would take no disciplinary proceedings against any of the 21, but that as they left, new men would have to agree to obey the regulations. This was a typical Winnington-Ingram device to allow himself to be extricated from the situation without undue trouble, but actually having accomplished nothing. The fact was that matters went on much as before and the pro-Roman element had succeeded in retaining their position. The Protestant agitator J. A. Kensit was incandescent at the lack of control and himself wrote and published an open letter to the Bishop of London in 1929 entitled *Undiluted Romanism: A Call for Action*. In it he alleged that many churches which on the face of it accepted the Bishop's rulings on Reservation in fact evaded them by simple devices, such as calling the service of Devotions to the Sacrament 'United Prayer Meeting', as was apparently done at St Andrew by the Wardrobe.

After the Prayer Book episode, there were moves among some moderately minded Anglo-Catholics to encourage universal acceptance either of the 1549 Book or of the so-called Interim Rite devised by Bishop A. C. Chandler, formerly of Bloemfontein, which was put forward on 2 January 1931. Fynes-Clinton and his associates were

39 Shaw: *The Transactions of the 21*, p. 32.
40 Ibid., p. 41.

strongly opposed to that course of action, and the Catholic League and the Sodality of the Precious Blood, at a joint meeting on 1 July 1938, passed a resolution deploring any attempt not to use the Roman canon and further deploring such practices as evening communion and the ministration of Holy Communion to Nonconformists.[41]

On Winnington-Ingram's eventual retirement, he was replaced by Fisher, whose stay in London in the event was to be cut short by the early death of Temple and his own consequent elevation to the See of Canterbury. Fisher had no sympathy for Anglo-Catholicism and lacked the benevolence which had led his clergy to refer to Winnington-Ingram as Uncle Arthur. Fisher determined to take strong action against recalcitrant clergy, and continued with that resolution even during the years of war. Although it did appear that some form of agreement had been reached at a meeting on 18 December 1944, and the *Church Times* carried details of it, no real compromise had been effected before he moved on.

It may well have been that much more effective action would have been taken against the Papalists in London had Winnington-Ingram retired ten years earlier than he did, and been replaced by Garbett or Fisher. As it was, a combination of his lax regime and the decline in episcopal confidence brought about by the defeats of 1927 and 1928 allowed the more ultramontane forms of Anglo-Catholicism to continue to flourish despite continued disapproval from above and widespread general unpopularity.

Other bishops attempted to enforce disciplinary measures against the Papalist clergy, with varying degrees of success. Hope Patten established the Shrine of Our Lady of Walsingham on private land held by trustees precisely in order to preclude interference by the Bishop of Norwich.

Bishop Bell in Chichester was faced with a diocese in which in 1929 about 50 churches out of about 400 had permanent Reservation. He held a meeting at St Martin, Brighton, on 3 December 1930, after which he issued regulations to the effect that there was to be no form of Benediction or Exposition, but pending final settlement of the issue he was prepared to dispense from a further rule prohibiting any services in connection with the Reserved Sacrament in cases where Devotions (i.e. without a monstrance) had been held in the past. An anonymous author

---

41 Doolan, *The First Fifty Years*, p. 24.

calling himself 'Watchman' strongly attacked this policy in a pamphlet entitled *The Bishops and the Prayer Book*, but the bishop did appear to be more flexible than some.

The most heavy-handed attitude was taken by the modernist Bishop Barnes in Birmingham. His views over the years frequently embarrassed his fellow bishops, and he was small-minded and unforgiving so far as Anglo-Catholics in his diocese were concerned. He issued directives against Reservation and Benediction on his appointment in 1924 and again in December 1925, which resulted in a rebellion rather similar to that in London, but which ran for far longer. There were 12 to 15 rebels, led by the able Revd G. D. Rosenthal of St Agatha, Sparkbrook. Barnes wanted to squeeze them out of the diocese by depriving them of any material aid and by refusing to institute replacements of a similar inclin- ation. The Bishop refused even to meet Father Rosenthal, and priests such as himself and Father Langford-James of St James, Edgbaston, were ignored by their diocesan for many years. They instituted what was in effect their own Finance Board, since as they were not receiving diocesan grants they refused in return to contribute towards diocesan funds. The 'So-called rebels' (the title of a justification published by Rosenthal and another in 1930) agreed between themselves not to move or resign benefices while the policy of Barnes was in force, but of course in some cases death or illness supervened. When Father Barlee of St Aidan, Small Heath, was forced by ill-health to resign, Barnes refused to institute a successor and proceedings for an order of mandamus had to be taken in the High Court to compel him to do so, an episode which reflected no credit on him at all. Rosenthal (1881–1938), whose father was a convert from Judaism who exercised a ministry in the East End of London, was a prominent figure in the Anglo-Catholic Congresses but was by no means an extremist liturgically, using the Prayer Book and supporting the Interim Rite. However, he was moved to write that 'The Bishop [i.e. Barnes] rules his diocese, not as an official of the Church, but as an officer of the State; and this, we would contend, robs his directions of any moral value.'[42]

Rosenthal refused to leave his parish despite increasing ill-health, because he knew that if he did so the Bishop would refuse to permit Reservation of the Blessed Sacrament in the church. He died in harness

---

42 Russell: *Rosenthal*, p. 80.

in 1938, still a young man. Barnes was unable to attend his funeral because of ill-health, but in an act of insensitivity and vindictiveness, insisted on visiting the church two days later to confirm that the Sacrament had indeed been removed from the tabernacle.

In 1947 Barnes published *The Rise of Christianity*, in which he dismissed both the Virgin Birth and the Resurrection and discredited the crucifixion narrative. Fisher told him that if his views had been those expressed in the book, he would not have been able to continue in episcopal office.

In the post-Second World War period, although there were occasional outbursts, such as the conflict in 1959 between Bishop Stockwood and Father Rice Harris at Carshalton, matters generally settled down and Anglican Papalism was left to decline at its own pace rather than being bolstered by the inevitable reaction to attacks from above.

5

THE DEVELOPMENT OF RELIGIOUS COMMUNITIES 1900–1960

A great deal has been written about the growth and early development of religious communities in the Church of England, although rather less about their position in the 1900–60 period and then their steep numerical decline since about 1960. There are, however, certain trends in relation to the 1900–60 era which are fairly clear.

Those trends include a fairly general move away from outside work which, particularly in the case of the women's communities, had been the reason for their original foundation and early growth. More communities turned to inward, contemplative forms of life. Another trend was the adoption by many older communities, even those among men, which had previously been very austere in their devotions, of Roman uses. The third was the establishment of several new communities along ultramontane lines.

By about 1900 the position of religious communities in the Church of England was well established, although their legal position remained somewhat anomalous. Because they had revived over a relatively short period commencing in 1845, and because they were originally treated with some suspicion by the authorities, there was no central control of religious orders. The Advisory Council on Religious Communities did not even commence existence until 1935.

Unlike the Roman Catholic Church, in which the religious are and were an integral part of the structure of the Church, the communities in the Church of England were, as it were, external and additional to the main structure. One consequence of that was that they were far less controlled in their devotional life than were parishes, and although the Protestant agitators were strongly opposed to the religious life in community, they often had little idea of what actually went on, especially in the enclosed orders.

The growth in numbers in religious communities reached its zenith about 1900 and those numbers were maintained until after the First World War. They did not vary much in the inter-war period, despite the growth of Anglo-Catholicism during that era, and then there were modest increases, particularly among the men's orders, in the period after the Second World War before a steep decline, particularly affecting the women's orders, after that time. In recent times many orders have gone out of existence altogether, or been amalgamated with larger communities, and many have moved from the very large establishments which they once had.

In the early part of the century some of the older established orders for women were quite substantial: in 1913 the Community of St Mary the Virgin (Wantage Sisters) had 50 houses, the All Saints Sisters 33, the Community of St John the Baptist (Clewer Sisters) 40, the Society of St Margaret 40, the Sisters of the Church 30, and the Sisters of Bethany 13.

The Society of St Margaret was founded at East Grinstead in 1855 by John Mason Neale. In 1865 their mother convent, built on a huge scale, was begun, and although Neale died in August 1866 the order flourished. The St Margaret Sisters were in the late nineteenth century far more advanced liturgically than many of the other orders. The Wantage and Clewer sisters in particular had a most austere devotional life with very little ceremony. It appears that not only Reservation but also Benediction of the Blessed Sacrament had commenced among the St Margaret's Community about 1857/8, under Neale's own direction. In 1870 the Sisters opened a branch house known as St Katharine's Convent at Queen Square, Bloomsbury, where in the latter part of the nineteenth century and the early years of the twentieth those of a ritualist frame of mind could attend Benediction in Latin, which was not then found in the Church of England elsewhere in London. In 1908, however, the Sisters at that branch house made a corporate submission to Rome, one of the very few such occasions when this occurred.

It may be that thereafter the Community held back somewhat with its advances liturgically, and moved more into the Anglican mainstream. The same path was not taken by the Holy Cross Sisters at nearby Hayward's Heath, founded by Neale's sister, who are discussed fully in the next chapter.

The Bloomsbury secession was a blow to those who saw in the communities a means of leavening the Church of England in a Roman direction from within. So too was a wave of secessions in Brighton in 1910 in which both clergy and some of their parishioners crossed over. However, neither had anything like the impact that was caused by events on Caldey Island.

At the turn of the century, the male communities appeared totally loyal to the ethos of the Church of England. Their safety in the eyes of the establishment was well demonstrated by the elevation to the episcopate of Charles Gore, founder of the Community of the Resurrection, in 1901 and even more so later by that of Walter Frere CR in 1923; when the latter took up his bishopric he took with him a small number of the brethren from Mirfield and they established in effect a branch house at Lis Escop, the Palace in Truro.

The communities for men which were in existence in 1900 had generally been founded later than those for women. The main bodies at that time were the Society of St John the Evangelist, based in Oxford, the Order of St Paul, which then had a specific mission to seafarers but was based in Alton, the Community of the Resurrection in Mirfield, the Society of the Sacred Mission at Kelham, and the Society of the Divine Compassion, whose mother house was in Plaistow.

Of these, the SSM was the least influenced by Roman Catholic sources and remained so throughout. Its superior was the only one of the leaders of the main communities for men who did not sign the 1943 protest over South India. The SDC, although also definitely Anglo-Catholic in its outlook, was Socialist in its thinking and practice. Although now defunct, it had considerable influence for some years. One of its members was a former friend of Ronald Knox, Vernon Johnson (Father Vernon SDC from 1913), who in the post-First World War period was one of the most popular preachers in the Church of England. His unexpected secession to Rome in 1929 was brought about by reading the autobiography of St Theresa in 1924, followed by a pilgrimage to Lisieux in 1925. His was one of the most damaging single defections of the century from the Church of England to Rome. He set out his journey in *One Lord, One Faith* (1930) in which he described how his appreciation of the acceptance of suffering by Thérèse Martin led him to Rome: thereafter he had a great devotion to the French saint.

The respectability of those orders was not much damaged during the nineteenth century by two more exotic organisations. One of these was the Order of St Augustine, the foundation of Revd George Nugée, which had a priory in New Kent Road, the decor of which represented one of the early attempts to break away from Gothic in favour of more Roman models. The order was secretive, ritualistic, and regarded with disfavour by those outside the Anglo-Catholic underworld: it died out quickly after the death of the founder in 1892. The other was the quasi-Benedictine order, if that is the appropriate word for one whose life was filled with disorder, associated with the extraordinary Father Ignatius (1837–1908). Although Father Ignatius (Joseph Leycester Lyne) was in some ways ahead of his time in seeking the revival of Benedictinism in the Church of England, his methods were somewhat chaotic and he had no judgement in relation to those who wished to associate with him. He had little support from any of those in authority in the Anglo-Catholic Movement and his monastery at Capel-y-Ffin in South Wales represented a high flowering of the Romantic feeling behind much of the nineteenth-century Revival.[1]

It was against this background that a young medical student, Benjamin Carlyle (1874–1955), who took the name in religion of Aelred, began his own attempt to revive the Benedictine spirit in the Church of England, although in fact his community on Caldey Island as it developed was more Cistercian in its ethos.

Carlyle demonstrated to an extreme extent that feeling, often found among Anglican Papalists, which required that in order to show that the Church of England was truly part of the Catholic Church it should demonstrate so by its outward manifestations, such as religious communities, shrines and the like. He had from an early age a thoroughly romantic view of monasticism, which must have been partly tempered by the privations which his little community endured in the years between 1898, when he received a letter from Archbishop Temple approving his profession, and 1906, when they moved permanently to Caldey.

One of Carlyle's problems was that, although some qualified approval had been given to his plans by the Archbishop of Canterbury in the form of the letter to which reference has been made, no bishop in England would ordain him priest. In 1904 he was, however, ordained by Bishop Grafton of Fond du Lac, Wisconsin: he was another bishop who was

---

1 It is an interesting reflection that while Father Ignatius' church is now ruined, Mass [sic] is now advertised (2003) at the tiny chapel in the hamlet of Capel-y-Ffin, very near the monastery.

sometimes gullible where the conferring of orders was concerned, although Carlyle had a genuine vocation, as his later life showed. The fact that he was ordained abroad meant, however, that Carlyle was subject to the Colonial Clergy Act 1874, and therefore required permission before he could officiate in England.

The Community were itinerant for a number of years, spending time on the Isle of Dogs in the East End of London, Guiting Power in Gloucestershire, Milton Abbas in Dorset, and then from 1902 to 1906 at Painsthorpe, Yorkshire, in a property owned by Lord Halifax. At the commencement of that period, Archbishop Temple approved the community, without perhaps understanding the tendencies which it had towards Rome. From early days the Benedictines had strong connections with the nascent Papalist party in the Church of England, and while they were still at Milton Abbas (1899–1900), Father Alban Baverstock used to come over from his parish at nearby Hinton Martel to hear their confessions and to say mass for them.

In 1906 the prospect of the brothers moving to Caldey Island, off Tenby on the Pembrokeshire coast, became a reality with an offer of a loan from a third party. They had already been to the island for a short stay, and nowhere could have appealed more to Carlyle's sensibilities than this place with its history and location.

When the monks took up residence on Caldey, Carlyle began to dream of a vast abbey with a church of cathedral-like proportions. In fact, the Community lived in a group of workmen's houses as a temporary measure, but in 1910 an abbey church was dedicated, built as a result of a very substantial donation. The Abbot, as Carlyle now was, had appealed for stones from pre-Reformation monasteries and these were incorporated into the altar. The reredos was Gothic in design and was the work of the conservative ecclesiastical architect F. C. Eden.

By this time, Caldey was exciting very many supporters of Anglo-Catholicism. It was Lord Halifax, however, who was to prove the Community's most loyal advocate. There was nowhere else in the Church of England where followers could observe such ultramontane spirituality, and a very large number of visitors arrived. Guests such as Halifax himself, the politician Samuel Hoare, Niall Campbell (later Duke of Argyll), Athelstan Riley and Samuel Gurney, all of whom were in a position to assist financially, came, as well as enthusiastic young devotees such as Ronald Knox and Vernon Johnson. Athelstan Riley gave a silver hanging pyx beneath a canopy of three crowns, designed by Ninian Comper, which is now in St Mary, Penzance, after a number of moves. Riley wrote in *Pax*, the magazine of the Community, that 'Caldey is to me the greatest phenomenon in the Anglican Communion at the present day'.[2] Gurney donated the bells for the tower, and Halifax, after being present at Exposition of the Blessed Sacrament and Compline in the chapel, wrote to his daughter, 'It really was the chief dream of my life realised.'[3]

The publicity surrounding the Community attracted many impressionable young men to it and it rapidly expanded so that the monks numbered about 40. The life was, however, not easy, and the quasi-Cistercian observances followed precluded meat being eaten at any time. After 1911 a group of Solitaries was formed within the Community, who never came to recreation save at Christmas and otherwise lived a hidden life of prayer. It was a particularly difficult period, not only because the growth of the order was so rapid, but also that the growth took place in circumstances where there was very little privacy for the Community to develop its own ways. The young Peter Anson (who had not in fact adopted that forename at that time) was a member of the Community from 1910 onwards and wrote extensively about it both in his ecclesiastical autobiography *A Roving Recluse* and in other books. He had adopted the name in religion of Richard Whytinge, last abbot of Glastonbury, whose supposed relics were removed to Caldey with great ceremony.

Anson says that by the time he joined: 'It was only on Sundays, when the *Church Times* was read aloud in the refectory, that we had occasion to recall any links with Anglicanism', although there was one caveat, in that Carlyle was a devotee of the cult of Charles King and Martyr and his observance was always kept.[4] For although the architecture was Gothic, the liturgy and the devotional life of the Community was entirely Latin in origin, and that language was used for worship.

From 1910 onwards Carlyle appears to have developed some delusions of grandeur. He was so convinced that his community reflected the future of the Church of England that he pressed on with his building programme, despite the fact that debts began to accrue. After 1910 there were normally 100 men or more at any one time involved in

---

2 Quoted in Anson: *Abbot Extraordinary*, p. 120.
3 Letter of about 1908, quoted in Lockhart: *Charles Lindley Viscount Halifax, Part Two*.
4 Anson, *Abbot Extraordinary*, p. 130.

the construction work, and after the chapel they constructed palatial apartments for the Abbot, which included a minaret-like tower, which almost immediately collapsed. Carlyle's reaction was to have the tower rebuilt and made even larger. He had plans for further foundations in places as diverse as the Isle of Man, Assisi, and Pershore, Worcestershire. There is no doubt however that he was a man of great personal charisma, and while he repelled some, he attracted many others. Anson, who knew him well, attempted to paint a complete picture of him in his biography, written after Carlyle's death, but although he said he had counted him as a friend throughout his life, the resulting portrait revealed previously unspoken flaws in the Abbot which he had avoided in his earlier general work on the Caldey Community, written while the founder was still alive.

The ostentation which began to form part of the Abbot's life, at least as shown to the outside world, was not thought appropriate by many of the supporters of the order. A silver monstrance was no doubt considered proper, but many drew the line at the private yacht owned by the Community, and by the fact that when the Abbot went on one of his frequent visits to the parallel Benedictine Convent, which had moved to nearby Milford Haven, he was transported by Daimler. The author Rose Macauley wrote in her introduction to Anson's biography of Carlyle, *Abbot Extraordinary*, that 'it was all like a fairy dream, an iridescent bubble blown by a dreamer who never paused to count the cost, an insubstantial bubble that must before long burst'.[5]

The bubble did indeed burst, but not for financial reasons, although there would no doubt have occurred a time when those matters became too embarrassing to ignore. Various members of the Community, including the Abbot, began to have doubts about their position within the Church of England. Those doubts were complicated by the uncertain legal position of the brothers and of Carlyle himself: they claimed to be extra-diocesan, but were rather at that time subject to no ecclesiastical control at all.

In August 1911 Halifax called his Hickleton Conference on Prayer Book Revision, which Abbot Aelred attended. Much of the time of the participants was spent in persuading the Caldey Benedictines that they should remain within Anglicanism, and for a time it appeared that they

---

5 Ibid., p. 8.

would: however, the problem would not go away. Father Langford-James came to lecture to the brothers in 1912 and 'did his best to prove that, although it was a clear duty to accept the Papal claims, yet at the same time this did not involve submission to the Holy See . . .', a constant theme among Anglican Papalists.[6]

The submission of the majority of the Caldey Community, including their Abbot, to Rome, which took place on 5 March 1913, was a seismic event within advanced circles of Anglo-Catholicism. It followed an attempt to regularise the position of the Community through Bishop Gore, who sent emissaries to discover the true nature of the spiritual and liturgical life of the order before agreeing to become Visitor, although that attempt was in fact prompted by a request to Archbishop Davidson that official recognition be given to the Abbot's ordination by including him in *Crockford*. Gore, although co-founder of the Community of the Resurrection, was narrow-minded and intransigent in his opposition to Romanism and in particular to the rite of Benediction and associated extra-liturgical eucharistic devotions. By asking Gore to be involved, Carlyle was ensuring that a blind eye would not be turned to the way in which the Community was organised. Carlyle was also under some pressure from the strong-minded Abbess Ewart of Milford Haven, the majority of whose nuns seceded at the same time.

Not surprisingly, the Roman Catholic authorities were anxious to make what publicity they could out of the situation, although they may not originally have realised the extent of the financial problems which they took on: the cost of the building work was about £68,000, but nothing like that amount had been raised. In addition there were rumours about the Abbot's over-familiarity with some of his younger oblates, and his interest in the occult. He was however reordained and reappointed as Abbot by the Roman Catholic Church with what some thought was indecent haste.

Relatively soon afterwards Carlyle left the religious life and had a long and hard-working career as a secular priest in British Columbia. Shortly before his death in 1955 he returned to England and renewed his vows as a Benedictine at Prinknash.

The debacle into which Caldey turned, so soon after raising the hopes of so many, was undoubtedly a serious setback to Anglican Papalists.

---

6 Anson: *The Benedictines of Caldey*, p. 154.

Those who had poured scorn on the Community on the other hand may have thought that its departure marked the final flowering of such exotic practices in the Church of England. Nothing could in the event have been further from the truth. Not only did the few from Caldey who remained in the Church of England rebuild the Community more slowly and upon surer foundations, but a number of other orders also developed on entirely Roman models.

The further development of the Benedictines of Pershore and then of Nashdom, as they became, is dealt with in the next chapter, as is the interrelated history of the women's Community of the Holy Cross at Hayward's Heath. The latter order exemplified the tendencies identified earlier, namely the move from external to internal work and the increasing Romanism of the devotions.

The collapse of the Caldey experiment had a profound effect on many individuals, but perhaps on none more than Father William Sirr (1862–1937), who was professed as a member of the Society of the Divine Compassion in 1903 and was Superior of the Society from 1906 to 1912. He was so affected by the failure of the Caldey Community that he offered his own life in reparation for it, and elected to follow a life of solitary contemplation. After some years preparing for this he took up the contemplative life at Glasshampton, Worcestershire, in 1918, initially in community but after 1930 on his own. The life of the Contemplatives of Blessed Mary at the Cross was too austere for others: it involved silence save for three periods of recreation each week, and for the celebration of mass. The importance of Father William was that many came to him for advice and counsel, including Stanley Baldwin. Thus in this unexpected way the influence of the more extreme forms of Anglo-Catholicism reached the centre of civil power.

The centrality of eucharistic devotion in the women's orders was also found in the Community of Reparation to Jesus in the Blessed Sacrament, founded in 1869 and which has recently become defunct. It was connected to the church of St Alphege, Southwark, which Betjeman described as: 'A wide, squat mission church furnished in the Belgian taste. Perhaps the most convincing Roman Catholic interior in the Church of England.'[7] The substantial convent was built in 1911 and Benediction was held at a time when it could rarely be found elsewhere;

---

7 Betjeman: *Collins Pocket Guide to English Parish Churches: The South*, p. 279.

the knowledgeable public could gain access to the service. The church has recently been demolished and services are held in part of the former parish hall.

The Milford Haven Benedictines had moved to Wales from Malling Abbey in Kent. There was another small community of Benedictine sisters in the Church of England who at the time of the Caldey secessions were at Baltonsborough in Somerset; they had moved there in 1906 after starting as an active order in Edmonton. In 1916 they in turn moved to Malling Abbey, where they have remained ever since. They were closely connected thereafter with the men's community at Nashdom. The West Malling nuns adopted a similar liturgical regime to Nashdom, with all services in Latin and the outward appearance of a Roman Catholic order. They rose at 4 a.m. to recite Matins and kept all the other offices with equal care. However illogical their position might have appeared to the informed onlooker, their loyalty to the Church of England did not waver and they remained as a small but real example of the Anglican Papalist ideal, namely an organisation within the Church of England indistinguishable from its Roman counterparts.

Another order which became allied to Nashdom was the Sisters of the Poor, otherwise known as the Benedictine Community of St Mary at the Cross. This order was founded by Father Henry Nihill in 1865 while he was vicar of St Michael, Shoreditch, and their mother house was originally adjacent to the presbytery and formed part of the splendid range of buildings adjacent to the great Brooks church. They too were originally an active order, but unlike many of the other foundations of that age they were influenced heavily almost from the date of their foundation by Roman sources. In 1877 they opened a daughter house in Edgware, also designed by Brooks, and took up work there for those who were then termed 'incurables'. In due course the sisters moved from Shoreditch and concentrated their work on Edgware, where the order still continues.

Almost from the date of foundation, the Community used the Brevarium Monasticum in Latin, although this was abandoned in 1905. In 1929 Revd G. A. C. Whatton was appointed chaplain to the Community, and from that date onwards all services were in Latin. In 1935 they adopted the whole of the Rule of St Benedict. By 1939 their devotions included Exposition of the Blessed Sacrament from Mass to after Vespers each Sunday, and a further insight into their spirituality can be gained from the naming of one of the wards of the hospital after the Little Flower of Lisieux. As with the West Malling sisters, the Community of St Mary at the Cross was, while loyal to the Church of England, cut off from it liturgically. However, any criticism from outside was tempered by the obvious devotion which the Community brought to its work for the severely handicapped and terminally ill.

Geoffrey Arundell Chatfield Whatton (1898–1977) was prominent in many of the organisations already mentioned, and was a prolific author. He was the son and grandson of priests, and his father had at one time assisted at St Michael, Ladbroke Grove, under Prebendary Denison. His maternal uncle was Lord Chatfield, from whom he derived his third Christian name. He went up to Keble College, Oxford, but financial difficulties prevented him proceeding to a degree: he went on to Chichester Theological College and was ordained deacon in Llandaff Cathedral in 1921. He served his title at the now demolished church of St Dyfrig, Cardiff, and was ordained priest in 1922, immediately joining the Sodality of the Precious Blood. In 1924 he tried his vocation with the Benedictines of Pershore, but soon went over to Rome and became a postulant at Downside. This too was not a success: the novice master took the view that despite his ultramontane views he remained an Anglican at heart. He was prevented from rejoining the Nashdom Community (see next chapter) but became an oblate, and then in 1927 went to be curate of St John, Limehouse. He remained there until taking up the position at Edgware, where he stayed until 1960.

The rather lonely position of chaplain to the Community allowed Father Whatton the time to write a number of books, the best known of which was *The Priest's Companion*, first published in 1939 and reprinted in 1946 and 1960. In 1946 a much expanded version of part of the original book was released, entitled *The Priest and His Life of Prayer*. Whatton wrote a number of pamphlets, including a strong defence of clerical celibacy, based on earlier work by the Society of the Holy Ghost, which was an association for celibate priests promoting a disciplined clerical life.

He was Master of the SSC from 1947 to 1950 and again from 1953 to 1956, and also Director of the Order of Charity of St Francis, based in Haggerston, which required its members to recite the Little Office of Our Lady in Latin. It is interesting however that Whatton, like Fynes-Clinton, supported the relaxed views on fasting emanating from Rome in the 1950s, and he commended evening masses very early. He was instrumental with his friend Revd E. Bowtle (parish priest of Hinton Martel 1935–53) in reviving the pilgrimage to the pre-Reformation shrine of St Wite at Whitchurch Canonicorum, Dorset.

Father Whatton was taken seriously ill in 1960, which precipitated his retirement. He was not expected to survive cancer, but in fact lived another 17 years, which he attributed to the administration of a sacramental known as the Sign of St Maurus the Abbot, which involved a blessing with a relic of the True Cross, by Dom Godfrey Stokes of Nashdom. After a long retirement assisting at various churches and communities, he died in 1977 and is buried at Hinton Martel.[8]

A third woman's order with links to Nashdom was the Society of the Good Shepherd, established at Walthamstow in 1909, which later had its mother house on Canvey Island, Essex. They were directed by the SDC, which had its novice house at Stanford-le-Hope, near Canvey. However, in 1936 the Abbot of Nashdom became the warden and the sisters adopted a modified form of the Rule of St Benedict. In 1939 they moved to Twyford, Berkshire. The order is now defunct.

The Society of the Precious Blood began as an active community for women in Birmingham in 1905 under the guidance of Revd Arnold Pinchard. Arnold Theophilus Biddulph Pinchard was the parish priest of St Jude in that city, a leader in the Anglo-Catholic Movement of the time, and also a supporter of the Church Socialist League. He had taken on the inner-city parish because his wife's health had required a return from Argentina, where he had been vicar of a church in Buenos Aires and later a canon of Stanley Cathedral in the Falklands. His younger half-brother, Revd John Lester Biddulph Pinchard, was also much concerned with the Sisters, especially after Father Arnold Pinchard's death in 1934, and Father Lester Pinchard frequently visited them when parish priest of St John, Holland Road, Kensington, from 1921 onwards.

The sisters in the small community, founded and led by Mother Millicent (Taylor), a strong-minded woman with clear views, were initially required to work amid great poverty, and many failed to stay the course. As time went on, the Reverend Mother felt herself called towards a more inward-looking existence, and after many troubles, and the near

---

8 For information on Whatton I am indebted to Revd Robert Farmer, who supplied me with an updated version of his article in *The Messenger* of the Catholic League, June 1994.

demise of the Community, in 1916 they moved to Burnham Abbey, Buckinghamshire, so that after the Benedictines later moved to Nashdom the two communities became close neighbours and for many years the monks acted as chaplains to the SPB. In the meantime however, yet a further period of uncertainty followed in which Father Lucius Cary of the SSJE, who became warden, tried to persuade them to merge with the Society of the Love of God in Oxford, whom he was also assisting.

The Community on the other hand persisted on their own line and Father Pinchard resumed the wardenship: this was made easier for him when he was appointed Secretary to the English Church Union in 1920 and left Birmingham. In the late 1920s and again in the early 1950s the Community increased substantially in numbers. They adopted the Latin breviary and their life involved perpetual intercessory prayer with an unbroken watch before the tabernacle and Exposition on Thursday nights and all through Friday. The Sisters aimed at reproducing the way of life of the Canonesses Regular who were at Burnham Abbey from 1266 to 1539: that too was a characteristic Papalist desire, namely to attempt to establish continuity from the pre-Reformation Church to the present. It was this Community which prayed all night for the rejection of the 1928 Prayer Book, not least because they had taken the view that if Reservation of the Blessed Sacrament were really to be banned, they would have to move outside England, and had actually made contingency plans to go to Scotland. It is, however, an interesting reflection on the diversity found within the Church of England at that time that while the House of Commons was voting down the new Prayer Book on the grounds that it moved the liturgy away from what was seen as the Protestant heritage of the Church, on the other hand the Sisters were living a way of life which was entirely based on a Roman model. Indeed, in 1930 Sister Dorothy Mary elected to try her vocation as an internal solitary within the Community: by 1932 this appeared to be the way in which she wished her life to go forward and new quarters were converted for her. It would be interesting to know if the Protestant Truth Society and its allies were aware that on 15 August 1932 not only did the Community celebrate the Assumption, which was the feast of title of the original Abbey, but also they formally enclosed the solitary as an anchoress, using an ancient rite for that purpose, celebrated by Father Arnold Pinchard and Revd S. Menteath, chaplain 1925–34, who curiously does not appear in *Crockford* for the time. It was thought that this was the first occasion within the Church of England that the rite of enclosure had been carried out. Sister Dorothy lived in almost perpetual isolation until in 1947 she became so ill that she needed full-time care: she died in 1948.

The Society of the Precious Blood remains in existence and has now spread abroad, with an independent house in Lesotho being founded in 1957.

It was however not always the case that closed communities were Papalist in tone. In 1921 the Servants of Christ, who had been established in 1897 in Upton Park, East London, as an active community, and then spent some years at Pleshey in Essex in a life of prayer, also moved to Burnham, in close proximity to the SPB. Although enclosed and living a life of silence, solitude and prayer, they tended towards more English usage than other such orders. In 1935 Comper provided them with a striking chapel, but more recently the Community has become defunct. Similarly the Community of the Sisters of the Love of God, which was founded in 1906, moved in 1922 to its present premises, the Convent of the Incarnation, Fairacres, Iffley Road, Oxford. They too are engaged in prayer and contemplation, but have never been Papalist in ethos, although rather ironically their buildings, designed by Paul Waterhouse, are in a modified Spanish baroque redolent of the Counter-Reformation.

There were other established orders for women which did not identify themselves as thoroughly with Roman devotions, but remained committed to the unity of the Church: for example the Sisters of Bethany, based in Bournemouth, always said prayers for that object throughout their existence. Also, the attraction of Roman systems caused tensions within communities, with older sisters often wishing to retain a more restrained liturgy. Such problems led for example to a split in the old-established Sisters of St Peter in Horbury, Yorkshire, in 1932, when a substantial dissident faction left and formed the Community of St Peter at Laleham, Surrey, which was considerably more baroque in decor and more ultramontane in theology. Curiously, the original community survives still while that at Laleham is extinct.

The pattern among the much smaller number of men's communities had certain similarities. The Society of St John the Evangelist (Cowley Fathers) had always been very conservative in their devotional life, and were never regarded as leaders of Papalism, yet it was their Superior-

General, Father O'Brien, who took the lead in opposing the Church of South India.

It was, however, the Community of the Resurrection which saw the most extensive changes in ethos, particularly under the leadership of Raymond Raynes (1903–58), who was Superior from 1943 to 1958. Raynes was a complicated, somewhat difficult man who excited strong emotions. The portrait of him in Nicholas Mosley's 1961 biography, spending hours in silent prayer before the Blessed Sacrament in the mission house in South Africa while existing on a diet consisting mainly of tinned sardines, was one side of the man: the other was his increasing need as he grew older to find relief from the monastery in the luxurious surroundings of rich friends. His political views were well to the left of centre, and he sought to disassociate Anglo-Catholicism from the rather wishy-washy pleasantries to which some used to resort. He drove himself very hard indeed and expected others to be so driven, although he disliked opposition to his views and was an exponent of the hierarchical nature of the Church rather than the social democratic, despite his political views.

However, there is no doubt that in the inter-war period and immediately after the Second World War the liturgical life of the Community moved very considerably towards Roman models and away from the austere religion of its founders. Indeed, by the late 1940s Mirfield was much nearer to Benedictinism than to its traditions. This was a trend even before Raynes was elected as Superior, particularly under the influence of Father Hubert Northcott (Novice Guardian 1922–37). The priest members of the Community began to celebrate their own private masses most days, and the importance of communal worship was reduced. The Sunday High Mass became non-communicating although Anglican forms were always used.

When the Superiors of the men's communities met at the Community of the Resurrection retreat house at St Leonards on Sea in 1943 in order to formulate opposition to the South India scheme, Raynes found that there was an English altar in the chapel, and had it demolished even before he left the conference. In 1944 the Community opened their Priory of St Paul in Holland Park, Kensington, the interior of which was designed by Martin Travers in classical style with baldachino over the altar, in sharp contradistinction to the restrained Anglicanism of Mirfield. The historian of the Community, Alan

Wilkinson, is scornful of this period in its history, writing: 'Many Anglo-Catholics, especially in the religious orders, . . . made a fatal mistake. Instead of using their freedom to interact creatively with Eastern Orthodoxy and Protestantism, as well as Roman Catholicism, they lost the proper confidence that Gore and Frere had in the Anglican right to be different and locked themselves up in a quasi-Roman prison of their own devising.'[9] Father Harry Williams CR in his autobiography is scathing about Raynes' authoritarianism and lack of sympathy for the Anglican tradition at Mirfield. He records, 'Gore wasn't an Anglo-Catholic in the sense that he didn't think it necessary to imitate Roman Catholic structures. Quite the opposite – so much so that . . . in the 1940s . . . Raymond Raynes ordered a whole trunk full of Gore's papers to be burnt because he thought them heretical (i.e. the views which they expressed were not Roman Catholic) . . .'[10]

The Mirfield Community had its own serious problems in the light of the post-Vatican II changes, which came to a head in 1974 when the Superior, Hugh Bishop, not only left the order but did so to cohabit with another man. However, after a period of consolidation and readjustment, the Community has weathered those storms.

The Society of the Sacred Mission was almost unaffected by the trend towards Rome, and indeed Father Gabriel Hebert of that community was an early and influential advocate of the Parish Communion, as early as 1929 referring in derogatory terms to the non-communicating High Mass beloved of Anglican Papalists. In 1935 he published *Liturgy and Society* and in 1937 a book of essays entitled *The Parish Communion* which was a forerunner of much that was to take place in the Church of England after the Second World War.[11]

The third trend identified above was the establishment in the middle years of the twentieth century of a number of new communities, some of which were directly identified with the leaders of the Anglican Papalist party.

Fynes-Clinton himself was instrumental in the formation of two orders, neither of which was in the event very successful. In 1911, while a curate in Shoreditch, he started the Society of St Augustine of Hippo, which was placed under the Patronage of Our Lady of Good Counsel. In

---

9 Wilkinson: *The Community of the Resurrection*, p. xiii.
10 Williams: *Some Day I'll Find You*, p. 330.
11 See Chapter 11, footnote 12.

1920 its name was changed to the Servitors of Mary and St Austin, but its object remained the same, namely to foster the religious life among men who were debarred from leaving worldly life by obstacles of moral binding force and who could therefore work outside in ordinary employment while living in community. The aim was to set up retreat houses and hostels in which the members could live, with priories attached, the special intention being the reunion of Christendom. The order published a magazine entitled *The Disciple*. The priest director in the early days was Revd Austin Taylor, but he died suddenly in 1918 and later Fynes-Clinton himself became the warden. On 5 June 1920 he received the profession in life vows of one Brother Ignatius during a Catholic League festa. The order maintained Priory House, at 76 York Road, Walthamstow, at least from 1917 until 1924,[12] and until about 1920 also had a house at 58 Pedro Street, Clapton, which then moved to 38 Union Grove, Clapham.[13] However, the Community became extinct through lack of vocations in about the mid-1920s.

The other religious order founded by Father Fynes-Clinton was the Community of Our Lady of Victory. It proved more long lasting than the Servitors but scarcely more successful. Fynes-Clinton had clothed Sister Mary St John Watson as a novice in the new community in the chapel of the Sisters of the Poor in Shoreditch, when he was still a curate at the adjacent church of St Michael. On 1 July 1915 he professed her as Canoness Regular at the Sisters' other house in Edgware, after which High Mass was celebrated. The purpose of the order was to follow the rule and ideals of the former Order of Canonesses Regular of the Holy Sepulchre, with a life centred on the Divine Office from the Brevarium Romanum and offering intercession for the restoration of the Holy

---

12 The Walthamstow Priory was near to the church of St Oswald, York Road, built on land given specifically for the purpose of furthering the Catholic Faith in the Church of England. Father Taylor was the priest in charge of the church: he did not live at the Priory, which was a small terraced house. The church was closed for a time in 1917–18 because of a dispute over the ritual used and the furnishings which had been installed, which reflected practices which were barely tolerated in the Diocese of Chelmsford, and was reopened in 1919 after Father Taylor's death and after it had been refurnished on the orders of the Bishop, but it was then bombed in the Second World War and not rebuilt.

13 Anson, in *The Call of the Cloister*, p. 218, appears to have thought that the Clapton and Walthamstow communities were separate organisations, but that seems unlikely.

Places of Palestine to Christian sovereignty. Again, the idea of reaching back to the past is demonstrated by this foundation.

The new order then established itself at the Priory of the Holy Sepulchre in Shepherdess Walk, Hoxton, a building which they apparently found after being given directions in a dream. This was in the parish of Holy Trinity, Hoxton, the parish priest of which was then Father H. W. G. Kenrick, the translator of the Missal, and they were made welcome there.

The Community did not grow, and in any event was handicapped by the continued illness of Sister Mary St John. In 1921 they moved to Edgware for a time as guests of the Community of St Mary at the Cross, and then in 1923 to St Joseph's Cottage, in the small and remote Essex village of Stow Maries. They then moved to Beckenham, and had a period in Scotland, by which time there were only two Sisters remaining. In 1928 they returned to Edgware where Sister Mary St John and Sister Martha Mary lived in a bungalow in the garden of the convent. They continued so to live for many years: Sister Martha Mary died in 1950 and Sister Mary St John (despite her earlier ill-health) lived on to 1961. With her death the Community came to an end. An icon which had been presented to the Sisters by Fynes-Clinton was returned to St Magnus in 1921 and is on the north wall of the church. At Edgware they were assisted by Father Whatton, who was resident there.

So far as other Papalist leaders are concerned, Father Hope Patten was concerned with various orders of his own and other foundations, and these are dealt with in Chapter 7. Father Alban Baverstock had, as already mentioned, been an early supporter of the Benedictines when they were in Dorset. In 1918 he founded the Sisters of the Transfiguration, whose aim was to work for mentally handicapped girls, thus continuing the tradition of the nineteenth-century sisterhoods in identifying gaps in the state provision for certain people. The first Sister was professed by Baverstock in November 1919 and took the name of Sister Mary Frances of the Holy Crown of Our Lord. Her name in religion reflected the earlier history of the organisation from which the Community grew: the secular Society of the Crown of Our Lord was founded in 1895 and Father Baverstock had become its Warden in 1909. The Community moved several times, including a spell in Basingstoke when Baverstock himself acted as chaplain (1932–3), but finally established itself at Wingrave, Buckinghamshire. They held a devotion of Holy

Hour every fourth Sunday with the specific intention of the reunion of Christendom. The Abbot of Nashdom became visitor in succession to Baverstock and Dom Gregory Dix was for a time the warden. The order diminished in size and there was increasing state provision for those among whom they worked, and in 1952 it was merged with the Community of St Mary at the Cross in Edgware, who took over the property at Wingrave.

In about 1920 Revd T. A. Lacey founded the Sisters of Reparation to Our Most Holy Redeemer, whose devotions were centred on perpetual adoration of the Blessed Sacrament. The convent was in Hayes, Middlesex, but the order had a short life.

Another foundation from the inter-war period was the Servants of Christ the King, named after the feast instituted by Pope Pius XI in 1925. What was originally called the Brotherhood of Christ the King was started in about 1928 at Staithes, Yorkshire, but they soon moved to Pershore after the Benedictines had moved on to Nashdom. They took as their vocation work for mentally handicapped boys to complement that carried on by the Sisters of the Transfiguration and in August 1931 moved to Mount Olivet, near Farnham in Surrey.

The spirituality of the small community was always ultramontane and they had baroque furnishings in their chapel with a crowned tabernacle. The brothers had close links with Nashdom and were under their direction: there were no priests among the professed brethren, the leader of whom was Brother Joseph Gardner, who spoke on the subject of 'Dogmatic Agreement' at a CPCU meeting at the Caxton Hall on 1 July 1935. Although *Reunion* in 1934 described the SCK magazine *Christus Rex* as 'always a good read' and although the *Anglo-Catholic Annual* for 1935 praised the unique work of the community within the Church of England, at Easter 1936 they made a corporate submission to Rome. Gardner (1908–47) was a man of notoriously short temper, who left Staithes after an incident in which he had assaulted several hecklers with a large crucifix. In 1935 he was suddenly moved to denounce Anglo-Catholicism at a pilgrimage at Frensham presided over by Dom Martin Collett: hence the move to Rome the following year, by which time there were only three brethren. The chaplain, Revd W. F. Wyber, moved to the Convent of St John, Sandymount, Dublin, where he was able to continue to use Latin for his services, uncommon in the Church of Ireland. The order continued only until 1938 and was then disbanded. It is said that after the example of Caldey the Roman Catholic Church had decided not to accept any more communities as an entity, but rather to disperse the members among existing orders, but this did not happen here, perhaps because of the specialist nature of the work undertaken.[14]

There was more Anglican Papalist influence in the Third Order of St Dominic, which was formed by Silas Harris with the assistance of Revd G. Hargrave Thomas, for many years vicar of Needham Market, Suffolk. Harris wrote that by 1923 his own outlook was almost entirely Dominican, and in 1925 the Order was set up with himself as Prior General: a rule of life was drawn up under which members lived in the world.[15] There was a Council of Priest Tertiaries to assist the Prior General. After Father Morton Howard moved to Hull, he organised in the 1936–8 period another group which joined that already in existence.

The declaration of the Third Order was uncompromising:

> Desiring to live the Dominican Life in the Third Order in all its fullness and reality and lamenting with sincere heart the conditions which cause our outward separation from the historic Order of Friars Preachers organized under its Master General, we declare that we accept the above necessary arrangement only in default of the normal organization of the Order and we pray for the time when we shall once more be in communion with it and with the Holy See.

Yet again, a community was looking backwards to its pre-Reformation origins and accentuating its links with that period. Harris referred to it as being the Congregation Anglicane of the Third Order and it was organised as if it were Roman. In 1928 a diary was published for the members by the St Dominic's Press at Ditchling, which was part of the craft community in that place associated with Eric Gill. The Order used its own book of Dominican Devotions, but they were simply copied from Roman sources.

There were about 80 to 90 professed members of the Order in all, some being in the United States and Canada. Revd Douglas Carter, later General Secretary of the Church Union, tried his vocation with the Dominicans as a young man, but did not proceed to profession. Others joined but seceded to Rome in due course.

---

14 For further information see B. Sewell: *Cancel All Our Vows* (Aylesford Press, 1938).
15 See the uncatalogued Harris papers in Pusey House for much information on the Order.

There was interest after Peter Anson published the first edition of his *Call of the Cloister* in 1955, but then numbers fell away again and Harris, by then a very old man, disbanded it after the death of a long-standing and devoted American member, Paul James Colby, about 1980.

Another very small Benedictine community for women, with a tangled history, established itself under the name of the Order of SS Mary and Scholastica at Kettlebaston, where they assisted Father Butler in his attempt to establish an ultramontane parish in the depths of Suffolk, but it did not flourish. They took over a cottage, now known as 'The Old Convent', in the village.

In other places, Roman models were also adopted, without any specific Anglican Papalist influence. The Benedictine Community of the Salutation of St Mary the Virgin began in 1941 as an offshoot from the Wantage sisters in an Elizabethan mansion in Burford, Oxfordshire. The Sisters immediately adopted the same Latin use as their opposite numbers in the Roman Catholic Church. Raymond Raynes was the first warden, but in 1952 he was replaced by the Abbot of Nashdom. This community still exists, but in more recent years has accepted men as well as women. Another community from the same period is that of St Clare at Freeland, near Oxford, established with assistance from other sisters in 1950. Their life was entirely enclosed and contemplative. The male contemplative community of the Servants of the Will of God, founded in 1938 by Revd R. C. S. Gofton-Salmond of St Clement, City Road, lived a hard life of solitude, but although they were Catholic in tone, and drew on Roman models, they always used English for their services. They too still exist and in recent years have also become mixed.

Other communities which date from the period in question were organised on far more traditional Anglican lines. So far as men are concerned, the Brotherhood of the Holy Cross, which functioned in Peckham from 1924 to 1963, was Socialist in inspiration and Anglican in tone, rather as was the SDC. The Franciscans, who were brought together from several groups in 1921 and have since flourished in various parts of the world as well as in England, used the Book of Common Prayer although with variations. In women's communities, the Society of the Sacred Cross, at Tymawr, Gwent, which was established in 1914 but did not move to Wales until 1923, and the Order of the Holy Paraclete, established at Whitby, Yorkshire, in 1917, were also much more English than Roman in their spirituality.

The Anglican Papalist movement is shown at its most characteristic in the development of the various religious communities, particularly in the changes which occurred to the older orders. The newer orders founded specifically in order to propagate Papalism were not successful.

The developments set out in this chapter well illustrate that during the period from 1900 until at least 1940 Anglo-Catholicism was a dynamic force – indeed the most dynamic force within the Church of England at that time. Although there was great opposition to it, and although some positions were only captured after much struggle, the expansion of the movement clearly took it with more ease into places where there was a vacuum of power. The religious communities were precisely such a place, because they were ignored by many in the Church of England, and because very little was done to impose discipline within them. Thus islands of Anglican Papalism developed, perhaps most notably in the case of Nashdom and of the various communities which were directed by or connected to that order.

It is difficult in fact to avoid the conclusion that completely different standards were applied by the bishops to the control of worship in the communities from those applied in parish churches. A blind eye was turned to much of what occurred, and it was only deliberate disloyalty, such as at the Community of the Holy Cross in Hayward's Heath, described in Chapter 6, which provoked retaliation. There were occasional forays by the episcopate into regulation, such as in July 1930 when a conference was arranged at Keble College, Oxford, to set up regulations for all the communities: there appears to have been a serious proposal that the communities should all use the Book of Common Prayer, whereas in fact by 1920 many had moved so far in a Roman direction that they were effectively out of the orbit of ordinary parochial life.

Following the institution of the Advisory Council in 1935, a certain amount of co-ordination of the communities took place, but by then their character was well established. It was not in the end to be the bishops, but rather the changes in the Roman Church, followed assiduously by the religious in the Anglican Community, which brought back those who remained into the mainstream.

In more recent years a number of nuns have been ordained as priests, and the number of communities which have stood out against that development has been remarkably small viewed against their history.

6

THE OUTER FRINGES OF THE CHURCH OF ENGLAND

Father Victor Roberts and Dom Gregory Dix

The ecclesiastical views of Revd Thomas Victor Roberts, for many years warden of the Community of the Holy Cross at Hayward's Heath in Sussex, have already been mentioned in the first paragraph of Chapter 1.

The author's attention was first drawn to Father Roberts many years ago when in a letter responding to an undergraduate interest in the matters set out in this book, the late Peter Anson referred him to Roberts' 'stratospheric Papalism' while warden of the Sisterhood.

That attention was further aroused when perusal of the history of the Community, written by Alan Russell and published in 1957 to mark the centenary of the order, showed that the book was very reticent about Roberts, but on the other hand was very fulsome in its praise of Bishop G. K. A. Bell of Chichester, who, although distinguished in many different ways, would not normally be considered as a supporter of a sisterhood with a very distinct Roman devotional life.

In due course, however, a number of files in the Bell papers in the Lambeth Palace Library made the situation very much clearer, and incidentally threw a great deal of light on some unusual episodes in the history of Anglican Papalism.[1]

Victor Roberts was a non-collegiate student in Oxford in 1913, and then went to St Stephen's House. His father was also in holy orders. He was ordained deacon in the Diocese of Lichfield in 1916 and priest the

---

1 All the letters in relation to the Community of the Holy Cross and the dispute with the Benedictines of Nashdom unless otherwise indicated are contained in the Bell papers in Lambeth Palace Library.

following year, and served curacies at Holy Trinity, Sneyd, Burslem, from 1916 to 1919, and at St George, Wolverhampton, from 1919 to 1921, before joining the Benedictine Community then at Pershore, Worcestershire.

Both those curacies have some interest. At that time, there was a strong move among those churches where the English Use had been adopted to move over to the Western or Roman Use. While Roberts was at Sneyd, the Western Use prevailed, but subsequently that church was one of the few which moved in the other direction: this was under the influence of Revd Harold Mason, who became curate there in 1923. He had been converted to the English Use by Conrad Noel at Thaxted, and persuaded his vicar to adopt it in Sneyd.

In Wolverhampton on the other hand the interest was more personal. One of Roberts' parishioners there from 1919 to 1920 was Constance Young, who had been brought up as a Roman Catholic and educated in a convent, but for some now unknown reason had then attached herself to the Church of England. She was to have an enormous influence on his later life.

In 1921 Roberts left Wolverhampton and joined the Benedictines. Following the debacle of the Caldey secession, the remaining remnant of the Community consisted of one monk in vows, Dom Anselm Mardon, and two internal oblates, Father Denys Prideaux and Brother Charles Hutson. In September 1913 they went into residence at Abbey House, Pershore, which was solemnly blessed by Bishop Yeatman-Biggs of Worcester on 1 May 1914; in 1919 Bishop Pearce replaced him as the local diocesan and was noticeably less sympathetic to the Community's aspirations. Those who had assisted before rallied round: Lord Halifax became the chairman of the Pershore Helpers' Committee, and Athelstan Riley and the Dukes of Newcastle and Argyll also lent their support.

Dom Anselm soon followed his brethren to Rome. The survival of the nascent community was only secured when Father Denys finally agreed to enter the religious life. He was professed on 18 February 1922 and installed as Abbot the following day. Others who were to be of influence in the development of the Community also joined at about this time, including Martin Collett, who was to succeed Prideaux as Abbot, and Bernard Clements, who was later to act as a parish priest in London.

Abbot Denys had been a curate at St Cuthbert, Philbeach Gardens, when he was still known by his baptismal name of William. He then suffered a breakdown in health, and moved to Caldey in 1907. Throughout his life he was prone to periods of depression, was a poor chairman, and found it difficult to delegate. On the other hand he was a man of immense learning who re-established the Community on much stronger foundations than had been the case before. These were made even firmer when in 1926 the brothers left Pershore and moved to the Lutyens house at Nashdom, Burnham, Buckinghamshire, which they were able to adapt in an entirely Italianate way for their use. The Community was established on purely Benedictine lines, and the entire Rule of the saint was followed after 1920, whereas Caldey had been quasi-Cistercian in observance.

Father Roberts was at Pershore as a postulant for only three to four weeks, and then as a novice for one year, before taking his final vows. He was subsequently to assert that he took those vows without proper preparation or thought, and subject to an express condition, agreed by Abbot Denys, to the effect that he might assert any matter of conscience even if in disagreement with the other members of the Community. He alleged that the order was so short of priests that pressure was placed upon him to make his commitment, and he went so far as to suggest that the inducement of ordination was held out to some aspirants, as well as financial offers such as the payment of debts owed by some postulants.

These apparently wild allegations receive considerable support from contemporary assertions to a similar effect made by Father Donald Rea, who was later to play a significant part in this episode and who has already been noted for his part in the wider history of the Papalist Movement in the Church of England. He was in a particularly vulnerable state at this time, as he had suffered from what was then known as shell shock following his experiences in the trenches in the First World War. In 1921 he was encountered on Herm by Compton Mackenzie. Rea had been sent to the island to cut bracken in a successful attempt to recover his health after a breakdown, and he was able to assist the author with *The Altar Steps*, the first volume of his ecclesiastical trilogy. Rea corroborated Roberts' allegations to the extent that he alleged that, while he had visited Pershore and had been interested in the life there, he had never wanted to take vows: however, the Abbot appeared to assume that he would be joining and pressed him quite hard so to do.

Abbot Denys is usually portrayed as a somewhat unworldly character, but his dealings in relation to this episode perhaps show him in a different light. It is however perhaps a mark of the flights of fantasy to which some on the ultramontane wing were concerned that Father Maltby suggested (in a letter dated 25 July 1927) that Denys should be consecrated as Bishop of the English Catholics, so as to be able to 'regularise' the orders of Anglo-Catholic priests and form a bridge to Rome.[2] Although Denys had many talents, the proposition that he should join the episcopate is difficult to take seriously.

It does not appear that Dom Victor, as Roberts became, was an entirely easy colleague. When Father Whatton returned to the Church of England after his brief sojourn in the Roman Catholic Church, Roberts was the only member of the Pershore Chapter who refused to agree to his readmittance to the Community.

In about 1923, however, Roberts was permitted to leave Pershore on a temporary basis in order to act as chaplain to the Sisters of the Church in Kilburn. Abbot Denys later alleged that while he was there one of the Sisters began to experience visions, which however were said to have suddenly ceased after Roberts left.

In about late 1924 Roberts was sent to be warden of the Holy Cross Sisters at Hayward's Heath, initially as a part-time appointment and on the basis of course that he remained a member of the Pershore Community. He was granted a formal licence so to act by Bishop W.O. Burrows of Chichester on 28 March 1925.

The Holy Cross Sisters were founded by Elizabeth Neale, the sister of the hymnographer John Mason Neale, who was himself the founder of the Sisterhood of St Margaret at nearby East Grinstead. The Holy Cross Sisters had always been more Roman in their outlook than many of the other orders founded at that time, and in particular had worked in the parish of St Peter, London Docks, under the legendary Father C. F. Lowder, where they had distinguished themselves in a cholera epidemic. In company with many such orders however, by the end of the First World War they had drawn back from much outside work and become more contemplative in outlook. Their convent at Hayward's Heath was very large and possessed extensive grounds: in addition they had a branch house at Limpsfield, Surrey. Retreats were organized at both houses.

---

2 This letter is in the uncatalogued Rea papers in Pusey House.

The visitor of the Community at the time of Roberts' appointment was Father Darwell Stone of Pusey House, who held other such positions elsewhere. There was no-one more qualified to act tactfully and wisely should difficulties arise.

There were frequently tensions between such communities and the local diocesan, as practices were introduced, and sometimes tolerated, which would not have been allowed in a parish church. Neale had for example introduced his nuns to Exposition and Benediction of the Blessed Sacrament at a very early date.

On 21 July 1921 the disciplinarian Bishop of Southwark, Cyril Garbett, wrote to Burrows complaining that the rite of Benediction was regularly being performed at Limpsfield, which was within his diocese. Burrows wrote to Darwell Stone, who said that the Sisters had had Reservation of the Blessed Sacrament for as long as he could remember, and then took it up with the Warden, Revd W. Astley Cooper. The latter replied on 26 December 1921 asking not to have to give up the practice, and justifying it. This was followed by a petition dated 13 January 1922 from Mother Ida and all the other Sisters, asking the Bishop not to prohibit the devotion. Benediction of the Blessed Sacrament was however a service which was so explicit in its meaning that at that time no bishop in England was prepared to sanction it, and Burrows was no exception. On 24 January 1922 Father Cooper wrote back to say that, with reluctance, he would accept his ruling. Cooper was Roberts' immediate predecessor, and he died in 1925.

One of the signatories to the petition was Father Roberts' former parishioner, Constance Young, who had in the meantime joined the Community and had adopted the name of Scholastica in religion: this name itself had unfortunate overtones within the Anglican Communion, as it was the name which had been taken by Abbess Ewart of Milford Haven, who had defected to Rome at the time of the Caldey secessions. Sister Scholastica Young took her final vows in May 1923.

From 1925 to 1927 Sister Scholastica was reported to have had a number of visions and other spiritual experiences, which Roberts described enthusiastically as 'ecstasies'. Abbot Denys later alleged that these tended to occur conveniently whenever Roberts was expected to return to Pershore, and he certainly produced the transcripts of a number of letters from him in which he put off his return because of the condition of his protegée. Roberts himself reported in writing that Sister

Scholastica had received the stigmata of Christ on one occasion, and then on another had been marked on her head as if by the Crown of Thorns. He also said she had cried tears of blood, as well as seeing visions of Our Lady, St Teresa of Avila, St Theresa of Lisieux, and others. She underwent paranormal experiences such as being hurled from her bed across the room in such a way that the cord which all the sisters wore around the neck cut into her. In addition to those happenings, which are recorded by Roberts himself and by Sister Scholastica, Abbot Denys said that Roberts had reported that he himself had received the stigmata, and had seen rays of light emanating from the Blessed Sacrament and illuminating Sister Scholastica. Denys also said that he had been told that Scholastica had had a vision of Our Lady, who had told her that Roberts' orders were valid and there was no need for him to go over to Rome. Roberts never, however, accepted in writing to the authorities that that or any other experiences relating directly to himself had happened.

The manifestations were the subject of debate in the Community: in July 1926 however, in the middle of the sequence, Sister Scholastica became novice mistress.

It does not appear that these matters were reported to Bishop Burrows. He, however, did have cause to write to Roberts on 3 March 1926, asking whether it was true that services in Latin were being held in the convent. The reply was somewhat equivocal, with an indication that the Mass was partly in Latin, but it is interesting that in Russell's history he dates the introduction of Latin as at exactly this time, namely March 1926.

The Benedictines moved to Nashdom in 1926 and were again short of priests. Both for that reason and (as he later admitted) because he was extremely unhappy about the spiritual life of the Holy Cross Convent in the light of the visions, Abbot Denys decided to recall Roberts to the Community. Roberts at first deferred his return, and eventually refused to go back. He was formally recalled on 26 July 1928, and then given a peremptory order to return on 25 August of that year. On 12 November 1928 the Chapter of the Community met and again he was told to return: his response was to write on 4 December 1928 to the effect that his profession had been a mistake, it was done too quickly, and was made with reservations, and that he therefore regarded it as a nullity. However, on 10 December 1928 he was expelled and on 6 January 1929 an instrument of formal dismissal was drawn up.

On 7 January 1929 Darwell Stone resigned as visitor to the Holy Cross Sisters. He was later to explain to Bell, in a letter dated 16 July 1929, that he did so not only because he thought that the position of Roberts was impossible in retaining the wardenship while being a dismissed member of a religious order, but also because there was in the devotional life a 'sentimentality and unhealthiness which seemed to [him] dangerous', by which he clearly meant the visions together with the strong promotion of the cult of the Little Flower of Lisieux.

It is ironic in the light of that resignation to appreciate that the Nashdom Community itself did not have a visitor until October 1928 when they appointed Bishop Frere CR, whose knowledge of monastic life was unrivalled, but who had little sympathy with their own interpretation of the faith. They did so precisely in order that he might advise them over the Roberts affair.

Throughout the first half of 1929 the dispute over Father Roberts became a matter of bitter debate in Anglican Papalist circles. A large number of retreats which had been booked to take place at the Hayward's Heath convent were cancelled. Father Fynes-Clinton, who was a regular conductor of such retreats, wrote on 11 August 1929 that he personally would find it difficult to take retreats while the warden was a dismissed monk. On the other hand Father Langford-James, the co-founder with Fynes-Clinton of the Catholic League, strongly supported Roberts and eventually insisted on going to see Frere in Truro, to the latter's considerable annoyance. More support was given to Roberts by Father Roger Wodehouse, the flamboyant and well-connected vicar of St Paul, Oxford.

George Bell was installed as Bishop of Chichester in June 1929: Bishop Burrows had died some months before. One of the first matters with which he had to deal was an urgent appeal from Mother Mabel of the Holy Cross Sisters for 'protection' against the campaign being waged by the Benedictines of Nashdom. Bell began making investigations, and it soon became clear to him that a real hornets' nest had been stirred up. It is apparent that underlying the various accusations which were flying about was the unspoken assertion that Father Roberts and Sister Scholastica were rather more friendly than they should have been, bearing in mind their respective positions. Abbot Denys at one point asserted that Roberts had a picture in his study which he claimed was of his sister, but was in fact of Scholastica. It was even rumoured that the two had

1. Revd H. J. Fynes-Clinton (1876–1959), the leading Anglican Papalist of his generation. (*Catholic League*)

2. Revd Alfred Hope Patten, parish priest of Walsingham 1921–58 and refounder of the Shrine of Our Lady. (*Shrine of Our Lady of Walsingham*)

3. The interior of Father E. S. Maltby's mission church of St Mary, Erlam Road, South Bermondsey, about 1916. The church and indeed the road in which it stood have long since been demolished. (*English Heritage, National Monuments Register*)

4. Father Alban Baverstock.
(*Catholic League*)

5. Father Geoffrey Whatton. (*Catholic League*)

6. The genuine continental baroque high altar in St Michael, Ladbroke Grove, North Kensington, taken about 1965. (*English Heritage, National Monuments Register*)

7. The 'most convincing Roman Catholic interior in the Church of England', St Alphege Southwark. (*Michael Yelton Collection*)

8. The interior of the small back-street church of St Michael, Bingfield Street, Islington, taken about 1965. It has now been demolished. (*English Heritage, National Monuments Register*)

9. An unidentified bishop from overseas visits St Michael, Islington, probably in the 1950s. (*Richard McEwan Collection*)

10. The high altar at St Bartholomew, Newborough, near Peterborough, after refurbishment by Father Clive Beresford. (*Richard McEwan Collection*)

11. The Catholic League festa at Woodside, Croydon, Whit 1929: a relatively youthful Father Fynes-Clinton is sixth from the left in the back row. (*Revd A. T. J. Salter Collection*)

12. Altar of Father Corbould's church of All Saints, Carshalton, gilded by J. N. Comper. (*Michael Yelton*)

13. High Mass at St Thomas, Warwick Street, Toxteth, Liverpool (closed 1939 and later demolished). The celebrant is the veteran Father Ernest Underhill, with the deacon the lifelong Papalist Father Rice Harris. (*Richard McEwan Collection*)

14. Revd Rice Alforth Evelyn Harris, the so-called 'Martyr of Carshalton'. (*Michael Yelton Collection*)

15. Shrine of Our Lady Queen of Peace in St Saviour, Hoxton. (*English Heritage, National Monuments Register*)

16. (A) Revd Charles Chester Higgs, vicar of St Alban, Fulham 1939–59, taken at the time of his induction. (*London Borough of Hammersmith and Fulham*)

(B) Catechism certificate from St Alban, Fulham, signed by Fathers Higgs and Kewley. (*London Borough of Hammersmith and Fulham*)

This Certificate is awarded to Edith Brumpton for Regular Attendance, 417 marks, for the year Advent 1921–Advent 1922.

E. Hames.
Secretary of Catechism

Priests of Catechism. W. Kewley
C. C. Higgs.

been engaged to be married while they were in Wolverhampton. Roberts on the other hand alleged that Denys was mentally ill.

Bell decided that he should visit the convent himself in order to interview all the Sisters and get to the bottom of what was happening. That course was welcome both to the Community and to Roberts, whose letters to the Bishop at this time display an almost embarrassingly obsequious deference. Bell enlisted the assistance of Father Lucius Cary, who was to correspond at some length with him for many years over the affairs of the Sisters, and of Father R. H. Tribe of the Society of the Sacred Mission. The three men visited Hayward's Heath from 10 to 12 April and again from 26 to 30 May 1930, meeting all the Sisters privately as well as seeing Roberts.

The unofficial tribunal of inquiry was unanimous that 'the grave charges or insinuations which have been made against the moral character of the Convent have no foundation in fact'. Various drafts of a letter to that effect to be circulated to all the Communities in England were prepared, but in the meantime Bell insisted that the Sisters have an external confessor who would visit once a year in order that any who wished could speak to him in confidence. Revd T. Dilworth-Harrison of St Bartholomew, Brighton, was eventually prevailed upon to accept this post, which he did in December 1930. Roberts had said that the Sisters had access both to Father Rea, who was chaplain at the Limpsfield branch house from 1925 to 1934, and to Revd C. F. Hrauda, a priest of Austrian origin whose presence within the Anglican Communion sometimes appeared as surprising to himself as it did to outsiders, but both these were regarded as insufficiently independent.

In the meantime also, and before the formal release of the statement, the Sisters were told of the conclusions, and Bell was requested to become visitor to the Community, to which he agreed. At the same time he was asking the Nashdom monks to acquiesce in Roberts' plea of nullity in his profession, and wrote to them to that effect in June 1930: they finally, and with some reluctance, agreed to that course in December of that year.

It appeared therefore that Bell had managed to resolve the situation satisfactorily. On 29 December 1930 he made his first visit to the Community in the capacity of visitor, and read to the Sisters the statement which had been drafted for circulation.

However, matters were nowhere near as settled as Bell no doubt thought after that visit. He had exculpated the convent from the serious allegations which were being made against its moral tone, but he had not at that time really turned his mind to the liturgy which was being used and the teaching which the Sisters were receiving. It may also have escaped his notice that there was to be an election for the post of Reverend Mother on 6 February 1931, and there was some dissatisfaction with Mother Mabel, who was thought somewhat retiring in disposition.

This issue came almost immediately to Bell's attention. On 4 and 25 January 1931 Sister Harriet CHC wrote to him warning him of the possibility that Sister Scholastica would be elected, and complaining of her 'indiscreet familiarity with the Warden', the very matter he had just investigated and found to be without foundation. She also complained of the excessively pro-Roman tendencies of Roberts.

On 6 February 1931 the Sisters did indeed elect Sister Scholastica as their Mother: she was only 32 years of age and only just qualified on years of profession to accept the position. This decision did not meet with acclamation either from Bell or from his adviser Father Cary SSJE. Bell then began correspondence with Roberts in which he endeavoured to prevent the latter saying mass in Latin. Eventually he wrote on 25 February 1931 to the effect that he would acquiesce in the use of Latin in the mass, provided that the lessons were in English, and that the rite used was not the Roman rite. He also prohibited Benediction and Exposition. It is difficult to see whether Bell seriously envisaged that the Sisters would use the Book of Common Prayer or another Anglican rite in Latin. Roberts simply refused to comply and Bell did not press matters further. He had, however, to release his letter to all the Communities, which he had held back while he tried to settle the liturgical issues.

It is clear that once Father Roberts and his protegée Mother Scholastica, as she became, were the dominant forces within the convent outside influences were rigorously excluded. All the services were in Latin, the Sisters were strongly discouraged from attending local churches, and all the books in the convent had to bear the imprimatur of the Roman authorities. Father Dilworth-Harrison went to Hayward's Heath once a year, but did not actually see any of the nuns. The regime in the convent was based on the Rule of St Benedict, but Roberts took the view that they were not actually Benedictines as they were not founded from a foundation of that order.

There was, however, a certain amount of dissension within the walls of the convent which reached the ears of Bishop Bell. In October 1931 Sister Ruth wished to leave the order to look after her aged parents: she also complained about the 'Roman lines' upon which the order was being reorganised. In August 1933 a young female acquaintance of Bell tried her vocation with the Sisters for a short time. She reported to him that the 'whole convent had no use for Anglo-Catholicism but only for the Pope'. At this stage Bell had serious thoughts about withdrawing Roberts' licence, but in the event he did not take that step. Later he was even more disturbed to find, from an outside informant, that earlier that year some of the Sisters, led by Mother Scholastica, had gone on pilgrimage to Rome: on the boat out they had only attended the Roman mass, and had boycotted the services held by an Anglican parson who was also a passenger. In Rome they had stayed in a convent near the Vatican, had been to see the Pope in procession, and had apparently been approached by Archbishop Amigo of Southwark with a view to secession. Roberts, who does not appear to have gone to Rome himself, later said that he had seen the Bishop locally and had rejected his approaches because the Romans would not agree to reordain him *sub conditione.*

In November 1936 Sister Harriet, who had written the warning letters to Bell in 1931, ran away while being moved back to the mother house following the closure of the branch at Limpsfield. She again wrote to Bell, on this occasion asserting that the Sisters were being prevented from having any contact with him as visitor, and that Mother Scholastica had termed him the 'Protestant Bishop of Chichester', that Latin was being enforced even within the confessional, and that Father Wodehouse was being allowed to celebrate mass within the convent. The concern about Father Wodehouse resulted from the fact that in April 1935 he had been sentenced to a term of one month's imprisonment following his conviction for an offence of indecency with a male. He had had to resign his living and was temporarily precluded from parochial work.

The convent was not the only problem facing Bell. In 1937 Revd H. G. Davis died after a short incumbency of the Church of the Annunciation, Washington Street, Brighton. He had normally used the Roman rite, in English for those parts spoken aloud and in Latin for those which the congregation could not hear. This was unacceptable to the Bishop, and his successor Revd E. A. Power, who had some years earlier been a curate at St Bartholomew in the same town, was required to use more of the Prayer Book. Unfortunately, Father Hrauda, who had been rejected as an external confessor to the Holy Cross nuns some years before, was an honorary assistant priest at the Annunciation. It is said that he disturbed the 1662 rite with cries of 'Jezebel, Jezebel' and was only placated by being allowed to say his own Latin mass in a side chapel.

In the meantime, Bishop Bell assiduously carried out his annual visitation. On 28 December 1937 however he was somewhat disturbed to learn in conversation with Mother Scholastica that she thought that in the order 'we are all Romans now, for there are no Anglicans'. He noted that Roberts appeared to accept all the Roman claims save that he believed in the validity of his own orders.

The result of Bell's conversation with Mother Scholastica on this occasion was that he decided that his position as visitor was untenable: on 31 December 1937 he resigned. The response of the Community was to select Father Rea, who by this time was the parish priest of Eye, Suffolk, as the replacement visitor: his relationship with Father Roberts was such that he was unlikely to apply any great independent judgement to the affairs of the order.

In 1939 further reports reached Bell, as a result of which on 29 December of that year he interviewed Roberts. The latter accepted that he perceived himself as a Roman Catholic priest under censure, that he prayed for the Roman Catholic Archbishop of Southwark at mass (although he said that he also prayed for Bell), and that he referred to Bell as 'the superintendent', although he said that was only in jest. Bell recorded that Roberts even condemned the Belgian monks of Amay for their prayers for unity, because he took the view that there was in fact no Church of England which could submit to Rome. In that view Bell thought that he went even beyond the Anglican Papalist party. Roberts' theory was that the Community was part of a 'doorstep church' which was within the influence of the Holy See but not in communion with it because of external reasons which were not the desire of the sisters.

By this time Bell was extremely concerned about the position of the Community within the Church of England. He repeatedly pressed Father Roberts for a statement of his allegiance and eventually, on 21 January 1940, received a definitive reply. Roberts wrote:

I recognize that *de facto* I receive from the Bishop of Chichester such jurisdiction as he is capable of giving me and that this is the only jurisdiction to which I have access. I further recognize my duties of giving to the Bishop of Chichester canonical obedience, i.e. obedience to his authority in so far as that authority is itself exercised in obedience to the Catholic Church. This also represents the position of the Community.

This communication was too much for Bell. After consulting Archbishop Lang he withdrew Roberts' licence of 1925 and indeed requested its return. The withdrawal of the bishop's licence did not, however, prevent Father Roberts from continuing to minister to his Community. It meant only that thereafter the Community of the Holy Cross was regarded as a private association outside the Church of England.

In this somewhat twilight zone the Community continued throughout the war: in fact in it the convent was used for some years as a hospital. The ecclesiastical isolation of the sisters was, however, almost complete.

In 1947 there was a wholly unexpected twist to the story. Mother Scholastica had apparently become more autocratic over the years, and is said to have turned on her former patron, Father Roberts, and become abusive towards him. In February of that year she had a nervous breakdown, following which she announced her intention of re-adopting the style of Miss C. M. Young: she moved into a cottage in the grounds, wore secular clothes, and said that she intended to return to the Roman Catholic Church.

When Bishop Bell was told this news, he held out to Roberts an olive branch of reconciliation, but the latter refused to respond in any way. Mother Mary St Anthony was elected as Mother Superior and the convent continued along its chosen path, although it appears that in those later years the services, although entirely Roman, were much less elaborate than had been the case in earlier times. Roberts seems to have been regarded by most of his former associates as awkward to deal with: at this period he refused to release for publication some work which Father Hrauda had written before his death: Roberts was his executor, and the thesis was only published in *Reunion* after his own death.

On 16 February 1954 Father Roberts died in his sleep. His Community was by then wholly schooled in the ways of Rome, but their influence outside had dwindled very considerably. There were only 39

Sisters, whereas in the early 1920s there had been 70. There had been no new novices for ten years and Mother Mary St Anthony told Bishop Bell that she thought that it was a dying order. It is clear also from Rea's written reports to Bell that at about that time the last of three written invitations to secede came to the Sisters, this being from the Abbot of Downside.[3]

Bell saw the death of Roberts as a further chance to bring the order back within the mainstream of the Church of England, and on this occasion his approaches met with a more positive response. He decided to ask Father O'Brien of the Cowley Fathers and Dom Benedict Ley of Nashdom to enquire into the present situation of the Sisters vis-à-vis the Church of England. Whether or not the irony of asking for the co-operation of the Nashdom Benedictines in this task was apparent to Bell is not clear. However, as Father O'Brien warned him, the Nashdom liturgical regime was in fact very similar to that of the Community of the Holy Cross.

The reporters duly indicated that progress was possible, and the Community came back into the diocesan fold, although Bell realistically appreciated that after their 25-year period of quasi-Romanism the Sisters would not change their liturgy. The solution which was devised was that Father Rea would become temporary warden of the Community, because without a warden the statutes could not be changed: they were then altered to exclude the specific acceptance of the teachings of the Holy See. Bell was reinvited to become visitor and accepted.

It was in that context that Russell wrote his history. The references in it to Father Roberts are noticeably lukewarm, although he did say the Community hoped at some time in the future to replace the Gothic fittings by 'a proper liturgical altar' (presumably baroque in decor), in order to fulfil a hope of his.[4] Bell was reluctant to write the foreword, and it was eventually written by Rea himself, although Bell became more friendly when convinced of the uncontroversial nature of the contents of the book.

Mother Mary St Anthony was unduly pessimistic about the prospects for the order. The Community continued in existence, and continued to use Latin for all liturgical purposes. Rea continued as warden until 1961.

---

3 Rea Papers, Pusey House.
4 Russell: *Community of the Holy Cross*, p. 47.

In due course however the revolution from Rome which affected all communities in the post-Vatican II era made its mark here as well. Numbers declined, and in 1979 the vast premises at Hayward's Heath were vacated and the Sisters moved to Rempstone, Nottinghamshire, where there are now about ten in the Community. It is one of the very few Anglican communities which does not accept the ministry of women priests, so its traditions have not been entirely lost.

The development of the Benedictine Community at Nashdom after Roberts left it had certain similarities to that of the Holy Cross Sisters, although despite an attitude of extreme ultramontanism they were never as isolated within the Anglican Church.

Once the Community had moved to Nashdom they were able to move forward. Martin Travers designed baroque fittings for the ball-room, which became the chapel, and the adjoining billiard room became the sacristy. In 1930 daily High Mass began, and the general liturgical pattern thereafter was for there to be a private mass at 6.45 a.m. for all priest monks, with another monk acting as server, and then at 9.45 a non-communicating Conventual High Mass. All the services were in Latin according to the Roman rite and there was nothing at all in the devotional life of the Community to distinguish it from a similar house in the Roman Communion. In fact Abbot Denys specifically saw the growth of that form of worship in his community and also the women's orders at Edgware and West Malling as showing continuity with the pre-Reformation period and as reaching back to the Pope himself. There is no doubt that the Community was Papalist, in that all the members saw as their long-term objective the return to Rome of the entire Anglican Communion, and as their short-term aim the assimilation of the Church of England to Roman practices. The brothers saw themselves as the vanguard of that movement.

In 1930 close associations began between the Community and the Shrine at Walsingham and also with the convent of St Mary at the Cross, Edgware, of which Abbot Denys became major superior and Father Whatton chaplain. Nashdom also wanted to establish its own seminary at that time, but could not fulfil the required conditions: there were, however, occasional ordinands until about 1945.

In 1934 Dom Bernard Clements was offered the living of All Saints, Margaret Street, which he accepted and filled until his death in 1942. This was an extraordinary offer, bearing in mind that although many outsiders thought that All Saints was in the forefront of Anglo-Catholicism, in fact both the liturgy and the teaching were far from advanced. The appointment caused widespread protests among Protestants, and police were required at the Institution, but Clements became a successful broadcaster and well-known thinker.

In November 1934 Denys Prideaux died and was replaced as Abbot by Martin Collett, a far more effective administrator, who became a very strong supporter of the Walsingham devotion, and was much concerned with reunion societies. The Church Unity Octave became a central feature of the life at Nashdom.

In the late 1930s the community at Nashdom had contacts with Abbé Couturier, which have already been described, and these involved particularly both Dom Benedict Ley and Dom Gregory Dix.

It was Dix who was to have a much wider impact on the Church outside than almost any other religious in the Anglican Communion in this period.

George Eglinton Alston Dix (1901–52) took the name in religion of Gregory. He came from an Anglo-Catholic background: his father was himself ordained later in life, and his brother Ronald was a parish priest who took a prominent part in the 1948 Congress. Dix was a fellow of Keble College from 1924 to 1926. He was ordained deacon in October 1924 to the title of his fellowship, but in 1926, by then a priest, he left Keble for the Benedictine Community.

Dix was a man of mordant wit whose tongue offended many. He was also an original thinker, who often took some considerable time to come to a conclusion, but once he had reached his final position would defend it with great vigour. For many years he found himself unable to commit himself completely to Nashdom and was simply an internal oblate. It appears that at one point between about 1928 and 1932 he very nearly went over to Rome, but eventually he held back. However, his recent biographer, Simon Bailey, correctly says that he was 'distinctly reluctant to criticize Rome and always ready to make concessions [in that direction]'.[5] In 1936 he re-entered the noviciate and in 1940 took his final vows, although even in that year he wrote that staying in the Church of England required arresting the liberal tendency in it, disestablishment, 'regularising' Anglican orders, and convincing the Roman Church that

---

5 Bailey: *A Tactful God*, p. 98.

Anglicanism is fit for unity and the Anglican Church that it needed Catholic communion.[6]

By this period Dix had become much involved in literature supporting reunion: as already mentioned, he and Father Ivan Young, parish priest of Kensworth near Dunstable, edited *The Pilot*, the magazine of the Society for Promoting Catholic Unity, for a time. Some criticised the tone of the articles for their negative attacks on the episcopate, but Dix enjoyed using the rough edge of his tongue. The magazine was published by the Dacre Press, in which Dix co-operated with Mrs Berta Travers (who despite widespread belief to the contrary was no relation of the designer Martin Travers). In due course Dix did convince himself of the validity of Anglican orders, and wrote *The Question of Anglican Orders* (published by Dacre in 1944) to show the argument.

Dix himself drafted and ensured that the Dacre Press published the stern warnings over South India which were published in 1943 under the title *Open Letter of Superiors of Religious Communities to the Archbishop of Canterbury*.

It was also during the war years, largely while he was acting as chaplain to the Edgware nuns, who had been evacuated with their patients to Nashdom, that Dix wrote his masterpiece, *The Shape of the Liturgy*, which was published by Dacre Press in 1945. Although on the face of it an unlikely subject for a bestseller, it was an enormously influential book, and not only in narrow church circles. The lucid style and comprehensive coverage made previously esoteric matters comprehensible to the educated lay person. It began to sell very well immediately, and continued to sell in substantial numbers. The book remained in print for many years, although some of its scholarship has of course been overtaken by more modern research. One of the aims of the book was to demonstrate the continuity of the liturgy of the mass, the very principle upheld at Nashdom. It was an interesting contrast to the path which Father Roberts had chosen: while Roberts was isolated and inward-looking, Dix, from a similar position within the Church of England, spread his message out to the world.

The assurances given by Archbishop Fisher over South India in 1948 enabled those in the Church of England who were unhappy with the establishment of the new church to remain without too much loss of

---

6 Ibid., p. 48.

face, although Dix is reported to have said that one should not be surprised at the conduct of his fathers-in-God, commenting: 'After all, the sign of a Bishop is a crook, and of an Archbishop a double-cross.'[7] He then became a member of the group which drafted the *Catholicity Report* for Fisher. He contributed a chapter on 'The post-Tridentine Papal Communion', which was laudatory in its tone.

It is impossible to say whether Dix would have had an even wider influence had his life not been ended early by cancer, which killed him in 1952. His views were too extreme for him to be considered for a bishopric, and his tongue was so sharp that it offended many, especially among those whom he termed the NRE or 'National Religious Establishment', the vague centre of the Church of England.

The Nashdom Community flourished in the post-Second World War period, as did many other communities, while in the wider Church the influence of Anglo-Catholicism was declining. In 1964 the brothers published *The Jubilee Book of the Benedictines of Nashdom*, which is extremely optimistic in tone. However, it is now apparent that the Community had just reached its high-water mark of some 40 members. It was then almost overwhelmed by the waves emanating from the post-Vatican Council revolution as it affected communities. Latin was gradually abandoned from 1966 and had disappeared completely by 1970, and of course further liturgical changes came to Nashdom. There followed a serious crisis in the monastery and a number of brethren left; others had nervous breakdowns and in 1983 the then Abbot, Wilfred Weston, announced that he was leaving to marry.

The Community, however, survived. In 1987 Nashdom was sold at a good price and the Community moved to the much more modest surroundings of Elmore Abbey at Speen, near Newbury, Berkshire. There were nine members when the move was made, and that number has been slightly increased since then. Numbers still enquire about the noviciate but few stay the course.

Although the Elmore Community is still Benedictine, its tone has changed radically: the move from Nashdom was symbolic of an underlying shift in direction. It is no longer Anglo-Papalist in its direction: the Brothers are not even under alternative episcopal supervision and a majority does not oppose the ordination of women. On Sunday they

---

7 Ross Williamson: *The Walled Garden*, p. 144.

attend the Sung Eucharist in the adjoining village church. They have far more contact with evangelicals and other groups within the Church of England and are recognizably within that Communion rather than loosely attached to the edges of it. How Dom Gregory Dix would view the present position is perhaps difficult to imagine.

It is also interesting that while the call of the cloister has lost much of its force over the last 40 years, Elmore now has no fewer than 340 external oblates, of whom about 90 are priests: this is a form of commitment which has grown considerably in the Church of England in recent years while seldom found among Roman Catholics.

7

SHRINES OF OUR LADY
Walsingham, Egmanton and Middleton

The importance of the outward manifestations of Catholic faith in the growth of Anglican Papalism has already been noted. The proponents of that movement were most anxious to show that places of pilgrimage could spring up within the Church of England just as they had seen them abroad. There were two places where a significant revival took place of mediaeval Marian shrines, namely at Walsingham and at Egmanton, and one where more modern visions failed to produce any long-term consequences, Middleton. All, however, took place against a background of increased devotion to the Mother of Christ in the Church of England, and to a resultant striking change in the furnishings of many churches. In 1900 there were very few Anglican churches in which there stood a statue of Our Lady, whereas by 1960 they were commonplace.

The revival of the Shrine of Our Lady of Walsingham, Norfolk, was the single-handed work of Alfred Hope Patten, parish priest of Walsingham from 1921 until his death in 1958.

Hope Patten was an interesting and complicated man of whom there is as yet no full Life. His successor as administrator of the Walsingham shrine, Canon Colin Stephenson, wrote *Walsingham Way* (1970), which contains a significant amount of information about him, but is not referenced: further, many thought that it and his later book *Merrily on High* (1972) left a nasty taste in the mouth. Hope Patten himself wrote little save for his contributions to the newsletters from the shrine.

There is no doubt however that Hope Patten was a most significant figure in the Anglican Papalist movement, and that the restoration of the shrine was in many ways one of the quintessential representations of that tendency.

Alfred Hope Patten was born on 17 November 1885 in Sidmouth,

Devon, but was brought up latterly in Brighton. His birth certificate shows that he was actually born in the Town Brewery: his father was a gentleman brewer who enjoyed poor health, but ironically, bearing in mind his place of birth, Hope Patten rarely drank. He was an only child of parents who appear to have had no particular interest in church life, but he grew up as a somewhat introspective, perhaps lonely boy whose feelings of romance were solely channelled into religion. From an early age he was fascinated by mediaevalism and in particular by monasticism. The Anglo-Catholic movement as it was developing as he grew up entranced him almost immediately, and, living in Brighton, he was able to visit a wide variety of churches with the most advanced ritual of the time outside of London.

It appears to have been at St Michael, Brighton, that he was convinced of the truth of the faith and, in the same way as Father Sandys Wason (see Chapter 9) and others, he absorbed the Anglo-Catholic presentation of Christianity as a choate whole. He was never very interested in Roman Catholics, and had very little to do with any of them in England, although his spirituality was thoroughly ultramontane and derived almost entirely from Roman sources.[1] As with others, he was however devoted to the memory of King Charles the Martyr. It appears probable that he came across the young Fynes-Clinton when the latter was a curate at St Martin, Brighton (1904–6) and certainly the two remained close friends and allies throughout their lives.

At various times in his life Hope Patten had bouts of ill-health of nervous origin: he had an intense and powerful focus which bordered on tunnel vision, but this was coupled with a tendency to break down, particularly after sustained hard work. When he was still at home, his health gave way and he had no real education because he was unable to cope with the rigours of school life. In particular, he found it quite impossible to deal with the strain of examinations. This lack of educational achievement handicapped him thoughout his life and his general knowledge, although eclectic, had some surprising gaps. His grasp of

---

1 In the archive at the Walsingham shrine there is a copy of a letter from Hope Patten to Father Pierce dated 11 September 1930, the main point of which was to express strong views against birth control, but in which he floated the idea that it might be necessary for a section to break away from the Church of England and form a sort of Uniate Church if things deteriorated in that and other respects: that was not a view he usually espoused.

Latin remained so rudimentary that he was excluded from the Sodality of the Precious Blood, which always used that language for its communal worship, and he remained resolutely opposed to the use of Latin for worship at Walsingham.

At the age of 16 the young Hope Patten went to Belgium and was fascinated, as were other travellers of a similar frame of mind, by the ecclesiastical life which he saw, and in particular the devotions of the people. He was attracted most especially by the relics which he saw in every church. In 1906 he visited the Benedictines at Painsthorpe and met Carlyle, and it is interesting that when he built the shrine church at Walsingham he used stones from various ancient abbeys in the altars, just as Carlyle did at Caldey. There are many other striking parallels between the personalities of the two men: both were autocratic, charismatic, fascinated by the occult, and hopeless with money.

In 1910 Hope Patten, then still a layman, became a member of a small community started by the vicar and curate of St Mary, Aberdeen. The order was short-lived and even its name does not appear to have survived. The other two members later seceded to Rome. However, he then appears finally to have decided that he had a vocation for the priesthood and was accepted at Lichfield Theological College, which was prepared to take non-graduates. The system for training ordinands at that time was much less rigid than it later became, and a great deal depended on the views of the bishop concerned.

Hope Patten was unable to sit the General Ordination Examination because he suffered yet another breakdown and indeed was admitted to hospital. However, the ever kind-hearted Bishop Winnington-Ingram, after receiving a report from his Archdeacon, who interviewed Hope Patten at his bedside, decided to permit him to progress to ordination nevertheless, and he was made deacon in St Paul's Cathedral on 21 December 1913.

The young Hope Patten served his title at Holy Cross, Cromer Street, in a heavily populated area near King's Cross Station. The parish priest was Revd Francis Baverstock, brother of the better-known Alban, and who unlike him served his ministry in London; after Holy Cross he was for many years parish priest of St Clement, Notting Dale. He does not appear to have been the easiest of men with whom to get on, but equally he seems to have comprehended that Hope Patten had real gifts, and he appears to have been asked back to preach after he left. The clergy at

Holy Cross were all unmarried, and throughout his life Hope Patten had a strong belief in clerical celibacy. He regarded marriage by a priest as unlawful, although he was on the contrary always pleasant to clergy wives whose husbands he liked. It is also clear that from his ordination Hope Patten took his priesthood very seriously: he was not without a sense of humour, but that did not extend to jokes about the nature of the clerical state. Revd Derrick Lingwood, who knew him better than anyone else, was later to write that 'his greatest failing was not being able to see another person's point of view; to him black was black and white white and there were no shades in between'.[2]

There was one significant incident during Hope Patten's time at Holy Cross. Father Baverstock had served his first curacy at St Michael, Bingfield Street, in nearby Islington, from 1900 to 1905. During that time the vicar of that church was Revd A. H. Reeves, who moved to the living of Walsingham. Father Baverstock was involved with the League of Our Lady and on one occasion he showed to Hope Patten a small statue of Mary which he was about to send to Father Reeves on behalf of the League. It is inconceivable that Hope Patten did not know of the mediaeval pilgrimage to Walsingham, and he himself recorded that he passed a signpost to the village when he was cycling to Painsthorpe in 1906.

Curates at that time frequently changed parishes with some rapidity, and in any event the nature of the parish at Cromer Street imposed strains on Hope Patten. The story that he left the clergy house because it was haunted seems to be apocryphal, but certainly throughout his life Hope Patten was very sensitive to paranormal experiences of that nature. He moved in 1915 to St Alban, Teddington, an enormous church in a much more salubrious area near the Thames, but which always had a reputation for advanced Anglo-Catholicism, and then in 1919 to St Mary, Buxted, in Sussex. That church had been built by the munificence of Revd Arthur Wagner, who had built a number of churches in Brighton which were of course already familiar to Hope Patten. In fact Hope Patten was asked to go to Buxted by the vicar, Revd C. E. Roe, whom he had known when he was still a layman in Brighton and the latter was a curate at St Paul. Father Wagner seems to have chosen Buxted for this building project because he had a house in the

---

2 Lingwood, quoted in Cobb: *Walsingham*, at p. 12.

village, and was aware that the ancient parish church was some distance from the centre of what had become a substantial settlement. He had a chapel of Our Lady put in the church which was said to be of the same dimensions as the Holy House of Loreto, with a space within the screen to the east wall which equated with the ancient shrine of Walsingham.

In 1920 Hope Patten moved again, this time to act as curate to Father Corbould at Carshalton. He was placed in charge of the mission chapel of the Good Shepherd at Carshalton Beeches, which was later to be replaced by a striking quasi-baroque church designed by Martin Travers. Corbould had then just commenced his long incumbency at Carshalton, and it appears to have been under his influence that Hope Patten's thought became more specifically papalist. Thereafter he joined many of the societies and groups associated with the Papalist Movement, although he was too concerned with his own parish and shrine and too autocratic to involve himself in the detailed running of such organisations.

It was the following year, 1921, when the living of Walsingham fell vacant. There are various versions of how Hope Patten was offered the post, which was unattractive to many because of the remoteness of the location, the fact that there were three churches to serve, and the very small stipend. One is that Father Francis Baverstock recommended him; another is that Father Roe's brother, who was the local Rural Dean, consulted Father Roe and was given his name. Hope Patten himself said that it took him three months to decide whether or not to accept the offer, although on the face of it there was no parish in England which would have appealed to him more, particularly since there was already a tradition of Anglo-Catholicism at Walsingham before his arrival. The Lee-Warner family, who held the living, had adopted Tractarian principles and Reeves had been preceded in the village by Revd G. R. Woodward, who had been at St Barnabas, Pimlico.

When Hope Patten arrived in the village he very soon decided to revive the pilgrimage to Walsingham, which had fallen into desuetude at the Reformation. That was to form his life's work and he devoted himself to it with an intensity which came from the narrow but powerful energy which he brought to bear on it. It brought together two strands found elsewhere in Anglican Papalist thinking, namely the looking back to mediaeval precedents and the need to show that the Church of

England was a true part of the wider Catholic Church by its outward demonstrations of faith.

In 1922 Hope Patten arranged for a copy of a mediaeval seal of the Priory to be made at the Art and Book Shop near Westminster Cathedral, which has provided many Anglican clergy over the years with objects of piety meant for Roman churches, and on 6 July of that year it was solemnly installed in the side chapel of the mediaeval church. The design of the seal was researched in the British Museum and it was carved by a Carmelite nun. The preacher at that first great Walsingham event was Revd Archdale King, a well-known author on ritual, who in due course went over to Rome, a course which never seems to have crossed Hope Patten's mind, still less tempted him. Father Alban Baverstock blessed the statue.

The first pilgrimage was organised by the League of Our Lady for 24 to 26 October of the same year. It turned out to be a disaster when only two of the expected 40 pilgrims arrived. Hope Patten however, with his well-developed sense of the theatrical, transformed the event into a parochial festival and involved the villagers in the devotions.

There are conflicting accounts of the effect of the new priest upon his congregation. There is no doubt that the new Lord of the Manor, Eustace Gurney, who replaced the Lee-Warners as squire in 1922, was very hostile to Hope Patten's innovations, despite being the brother of the well-known Anglo-Catholic layman Samuel Gurney. The latter tended to keep away from Walsingham because of that family connection. Stephenson in his book said that Hope Patten was full of energy and enthusiasm when he went to Walsingham, and that he converted the village to his ways.[3] There seems little doubt that during those early years he made a profound impression on the local population: he was certainly different from the sort of vicar to whom Norfolk was accustomed. On the other hand, Peter Anson in his autobiography recounts how he went to Walsingham in the immediate pre-war years. He wrote that in 1934, 'Few of the natives appear to attend the parish church, for they had been alienated by the unfamiliar type of religion introduced by the present incumbent with the most laudable intentions.' He went on to say that the congregations were made up largely of pious old ladies

---

3 Stephenson: *Walsingham Way.*

attracted to Walsingham by the privileges available in the parish church.[4]

Peter Anson's quirky style of writing has illuminated many dark corners of ecclesiastical life during the twentieth century, but he was not always accurate, and his writing at this time (1946) revealed a great deal of anti-Anglican feeling which dated from his secession to Rome with the Caldey Community. His later work is less affected by this bias, while still poking gentle fun at the eccentricities of Anglo-Catholicism.

Immediately after Hope Patten's death Revd Derrick Lingwood and Sir William Milner both wrote reminiscences of him in the shrine newsletter, then called *Our Lady's Mirror*. They knew him better than did almost anyone else, particularly Father Lingwood (1910–72), who was a boy from the village who confessed with some trepidation one day that he thought he had a vocation to the priesthood. Hope Patten did not discourage him, but rather took him in to the vicarage and used his precocious financial expertise to organise the income and expenditure required for the burgeoning work of the pilgrimages. Hope Patten was unworldly with money and it is no exaggeration to say that Lingwood's contribution was of vital importance in the development of the revived devotion at Walsingham. In due course the friendly Bishop Blunt of Bradford ordained Lingwood, ostensibly to a title at Holy Trinity, Bradford, but in fact he returned to Walsingham to act as unpaid curate-cum-treasurer. He lived in the same property as Hope Patten for 32 years in total. His reminiscence does not pass over the faults of the vicar, but he is quite clear as to the impact on the parish which he made during his early years: he, after all, had been so attracted by the religion he saw as to look to ordination. Hope Patten in those first years visited assiduously and also had the servers round to the vicarage once a week. No doubt some stood askance, but it does appear that his personal magnetism, which was considerable, won over the majority.[5] There is further evidence to the same effect from Revd A. W. Leeds, a lifelong friend of Hope Patten's, who from 1926 to 1932 was curate in charge of Houghton St Giles, one of the three parishes of which the latter was vicar, who recalled the very large number of local penitents at Walsingham.[6] Interestingly he was married during this period, but Hope Patten then and later

4 Anson: *A Roving Recluse*, p. 201.
5 Lingwood, in Cobb: *Walsingham*, p. 8.
6 In the Walsingham shrine archive.

remained on very good terms with him. In later years another young local, John Shepherd, also went on to ordination under the parish priest's influence.

Sir William Milner was an architect and landowner who first met Hope Patten in 1923 and thereafter was a great supporter of the shrine in every way, including financially. He said specifically that the usual attendance at High Mass was 100–150 out of a population of about 1,000, which is a good indication that the parishioners did indeed appreciate what was happening in the church.[7]

After the statue of Our Lady had been erected in the church, the rosary was said daily and gradually the church was filled with statues, candles, *objets de piété* of various sorts and the like, so that it looked exactly like a French or Belgian interior – which of course is exactly the impression it was intended to convey. The erection of statues of Our Lady was still quite unusual at this time, and this made Walsingham the more exotic to most Anglicans. Initially, Hope Patten used the Book of Common Prayer for the mass, but inserting silently the canon from the Roman mass; later he adopted the same principle as Father Whitby, using the Book of Common Prayer but making it appear like the Roman mass. Still later in his life, he became convinced by Ross Williamson's book, *The Great Prayer*, that the Roman canon should indeed be used. The Sacrament was of course reserved in the church from the time of his appointment, and Benediction was a regular devotion.

From early on in his incumbency, Hope Patten began the foundation of organisations to support the work being carried out. In about 1925 he started the Society of Our Lady of Walsingham, which grew out of a local guild. Its members were provided initially with a blue scapular. In 1927 Priest Associates of the Society were separately organised, and by 1932 there were 125 in this category. Also in the 1920s the indefatigable Fynes-Clinton commenced an informal committee to support the work and in particular to supplement the modest stipend which Hope Patten received. By this time, Hope Patten was receiving a great deal of support from Bishop O'Rorke, the former Bishop of Accra. Mowbray Stephen O'Rorke was rector of nearby Blakeney from 1924 to 1935 and played a large part in the restoration, particularly in those years. By 1926 Milner had written the lengthy Pilgrim Hymn, sung to the same tune as at

---

7 Milner, in Cobb: *Walsingham*, p. 15.

Lourdes, which some regarded as doggerel but others enjoyed. A revised version was used after 1960.

After the debacle of the 1922 pilgrimage, groups did begin to arrive from London, particularly those organised by the League of Our Lady and the Catholic League, although everything was on a small scale and could only happen at all with the co-operation of the villagers. However, the ultra-Protestant Bishop of Norwich, Dr Pollock, began to be concerned at the growth of Mariolatry in his diocese, although strangely enough he and Hope Patten, from opposite sides of the spectrum, met several times in connection with their combined opposition to the Revision of the Prayer Book.

In about 1930 the Bishop came to Walsingham and asked to see the church. He asked whether the image could not be removed and replaced by a picture – one of those distinctions with no difference which were frequently urged upon Anglo-Catholic clergy. It appears to have been at that point that Hope Patten crystallised his thought that a separate shrine chapel should be erected on private ground so that the revival of devotion could continue unaffected by episcopal pressure. He was also very anxious that what was achieved should be preserved and not dismantled by a successor who was not in sympathy with his ideas.

Hope Patten went about this new project with characteristic energy. Romilly Craze, who was in an architectural partnership with Milner, designed a Holy House to the same dimensions as that which stood in Walsingham from 1061 to 1538, which in turn was the same size as the Holy House of Loreto. It was covered with a small chapel: the approximately £2,000 required for this building work was mostly lent by Milner. The building then erected was extremely small, but Hope Patten was convinced that it was on the site of the original shrine, particularly when, during construction, a spring was discovered and incorporated into the chapel.

The translation of the image of Our Lady from the parish church to the newly built Holy House took place on 15 October 1931, the feast day of St Teresa of Avila, although it was to be her namesake, St Theresa of Lisieux, who was later to be accorded a statue in the shrine grounds. The day of the translation was a triumphant celebration of Anglican Papalism such as occurred but rarely, and represented what the leaders of the Movement thought should happen across the country: a procession of the people in devotion with their priests.

At 7 a.m. that morning there was a votive mass at the new shrine, during which the deed of conveyance of the land on which it was built was presented to the celebrant and then given to Father Fynes-Clinton as representative of the trustees appointed to hold the property. Then at 11.30 there was a High Mass at the parish church at which Bishop O'Rorke pontificated and the sermon was preached by Father Underhill of St Thomas, Liverpool. He told those assembled: 'Today we are going to do something which will help towards making the worship of Our Lady of Walsingham no longer a parish matter, but something that will be national. Today we are taking her to a new sanctuary that is a copy of the Holy Home where was nursed the little Babe who is God Almighty. From henceforth Mary has come back into her own to show forth the incarnate life of her divine Son.'[8]

In the afternoon, Father Alban Baverstock preached, again at the parish church, following which the procession formed up. The contemporary account in *Our Lady's Mirror* is worth setting out in full:

A perfect autumn day with scarcely a breath of air stirring, the trees clothed in glorious tints, and in their setting of old Tudor Houses and low, red-roofed ancient cottages, a procession with over a thousand people walking, each bearing his or her lighted taper; many women in blue veils, little children in white casting their flowers; dark habited religious, nuns and monks; over a hundred priests in cassock and cotta; the mitred Abbot of Pershore [*sic*] and Bishop O'Rorke. Behind streamed the many hundreds of other people, all singing the glories of Mary, and in the middle of this throng, high and lifted up upon the shoulders of four clergy in dalmatics, and under a blue and gold canopy fixed to the feretory, sat the venerated figure of our Lady, crowned with the silver Oxford Crown and robed in a mantle of cloth of gold.[9]

It was named the Oxford Crown because it had been the gift of Father Wodehouse and his congregation at St Paul, Oxford.

The foundation stone of the new shrine indicated that it was constructed in the pontificate of Pius XI, the episcopate of Bertram Pollock, and the incumbency of Hope Patten. Perhaps no inscription more

---

8 Quoted in ibid., p. 33.
9 Quoted in ibid., p. 35.

clearly set out the Anglican Papalist position, nor was more incomprehensible to contemporary Roman Catholics.

The trustees on whose behalf Fynes-Clinton received the conveyance were formally constituted in 1932 as the College of Guardians. There were 20 in number and Hope Patten became Master of the College as well as Administrator of the Shrine and parish priest. In fact, during his lifetime the Guardians generally acted in accordance with his wishes: the purpose of the College was more to provide for continuity than to question Hope Patten's strategies. Over the years regalia for the Guardians was devised: in 1933 Fynes-Clinton presented the Master with a silver gilt chain of office, in 1938 all the Guardians began to wear distinctive blue mantles and in 1947 they acquired stars which were worn around the neck. The Guardians could from the start be drawn from both laity and the priesthood: there was a rule that priests had to resign if they married, but some, such as Father Lury of St Peter, Limehouse, were chosen when already married, presumably because Hope Patten was very anxious for their presence in the College.

Many prominent supporters of Anglican Papalism were appointed as Guardians, such as the Duke of Argyll, Father Fynes-Clinton, Father Alban Baverstock, Father Wodehouse, Father Raynes CR, and Father Bennett, together with Sir William Milner, Father Lingwood, and others. In various ways others assisted: Donald Hole, for example, wrote a popular but scholarly introduction to the shrine in 1939, which combined history with information on the then current position, and this was updated several times thereafter.

Hope Patten had arranged from an early date that the religious orders were represented in Walsingham by arranging that a few nuns from the Community of St Peter in Horbury should live in the parish. In 1927 they began looking after the hospice of Our Lady Star of the Sea, which had been converted from three cottages bought with the aid of an anonymous gift. When that order split into two in 1932, it was the more ultramontane Sisters from Laleham who continued with the work in Walsingham.

Hope Patten had never ceased to believe that he had a vocation to the religious life, although in fact he was too authoritarian for his ideas on monasticism ever to work properly. In the early 1930s there was a short-lived attempt to set up a branch house of the Nashdom Benedictines in Walsingham, but that failed. However, following a dream in which

Hope Patten saw Augustinian canons in Walsingham, when Father Lingwood returned in 1934 after his ordination, the two of them set up an Augustinian Community. The College of St Augustine, as it was called, was never very successful because the founder's personality, which had driven forward the re-establishment of the shrine, made it very difficult for others to live with him in community. Although men came and went, the College never had secure foundations and its failure to some extent marred Hope Patten's later years. The reminiscences of those connected with the CSA show that in that regard Hope Patten was a poor judge of men, allowing anyone who appeared to be enthusiastic to join, although many were more interested in the exotic side of Walsingham than in the strictly devotional. Some stayed a very short time. John Shepherd, who has already been mentioned, stayed six years, starting from a time when he was still at school, and came in to the College every evening, changing his school uniform for the habits worn in the College. The canons also wore enormously tall birettas which were extremely distinctive.

In the years following the establishment of the shrine, Hope Patten lost some of his influence in the parish. He was simultaneously parish priest, administrator of the shrine, Master of the College of Guardians, and Superior of the Augustinian Community. In addition to these responsibilities, there were considerable problems in the late 1930s between the Anglicans and the Roman Catholics: the latter began to develop the Slipper Chapel just outside the village as a centre of pilgrimage, and matters were not aided in that the first resident Roman Catholic parish priest, Father Bruno Scott James, was a convert from Anglicanism and had indeed been a member of the Nashdom Community. The unpleasant intransigence which marked that period and later years has disappeared more recently, and the latest (1998) version of the Catholic Truth Society pamphlet *Message of Walsingham* bears tribute to 'Father [sic] Hope Patten's great work'.

The number of pilgrims to Walsingham continued to increase, although they were drawn almost exclusively from a very narrow band of Anglicanism. By 1938 it was clear that the shrine needed to be extended: this was made possible by a very substantial gift (accounts vary as to whether it was £4,500 or £6,000: Hole says specifically that it was £4,578. 4s), which arrived unexpectedly in the post one day.

The blessing of the extension was on 6 June 1938, Whit Monday, which thereafter became an anniversary used for the most substantial pilgrimage each year. It was again carried out by Bishop O'Rorke, and Father Alban Baverstock again preached. There was substantial participation by Orthodox clergy, and about 4,000 pilgrims are said to have attended that day. Approximately 15,000 had visited the shrine in 1936, and this number increased to 30,000 in 1938.

The extension of the shrine was ill-thought-out in the sense that Hope Patten was always anxious to proceed with great speed with any project once it had attracted his attention. The new chapel was conceived on too small a scale and there were too many altars crammed in, some in very confined spaces. It is said that the inspiration for the 15 altars contained in the church was the Rosary Church at Lourdes, and certainly the effect of the completed building was completely alien to its surroundings. It looked as though a modern ecclesiastical building from Italy or Spain had been dropped in the very English surroundings of Walsingham. It was indeed, as Anson later remarked, the culmination of the Back to Baroque Movement in the Church of England. The editors of the relevant volume in the *Buildings of England* series are predictably dismissive of the architecture, remarking disdainfully: 'It is a disappointing building of brick, partly whitewashed, and looking for all its ambitions like a minor suburban church.'[10]

As already mentioned, Hope Patten used the device of incorporating stones from other sources into the altars. The altar of the Holy House, erected in 1931, was constructed mainly of stones from the ruined Priory of Our Lady of Walsingham. Stones from Augustinian houses were then incorporated into the north wall of the Holy House, and from Benedictine into the south wall. In the high altar of the pilgrimage church, dedicated in 1938 when the extension was built, there were built in stones from many cathedrals in England and abroad, and from former and existing religious houses, not forgetting those of modern foundations such as Mirfield and Kelham.

During the war, Walsingham was in a restricted area and pilgrimages all but ceased. However, it was in 1943 that Father Fynes-Clinton's unofficial committee was reconstituted more formally as the London Committee for Walsingham, under the chairmanship of Revd

---

10 See N. Pevsner and B. Wilson: *The Buildings of England: Norfolk 1: Norwich and North-East* (Yale University Press, 2002), p. 595.

J. H. C. Twisaday, the flamboyant parish priest of All Saints, Notting Hill. This later became the Central Committee for Walsingham and assisted with fundraising and increasing devotion to and interest in the shrine.

It was at about the same time that Hope Patten's authoritarian streak came to the fore again, and after a bitter quarrel with the Reverend Mother, the Laleham nuns were withdrawn. He then attempted to set up an autonomous order, the Community of Our Lady of Walsingham, but this again was not successful. Hope Patten's ideas about life in community were more theoretical than practical, and the order did not prosper. There were particular difficulties with Sister Benedicta, who became the Reverend Mother, for she was both authoritarian and difficult herself, and compounded this by being, it was said, chastely infatuated with Father Lingwood.

However, there was one aspect of the religious life which did persist. Sister Mary Phillida lived from 1934 to 1958 as a recluse or anchorite within the grounds of the shrine, very near to the crowds who came, but unseen to them. Her presence was no doubt another sign to Hope Patten that although some areas of his mission were not proving successful, Walsingham could still show the indicia of Catholic faith to the outside world.

After the war ended, the area was opened up again and pilgrims returned. There seems little doubt that by that time Hope Patten looked upon Walsingham as a sort of spiritual powerhouse for the rest of the Church of England. Although his attempts to stabilise the Augustinian Community were not any more successful, he took the sensible step in 1947 of asking the Reverend Mother of those Sisters of the Society of St Margaret who were working at Haggerston to send some of their number to work in Walsingham. This they did, after some hesitation, and that proved a far more productive method of progress than setting up a new community. The Sisters who arrived had an established ethos and, more importantly, were answerable to their own Reverend Mother, who remained away from Walsingham. In 1955, by which time the order was well established in Norfolk, the Walsingham Sisters were constituted an autonomous house of the Society of St Margaret, as they remain to this day.

In addition to that success, in 1939 the shrine took over the home for orphans which had been started by Father Bernard Walke at St Hilary,

Cornwall, and that functioned well for many years until in 1977 the need for it disappeared and it was closed.

In the war a branch of Quainton Hall School, Harrow, the head-master of which was Revd Montague Eyden, formerly assistant priest at St Mary, Somers Town, a well-known Anglo-Catholic parish, was evacuated to Walsingham after its previous location out of London was commandeered. The deputy headmaster who was in charge of this branch was an expert musician with a particular interest in plainchant, and thus the shrine acquired its own Choir School. Hope Patten, in addi-tion to his many other responsibilities, taught Divinity of a most definite type to the boys. Unfortunately however, his involvement did not end there: he had of course very little if any experience of education at all, and still less of running a school. He constantly interfered with the way in which the school was run, which led to successive masters in charge leaving after only short periods. In 1956 the Walsingham school was forced to close because of the fall in numbers, but the original school in Harrow continues to flourish.[11]

Hope Patten also converted part of the accommodation in the College of St Augustine to form a home for retired priests, but that too was unsuccessful, partly because of the difficulty of making provision for the residents when they became infirm. Hope Patten was also interested in fostering the work of artists in and around the shrine, and one, Enid Chadwick, became well known for her religious work at Walsingham and elsewhere.

The shrine in those post-war years continued to attract only those from a very small number of churches, mainly in London, although numbers did grow. In 1954 Hope Patten asked the then very elderly Sir Ninian Comper to design new fittings for the Holy House, perhaps influenced by Father Twisaday and Father Corbould, for both of whom Comper had carried out distinguished work. The refurbishment was not in fact completed until after Hope Patten's death, but added distinction to the original somewhat tawdry fittings.

Hope Patten was almost the equal of his great friend and collaborator, Fynes-Clinton, in the founding of organisations. In 1953 he named six women who had assisted with the work over the years as Dames of the Shrine. He had formulated a scheme to honour others who had led

---

11 See P. Miller: *Quainton Hall School* (school, 1997).

pilgrimages or otherwise promoted the shrine as Clerks or Lay Clerks, but this had not been put into effect when he died. It was his successor, Father Stephenson, who set up the Sacred Order of the Living Rosary of Our Lady of Walsingham to encompass these various groups.

By the mid-1950s Hope Patten was around 70 years of age. By that time also the strain of running the shrine and its various offshoots had told on Father Lingwood, who was in many ways the unsung hero of the entire re-establishment. Further, Hope Patten, never flexible where matters of faith were concerned, had by then become entirely set in his ways and Lingwood found himself increasingly out of sympathy with his mentor. It was, however, an enormous blow to Hope Patten when Lingwood left Walsingham in 1956 to take on a parish in Devon, although perhaps not so much a blow as when the younger man announced shortly after that that he was to marry. For Hope Patten, clerical celibacy was an essential and non-negotiable discipline. He insisted that on his marriage Lingwood retire as a Guardian, and although there was some rapprochement between the two of them before Hope Patten's death, it was an unfortunate episode. However, Lingwood wrote later that had Hope Patten given him more autonomy, particularly to look after the church at Great Walsingham (paradoxically the smaller of the two villages), he would not have left.

The loss of Lingwood also meant that for the last two years of his life Hope Patten was forced once again to involve himself more with his parishioners, and to re-establish the empathy which he had built up in the 1920s.

Hope Patten had throughout his life a very well-developed sense of the theatrical, but even he could not have stage-managed his own demise more dramatically. On 11 August 1958 he had received the first ever episcopal pilgrimage to Walsingham. After the evening torchlight procession, he gave Benediction in the shrine church, after which the Host was carried into the Blessed Sacrament chapel. As he finished locking the door of the tabernacle, Hope Patten fell back and collapsed, and later that evening he died.

Hope Patten had been preoccupied for many years by the thought that the work which he had begun would not be carried on if he were not able to lead it. Many of his arrangements had been made from exactly the fear that that would happen. His worries were in fact not to be realised and the shrine was to flourish in an unprecedented way thereafter.

Hope Patten's successor, Colin Stephenson, was a very different personality. He had had far more experience of the outside world, including a period as a naval chaplain, during which he suffered a very serious accident which resulted in him losing a leg. Immediately before taking over at Walsingham he had been parish priest at St Mary Magdalene, Oxford, with its eclectic congregation. Stephenson was criticised by some for the change in outlook which he brought to the shrine, but it is only fair to say that Hope Patten had been in something of an ecclesiastical timewarp since the Second World War. Stephenson's great contribution to Walsingham was to transform it from an exclusive devotion on the edge of the Church of England, apparently interested in only a small segment of that church, to a much more outgoing place, seeking contact with others within the same Communion instead of sheltering from them.

On Hope Patten's death, the position of Administrator was separated from that of parish priest, which inevitably cut off the village to some extent from what was happening at the shrine, although increasingly the local population became dependent on the income brought by pilgrims. From 1962 to 1984 the priests at the shrine took care of three small villages in the neighbourhood.

As if to symbolise the changes, in 1961 the parish church dramatically burnt down, and was rebuilt in a quasi-mediaeval style but with a much modernised interior. The original statue of Our Lady which Father Reeves had erected was among the losses in the fire.

In his early years, Stephenson continued with the attempt to live in community although not within the framework set up by Hope Patten, as the Community of St Augustine had come to an end on his death. He organised a community of Benedictine oblates, and in December 1961 there were no fewer than five resident at the shrine, but in June 1965 Stephenson announced in the *Walsingham Gazette* that he had decided that 'the attempt to have any sort of Community life in the College here is doomed to failure . . . It therefore seems to me much better to run the College as a clergy house and to have those who are prepared to come for a year or two, as to a parish.'[12]

Further, when Father Stephenson resigned as Administrator in 1968, worn out by his efforts, he remained as Master, rather than the new

---

12 Editor's letter in *Walsingham Gazette*, June 1965.

Administrator (Revd Charles Smith) holding that position as well. The concentration of power which had occurred in Hope Patten's time was therefore broken up.

The effect of these changes, and of the involvement of the shrine in diocesan and local affairs, was an increase in the number of pilgrims. In the 1950s the Whit Sunday national pilgrimage attracted 1,500 to 2,000; by the 1960s this had increased to 2,500 to 3,000, but by 1980 15,000 came. The shrine church was further extended in 1964, by the addition of the north cloister, in memory of Hope Patten, and again in 1972, by the addition of the corresponding south (Jubilee) cloister.

The further development of the Walsingham shrine is strictly outside the scope of this study, but it may be noted that nothing perhaps revealed its absorption into the wider Church more than the attendance of the Archbishop of Canterbury, Robert Runcie, to preach at the National Pilgrimage in 1980, and then the consecration in 1985 of David Hope, the Master of the College of Guardians, as Bishop of Wakefield, and his later translation to the Archbishopric of York. The Guardians were chosen from a wider spectrum of opinion, and included some well-known and sometimes controversial figures such as Bishops Trevor Huddleston CR and Mervyn Stockwood.

The shrine is now involved in ecumenical work to an extent which would have appeared impossible to earlier generations (although Hope Patten did appear on radio with the local Roman Catholic parish priest in the 1950s), and under successive Administrators has taken up an established position in the Church rather than being on the outside looking in.

The decision to ordain women, however, did have the effect here, as in other areas of Anglo-Catholicism, of reversing the trend to further integration and further isolating those who opposed that development. It is far too early to assess the long-term consequences of that decision either here or elsewhere. The interesting point about Walsingham remains that it managed to transform itself from a classic Anglican Papalist fortified position, looking inward on itself for the most part, into a much more dynamic and outward-looking centre.

Hope Patten was a man of his time, and must be regarded as such, but his vision was concentrated enough to ensure that it outlived him. His influence during his lifetime was very considerable within the restricted circles to whom the Walsingham devotion appealed, because he offered a picture of what could be achieved inside the Church of England. However, while there were others who were prepared to match his incessant hard work, there were few who had his charisma, and Walsingham remained unique.

The development of the only other significant Marian shrine in England, at Egmanton in Nottinghamshire, followed a very different course. Egmanton is a small village not far from the A1, near Newark-on-Trent, with a population of some 200. It had been a site of pilgrimage in mediaeval times, although not on the scale associated with Walsingham.

In the late nineteenth century the living of St Mary, Egmanton, together with that of a number of churches in the area, was held by the family of the Duke of Newcastle. The Seventh Duke was a committed supporter of the Catholic Revival in the Church of England, and his influence was directly responsible for the growth of a tradition around Newark which later gave birth to the Society for Catholic Reunion. In 1913 the patronage to the church was transferred to the Society for the Maintenance of the Faith.

In 1895 the Duke invited the then young Ninian Comper to restore the interior of Egmanton church. Comper's reputation at that time came from his research on the English altar, and particularly on his restoration of the church of St Wilfrid at Cantley, near Doncaster, where he had put into practice in 1893 the ideas set out in his paper *Practical Considerations on the Gothic or English Altars and Certain Dependent Rubrics of the Book of Common Prayer* (1889). His patron in that commission was a cousin of Lord Halifax.

The fashion for baroque had not then begun to influence the interior of Anglo-Catholic churches, and in any event it was never a fashion much espoused by Comper, whose great skill was in the reproduction of furnishings of opulence in the style of the Middle Ages.

Egmanton was one of Comper's finest interiors and was completed in 1897. He designed a large, vividly coloured rood screen across the chancel entrance, complete with loft, and with rood above surmounted by a canopy of honour. He also designed a pulpit and an organ case over the south doorway. A stone high altar was provided (as was the case with all the Newcastle restorations) with riddel posts and angels, and above it a typical example of Comper's mediaevalism: the Sacrament was reserved, not in an aumbry, still less in a tabernacle, which would have been very unusual indeed at that date, but rather in a hanging pyx decorated with angels, and covered by a canopy. He also designed the east window, showing not only Our Lady with the Holy Child, but also the Annunciation and the Assumption, and a magnificent thurible. However, the most interesting addition to the furnishings was an image of Our Lady and the Holy Child, painted and gilded in characteristic manner, which was set up above the organ. There is no record of the original figure, and Comper relied on his knowledge of precedents to create an image which was representative of what had been there before. The interesting point for the historian is that the shrine was re-erected as early as 1897, when very few churches at all in the Anglican Communion, and even fewer in the provinces, had statues of Our Lady. The guide to the church quotes an observer of the Palm Sunday mass in 1901 as indicating that by then there were six candlesticks on the altar, in Roman mode, and that the priest (Revd F. Harvey, who was vicar 1896–1912) wore full vestments and a biretta. Incense was used and in general the ceremonial was far in advance of that found in almost any other church in the country at that date.

By 1912, and possibly before then, a Guild of our Lady of Egmanton was in existence: this was a parish society with an obligation on its members to say prayers daily for the parish, including one Hail Mary. In 1926 Revd A. H. Manning was appointed as vicar, but he died shortly after and was succeeded the following year by Revd Silas Morgan Harris, who held the incumbency until 1959.

Harris was a well-known Papalist who, as already seen, was a prolific writer on reunion, a leading light in the SCR, and the founder of the Dominican Third Order. He was born in Brecknockshire and retained throughout his life a strong interest in his Welsh roots and in Celtic literature. He was admitted to the Gorsedd of Bards in 1908, and when at St David's College, Lampeter, in 1910, he and other students founded a new organisation. The St David's Catholic Guild was set up to promote Anglo-Catholicism in Wales: it published annual reports, later journals, entitled *The Faith in Wales (Y Ffydd yng Nghymru)*, written partly in English and partly in Welsh, to which Harris was a frequent contributor. In the 1914–15 edition Spencer Jones contributed an article entitled 'The Divine Ministry and the Ministry of Man'. A similar organisation, the Guild of St Patrick, was set up by others in 1912 to promote and maintain the Catholic Faith in the Church of Ireland, a more barren field to till.

Harris went from Lampeter for further academic studies at Keble College, Oxford, and was ordained deacon in 1916, priest in 1917. He served his title at St Mary, Bute Street, in the Cardiff Docks, and then in 1918 became a curate at St Stephen, Newtown Row, Birmingham. In November 1919 the vicar, Revd F. W. Chambers, suddenly seceded to Rome, and the churchwardens asked the Bishop of Birmingham to allow Harris to succeed him. He refused, because the church was under discipline for using Benediction, and Harris moved to be chaplain to the branch house of the Holy Cross Sisters at Limpsfield for a time. In 1921 he went to Rome and, by the introduction of some Roman Catholic acquaintances, met Pope Benedict XV. He then went in 1923 to be chaplain to another order of Sisters at the Convent of the Good Shepherd, Canvey Island, and had three years in the Scottish Episcopal Church, at St Columba, Newton, before becoming parish priest of Egmanton.[13]

It would appear on the face of it that when Harris moved to Egmanton, he was in a stronger position to develop the shrine than was Hope Patten at Walsingham, because the foundations had been more securely laid. Both places were fairly remote, and although Walsingham was nearer to London, Egmanton was readily accessible from Nottingham and the East Midlands. Like Hope Patten, Harris was involved with the religious life, with the Dominicans, but unlike Hope Patten, he had married.

However, whether because Harris lacked Hope Patten's charisma and drive or for whatever reason, the devotion, although constant, never developed in anything like the same way as at Walsingham. The first organised pilgrimage took place on Easter Monday 1929, with most of the visitors coming from Leicester but some from other places in the North and Midlands. A pair of silver candlesticks in memory of Father Manning was presented on that occasion. The following year Father Hope Patten and a group from Walsingham came to Egmanton and presented a Marian banner to the parish. At some point words were provided for the Egmanton Pilgrims' Hymn:

---

13 Although Pusey House has Harris' papers, as yet uncatalogued, they relate to his external work and not to the development of the shrine at Egmanton.

All glory we give to her Son, who's divine
As we offer our prayers at her Egmanton shrine.

A summer pilgrimage to Egmanton has been held every year since 1929, generally on the first Saturday in July, and in addition the parish celebrates its patronal festival on the Feast of the Assumption, at which time a further pilgrimage is held, together with one in October for the Rosary Devotion. These generally include an outdoor procession of Our Lady followed by Benediction. In more recent years a Society of Our Lady of Egmanton has been founded to continue the tradition.

No accommodation was ever developed at Egmanton for pilgrims and the pilgrimages remained as day events rather than residential. Father Harris held daily shrine prayers along the same lines as Walsingham, and until 1994 these continued weekly. Harris carried out little work to the interior of the church, which remains largely as it was at the completion of the 1897 restoration, but he did erect a statue of St Theresa of Lisieux, which looks somewhat incongruous amid the quasi-mediaevalism of the remainder of the furnishings.

After Harris' retirement from the parish, he moved to Cardiff and later to Bridgnorth, Shropshire. His interest in Welsh matters continued unabated and in the 1950s he had written two pamphlets on Welsh saints and shrines, dealing respectively with the devotions of Our Lady of Penrhys and of Cardigan.

Father Harris outlived all his contemporaries: he died aged 94 on 23 November 1982.

There was one other parish where a devotion might have started, but in fact no long-term results seem to have occurred.[14] Revd Frank Clive Luget (who always used his second Christian name) was appointed to the minute village of Middleton, on the Essex/Suffolk border but actually in the former county, in 1931, when he was 48: he had previously held no fewer than seven curacies in London and the surrounding area, lastly at St Michael, Walthamstow. The parish to which he moved had a population of only 94, but a large rectory, built in the nineteenth century by a member of the Raymond family, who provided five incumbents in the period from 1769 to 1929, one of whom

---

14 See Halliday in *Ecclesiology Today*, May 2003.

served the parish for 70 years, 66 as rector. There was also a tradition of Anglo-Catholicism: the last member of the Raymond family to hold the living went to be warden of the House of Mercy at Great Maplestead, not far away, which was run by the Clewer Sisters. One of Father Luget's curacies had been at St Stephen, Clewer, near the mother house of that order.

It was not untypical for a priest of that time to remain a curate until his forties. In addition, Luget was an uncompromising Anglo-Catholic whose views would have made him unacceptable to many patrons.

In 1931 Luget published a Gothic novel for children, *The Vision of Latton Priory*, which, as its name implies, featured both an apparition and mediaeval monasticism. He began to move the services at the church in the direction he thought proper, which included the restoration of a holy water stoup, the lavish use of incense of his own manufacture, and the replacement of the vernacular by Latin. He also became friendly with a resident of nearby Sudbury, Dr M. Thornber, who became the organist at Middleton. Thornber was regarded with some suspicion partly because his degree was thought to have been granted in Germany, but more so because he was said to have been involved with the Jesuits: on the other hand it was also said that at one stage he had been a member of a fundamentalist Protestant sect.

On 11 December 1932 a number of local residents saw what appeared to be a bright ball of fire moving around the village. Luget saw it in his large rectory garden, over a hillock known as the mound. He claimed that he saw the Crucifixion above the ball, with Our Lady kneeling before it. A servant boy at the rectory claimed that he too was able to see the vision as the priest described. Two days later, Dr Thornber and his young son Francis were at the rectory when another light appeared over the tussock. Dr Thornber approached it and then fell involuntarily to his knees, at which point the Virgin appeared and seemed to raise her hand in blessing.

Shortly after this Francis Thornber, then seven or eight, and described as resembling Little Lord Fauntleroy, told Clive Luget that he had seen Middleton church as it was in mediaeval times, with people looking though an opening in the wall of the chancel. Luget investigated and found a former leper squint buried beneath the plaster: he then uncovered it. The boy also had a number of visions of Our Lady in his dreams.

On 12 February 1933 Father Luget described these visions during his sermon at Sunday mass. He also said that since they had first occurred he had had many further visions of Our Lady as a young woman, sometimes dazzling white and sometimes blue, with rays of warmth apparently radiating from her. Francis Thornber was said to have dreamed that a spring in the rectory garden which had dried up would run clear again, although some reported this had happened before naturally. It also appeared that others in the congregation had seen appearances of Our Lady both in and out of the church.

The national and local press reported the events and Middleton became newsworthy. It also attracted the usual Kensitite protestors, although their activities were short-lived. The ubiquitous Father Fynes-Clinton was deeply interested in what had occurred and visited with the Abbot of Nashdom. In about the summer of 1933 Fynes-Clinton wrote a memorandum setting out all the facts, which has survived: typically, he recorded that the visions began in the Octave of the Immaculate Conception.[15] Unfortunately it seems that a collection of 12 witness statements from various other people who said that they had experienced visions at Middleton has been lost. Fynes-Clinton also recorded that there had been manifestations of Dominican monks in the grounds, and that a former priest, a member of the Raymond family from the nineteenth century, haunted a room in the rectory: the last Raymond rector however had no knowledge of any such haunting. In addition, there were reports of shaking of the house and of coloured lights above the mound: these last Fynes-Clinton himself believed he had seen. In September 1933 Revd J. E. Bazille-Corbin of St Mary, Runwell, also in Essex, who was later to become notorious in another context (see Chapter 10), visited the church and composed a Mariolatrous poem which has recently been sung at a revived pilgrimage to Middleton church: it starts:

> When the moon was hidden
> By the rising ground,
> We beheld her glory,
> On the daisied mound.

---

15 A copy was kindly provided by Robert Halliday, together with a copy of the letter from Fynes-Clinton quoted below.

The reference was of course to the first appearance.

Luget had none of the drive or charisma of Hope Patten and he was not forthcoming with the media. Interest by the outside world subsided and no long-term devotion ensued until the modern pilgrimages. He does not appear to have been anything but honest in his belief in the apparitions, but as time went by they became less credible to outsiders. He claimed to have almost daily visions of angels around the church, and also to have been visited by a Brother Bramate, who left messages in Latin on the walls of the rectory. On 29 July 1933 Fynes-Clinton wrote to Revd W. M. Raymond, the last of the family to hold the incumbency: 'I agree with you that the present Rector is decidedly excitable and nervy, but I cannot but believe that he is sincere though I equally believe that now, on the other hand, he thinks he sees a great deal more than he really does, even if we allow that some of the visions are genuine.'

Dr Thornber left the area very suddenly in mysterious circumstances in late 1933 and it is thought that a few years later he was killed in a road traffic accident.

As the years went by, Father Luget's eyesight deteriorated badly. He refused to have surgery, as he was convinced that in due course a spring would rise at Middleton and cure him, and he would then build a monastic establishment around it. However, although some parishioners retain fond memories of his children's parties, the congregation fell away and by 1948 was almost non-existent. The church was in need of urgent work, and the churchyard was overgrown. In 1951 the Bishop of Chelmsford called a public meeting in the village, which resulted in due course in the rector, by then an ill man, retiring. He died aged 69 on 28 April 1952. The living was united with other adjoining small parishes, and the rectory sold off. The mound was built over, and the leper squint reclosed.

Middleton is an interesting sidelight on the history of Anglo-Catholicism during this period. It was not the only small rural parish which found itself subject to a sudden change upwards in its churchmanship, but the visions were possibly unique. Clive Luget's patent sincerity took the sting from those who sought to attack him, but on the other hand the years of decline cannot have been happy ones either for him or for his people.

The casual visitor to the church will see nothing to draw his attention to the curious episode in its history which for a few months brought it in to the newspapers, although the recently revived yearly pilgrimage has at least kept alive the memory of what occurred.

8

ANGLICAN PAPALISM IN LONDON
St Saviour, Hoxton, St Alban, Fulham,
and The Annunciation, Marble Arch

The laxity of regulation which characterised the Diocese of London during the time of Bishop Winnington-Ingram has already been mentioned. However, even Winnington-Ingram's patience was tested by events at some churches within his area, particularly St Saviour, Hoxton, and St Alban, Fulham. On the other hand, although Fynes-Clinton's church of St Magnus the Martyr was consistently ultramontane in its teachings and liturgy, and although there were frequent complaints from Protestant campaigners over his activities, it does not appear that he and Winnington-Ingram were on bad terms. Fynes-Clinton, for all his extremism, had a strong establishment (in the wider sense of that word) streak in his character, which was shown for example by his involvement with the City in various regards. He also benefited from his aristocratic background, which counted for a great deal at that time in a church in which snobbery was commonplace.

The church of St Saviour stood in Penn Street and Hyde Road, Hoxton, in an overcrowded, entirely working-class, area of London which had originally been part of the Parish of Shoreditch. The imposing Gothic brick-built building with an apse at the east end and lancet windows was designed by James Brooks, whose work once dominated this quarter of London; he was also the architect of St Columba and St Chad in Haggerston and St Michael in Shoreditch. Brooks' churches here and elsewhere were generally designed for the ritual needs of the post-Tractarians, and this was the case with St Saviour. From its consecration in 1866 St Saviour offered services of a restrained and proper nature with sound teaching. However, for many years the ceremonial was very moderate and by the early twentieth century it lagged somewhat behind other similar churches, particularly the nearby St Columba, which was an early pioneer of perpetual reservation. In 1889 daily communion services began at St Saviour, but eucharistic vestments were not worn at that time. It was to that regime that E. E. Kilburn came as a deacon in 1891; he was ordained as priest in 1892 and stayed until 1896, when he left for a further curacy at All Saints, St Ives, which was then in Huntingdonshire and is now in Cambridgeshire. In 1899 he moved to the Missionary College of St Paul in Burgh, Lincolnshire, and then in 1903 to the well-known Birmingham church of St Aidan, Small Heath.

It is a matter of some irony in the light of the trouble that was to ensue that it was Winnington-Ingram himself who was instrumental in Kilburn being appointed to the living of St Saviour in 1907. The right of presentation was held by the Bishop and the Crown alternately. When the Bishop discovered that on the resignation of Revd G. W. Hockley the Crown intended to appoint a militant Protestant (who also happened to be a former Roman Catholic priest) he refused to accept Hockley's resignation until the matter was rectified, although he had already accepted the living of St Matthew, Westminster, and was about to be inducted there. Winnington-Ingram was able to deal with the problem with some alacrity, and in due course Hockley did move to Westminster, and the right of presentation became solely that of the Bishop of London. He therefore appointed Kilburn to the living.

The induction of the new vicar took place on 26 October 1907. The regime had changed somewhat since he was a curate, in that Hockley had introduced vestments, and had also begun to celebrate Corpus Christi Day. However, the observer at that time would have seen a fairly moderate churchmanship by the standards of contemporary Anglo-Catholicism, with the English Use being followed even by Kilburn initially.

What ensued is reasonably easy to follow, because fortunately there is a considerable amount of material available on St Saviour, as many of the parish magazines have survived and those which are available contain a serialised history of the parish written by Lawrence Jack, one of the last churchwardens, in 1938–40. The story has also been told in a recent pamphlet by Michael Farrer.[1]

---

1 Farrer: *St Saviour's Hoxton: An Extraordinary Story.*

It appears that fairly shortly after Kilburn's induction the services began altering both in tone and in content. In 1909 a new deacon, Revd J. Hampden Thompson, who later became a notable vicar of St Mary, Somers Town, arrived and he presented a small statue of Our Lady to the church. By 1910 incense was being used, and by 1911 the magazines refer to 'Mass' instead of 'Holy Communion'. The Western Use replaced the English, and as the First World War progressed so did the advance of Papalism at St Saviour.

The church had two curates at this time as well as Kilburn. Another new arrival in 1909 was Revd Magnus Laing, who stayed until 1920, when he moved on via a short spell in the Bahamas to St Mary, Bourne Street. He had a considerable reputation of his own as a preacher and had a particular influence on the young. Bruno Scott James says of him: 'He belonged to the extreme right wing of the Church of England, and there was no doctrine of the Catholic Church, and no extra-liturgical devotion of strongly continental, if not Mediterranean, flavour that he was not prepared to champion and adjust to the teaching of the Church of England.'[2] Despite his early prominence in Anglo-Catholic circles however, Laing left Bourne Street after a few years, married, and took a country living. The third curate at the outbreak of the war was James Burnes Holland, who was a curate at St Saviour, Pimlico, from 1908 to 1913, and then joined Kilburn and Laing at St Saviour.

Immediately after the commencement of the war, Kilburn left the parish in the care of the curates and became chaplain on a hospital ship in the Channel. His religious views must have been a considerable contrast to the ultra-Protestant regime imposed on most Army chaplains, which caused considerable resentment among others willing to assist. Michael Farrer discusses the theory that the curates pushed ahead with changes while Kilburn was away, but concludes that it was unlikely. He was away only a short time, and the moves towards Rome accelerated after his return in May 1915, although apparently there was trouble with a visiting priest from the Diocese of Zanzibar using a monstrance while he was away. That priest, Revd Robert Keable, later wrote a pamphlet for the SSPP on the Rosary.

The church was originally fairly plain inside. The high altar had an alabaster reredos by one W. R. Ingram, which was covered by later work.

---

2 Scott James: *Asking for Trouble*, p. 32.

In 1915 alterations were made, originally on a temporary basis for the Corpus Christi Day celebrations that year, by the exotically named Marquis de Tournay d'Oisy, representing the vestment makers Louis Grossé. He added a Sacred Heart motif on the figure of Christ, and some curtaining around the altar. Certainly by that time Winnington-Ingram was complaining about Exposition of the Blessed Sacrament at the church, and the position of St Saviour was the subject of widespread discussion among the more advanced priests in London, as reported by Ronald Knox.[3]

The following year, 1916, there was a solemn procession on Corpus Christi Day but this was only inside the church. During this time the liturgy became gradually nearer to that of Rome, and in due course Latin was used for some services.

The interesting aspect of these changes is that the parish magazines show a real concern for his people by Kilburn, who was much respected for that not only by them, but also by the diocesan authorities. His church was well supported, nearly entirely by those living round about in circumstances of great material deprivation. The fashionable swoonishness of some West End strongholds of Anglo-Catholicism was far distant.

In January 1917 the church began advertising in its magazines that Benediction would be held on Sunday evenings. That service was of course anathema to all diocesan bishops at that time, and Winnington-Ingram's prohibition was to no avail. On 10 June 1917, the Sunday within in the Octave of Corpus Christi, Father Kilburn held what was almost certainly the first public outdoor procession of the Blessed Sacrament in the Church of England since the Reformation. In fact, the day had begun with three low masses at 7, 8, and 9, followed by High Mass at 11 with a procession inside the church using an ombrellino over the monstrance. There was then Benediction, followed by Exposition from 12.30 to 6.30, at which time there was Evensong at which the preacher was Revd H. P. Denison, then vicar of St Michael, Ladbroke Grove, and previously for many years curate to his uncle at East Brent, Somerset. He had been one of the pioneers of the introduction of baroque furnishings in the Church of England: a very elaborate high altar 'fell into [the] fortunate possession' of his church in North Kensington early in the war.[4]

---

3 Waugh: *The Life of Ronald Knox*, p. 119.
4 Denison: *Seventy-Two Years' Church Recollections*, p. 85.

Following Evensong there was a second procession of the Blessed Sacrament, this time in the streets around, followed again by Benediction. This was accompanied by very considerable ceremony, including girls strewing the road with flowers, and it is said that nearby houses were also decorated. Kensit witnessed the events of the day, became almost apoplectic with indignation, and complained to the Bishop, who was more decisive on this occasion than on others. Having ascertained that the procession had indeed been held and that, more significantly, no undertaking was forthcoming that it would not be repeated, he placed the church under episcopal ban, refusing to visit it even for confirmations or to license curates: more importantly, diocesan grants to the parish were blocked.

The effect of this outside pressure was to remove any restraint on what occurred within the parish, because external checks were removed. Kilburn was not anything like as cut off as was Father Victor Roberts in later years at Hayward's Heath, but he was in a rather analogous position. He was also assisted by some sympathetic supporters: a fund to help pay for the curates was set up, of which the Duke of Newcastle became a trustee, and the omnipresent Father Fynes-Clinton, then at Lewisham, was the first donor. Some, however, stood askance, and much later Father Sturt wrote, with some exaggeration, that the bishops had broken the unity of the Catholic Movement over St Saviour by dividing the two camps.[5]

By 1919 all the services were in Latin and the Westminster Hymn Book was used. It was said that a notice was erected outside indicating that this was 'The Catholic Church of St Saviour'. There was nothing in it to show the outsider that the church had any connection with the Church of England, although there were references to it in the magazines. One of the consequences of the episcopal ban was that it was impossible for candidates to be confirmed in the church where they worshipped, and they had to be sent elsewhere when the Bishop visited. However, in late 1919 Kilburn was able to take advantage of the visit to England of many colonial bishops for the 1920 Lambeth Conference: they numbered some whose spirituality was far more Catholic in tone than any in England. On three successive days commencing on 14 September 1919 the church was visited by Bishop Hine of Northern

---

5 In *The Pilot*, Spring 1958, p. 5.

Rhodesia, Bishop Weston of Zanzibar, and Bishop Shedden of Nassau respectively. It was the visit of Frank Weston which aroused the most controversy, mainly because he confirmed some of the church's candidates, effectively contravening the ban of the diocesan. It is also said that he celebrated on this occasion in Swahili, since he did not feel able to use the Latin mass, but English was not used in the church.

Kilburn also moved forward with the refurbishment of the church. In 1919 he had Martin Travers design a new altar, but the parish magazine for August that year ('the month of Our Lady in Heaven') indicated that funds were too low for work to start. Then it was said that Travers had been too busy at Bourne Street. The work was quoted as costing £28 for a new tabernacle, £135 for a new stone altar with gradines and mensa of marble, £12 for steps to the throne, £15 for a plinth, £65 for removing the existing levels and £31 for new steps to the altar. This was a considerable sum for a poor parish, and the work had to be carried out in stages. The 1915 curtain screens were removed and a new altar was installed, which was first used for a Solemn High Mass of Exposition on 13 March 1920. In the parish magazine for April 1920 is a short note by the architect, pointing out that gilding and a new set of candlesticks was required to complete the work. He also explained that he had provided a proper Western Use altar, with a sepulchre in the centre for relics; the church indeed later placed in the altar relics of St Anthony and of St Francis. The altar was of characteristic neo-baroque sarcophagus form with gradine, and initially the original Gothic reredos was left in place.

In 1920 Father Laing moved to the Bahamas, although Father Holland remained. It appears that the parish was being assisted at this time by Revd William Lowndes, who is mentioned in a number of reminiscences of the time because he abhorred the use of the Prayer Book and had sworn never to take part in a service in which it was used. He is even said to have claimed that it was inspired by the Devil. In 1919 Revd Stanley Joad of Upminster, Essex, a former associate of Conrad Noel, was inhibited by his bishop from conducting any services in his church. He was referred to Lowndes for help, but decided that the Latin mass would be unacceptable in his suburban parish, and eventually was assisted by Revd D. L. Morse-Boycott from Somers Town, later well known as a journalist and writer.[6]

---

6 Groves: *Conrad Noel and the Thaxted Movement*, pp. 231–2.

Lowndes had been Vice Principal of Ely Theological College from 1884 to 1889, and then after short periods in Barbados and as a curate at St Michael, Shoreditch, he was parish priest of St Mary, Nassau, in the Bahamas from 1892 to 1915. Initially thereafter he is listed as living at Buxted, Sussex, but he then moved to 25 Alwyne Road, Canonbury, not far from Hoxton, where he had an oratory with his own relic of St Anthony of Padua. It may have been through Lowndes' contacts that Bishop Roscoe Shedden was invited to the church in 1919.

It was the devotion paid to the Blessed Sacrament which had caused Winnington-Ingram to intervene in the way set out, as was the case in other places. A conference was organised to discuss the question of Benediction, and this took place at St Saviour on 14 March 1918, organised by Lowndes and Revd R. H. A. Cotton, who was then a curate at another Brooks church, Holy Innocents, Hammersmith. That conference preceded the expulsion of Father Sandys Wason from his parish in Cornwall, which took place the following year, but it was in prospect at that time, and many of those who supported the conference also supported him: these included Kilburn himself. It appears that as many as 80 priests and 100 laymen attended, and a report of the conference was published in which it was argued that Benediction could not only not be lawfully prevented, but in fact was an obligation on a parish priest.[7] This argument was further developed in Baverstock's book *Benediction and the Bishops*, which has already been mentioned and which was published the following year, shortly after Wason was deprived of his living. It is interesting that one of the unnamed speakers at the St Saviour conference advised his listeners not to speak any more of the Church of England, but rather to refer to it as 'the Provinces of Canterbury and of York'.

The Conference Report is unsatisfactory in that the names of the speakers are not given, and some shorthand notes of other contributors' comments were apparently lost, but the tone of the meeting was in favour of strong steps to introduce, and then publicly to advertise, Benediction, to enter into no correspondence with bishops about it, and not to appear before the consistory court but to appeal to the canons of the Western Church and ask to appeal to the 'Western Patriarchate' (presumably the Vatican). The most important step was said to be to

---

7 See Anon.: *Report of the Conference on Benediction at St Saviour, Hoxton.*

stay in place in the parish whatever orders were made in the Chancellors' courts.

Although a Lay Federation was mooted at the meeting, and a sheet was circulated asking for a 'militant campaign' in favour of Benediction, no long-term organisation appears to have developed from this conference, but it was resolved to organise a series of 40 Hour Devotions to the Blessed Sacrament across London in the autumn of 1918. The fact that as many as 45 churches in the Diocese of London took part shows how eucharistic adoration had moved forward during the war years. It was while St Saviour was holding its own devotion in this sequence that the war ended, on 11 November 1918.

Cotton died young late in 1918. Lowndes is not listed in the 1920 or subsequent editions of *Crockford*, and it seems likely that he submitted to Rome, although no definite information has been found. In 1922 Kilburn himself resigned from St Saviour, as did Holland. It seems apparent from his valedictory messages in the parish magazine that at that time he was not intending to secede to Rome, but rather the prime cause of his departure was the enormous amount of hard work which he had put into the parish, accentuated by the strains brought about by the poor financial situation, which had meant that the unfortunate architect was not paid for his 1919–20 work until September 1922.

In the course of the next 12 months however, first Holland and then Kilburn did go over to Rome and both later joined the Oratory.

Kilburn was universally respected for his piety and his devotion to his flock, but even the sympathetic Dom Anselm Hughes in his personal account of the Anglo-Catholic Movement in the twentieth century, *Rivers of the Flood*, was moved to remark: 'occasionally an individual has made the mistake of moving too far ahead of the front line and so losing contact altogether. This is almost certainly true of E. E. Kilburn . . .'[8]

What happened on Kilburn's resignation appears somewhat peculiar. Winnington-Ingram held the right of presentation to the living, and after the trouble which the church had caused him it might have been expected that he would have chosen a safe and loyal Anglo-Catholic as Kilburn's successor. Instead it appears that the outgoing incumbent was permitted some choice in his replacement, or perhaps he agreed to

---

8 Hughes: *The Rivers of the Flood*, p. 44.

resign only if he was given that right. In any event, the new incumbent was Revd J. F. Bloxam, who had been a curate at St Mary, Bourne Street, or its mother church, St Paul, Knightsbridge, from 1905, and he continued the same liturgical regime as his predecessor.

Bloxam had been an undergraduate at Exeter College, Oxford, graduating in 1895. While there, he had been part of a homosexual coterie which strongly identified itself with Oscar Wilde, and the latter used his surname in *The Importance of Being Earnest*. Wilde was introduced to him in 1894 by George Ives, a propagandist for homosexuality, and found him an 'undergraduate of strange beauty'. Bloxam showed to the other men his story *The Priest and the Acolyte*, in which a priest who has become infatuated with his young server poisons the chalice before administering it to the boy and then to himself. Wilde encouraged Bloxam to publish the story in a new magazine which the latter started, the *Chameleon*, which appeared for the first and only time in December 1894. The story appeared unsigned, however, and was generally thought to have been written by Wilde: it was later to feature in his trials.[9] Another member of this group was the sinologist and fraudster Sir Edmund Backhouse, whose biographer also refers to Bloxam.[10]

There is no evidence that the wider world knew of these youthful indiscretions on the part of Bloxam. He was ordained deacon in 1897 and priest the following year, serving curacies at St Agnes, Kennington (1897–1902), and St Andrew, Worthing (1902–5), before moving to the West End of London. He was at Bourne Street for 17 years in all, although he served as an Army chaplain at the end of the war and was awarded the Military Cross in 1917 and a Bar to it the following year; these were unusual awards for a priest and must show that the authorities knew nothing of his rather outré past.

Apart from continuing the same liturgical practices as Kilburn, Bloxam continued with the scheme to refurbish the interior of the church. In 1924 Travers was called back to gild the altar, and this was prepared for Corpus Christi Day, 19 June of that year. The next stage was the erection of a new reredos and canopy, which was ready for the Midnight Mass in 1926. Interestingly, although there were no faculties

---

9 See R. Ellman: *Oscar Wilde* (Penguin, 1988), pp. 403–4.
10 See H. Trevor-Roper: *Hermit of Peking* (Penguin, 1978), p. 32.

for any of the work carried out in the church, the plans for this stage formed an exhibit at the 1927 Royal Academy show.

The conclusion of this work gave the interior of the church a characteristic look of the time, rather similar to the work carried out at St Mary, Bourne Street, itself, although on a less lavish scale. It appears that from behind the reredos packing cases could readily be discerned, which had been used to build it up. However, the reredos itself was impressive from the side seen by the congregation: it had a very large gilded rood scene within an ornate frame, and above was a chalice and host. The main set of six altar candlesticks on the top gradine was propped from behind, for cheapness, and were wooden, but in addition there were a further six candlesticks on the next shelf and a further four beneath that. Above the altar was an octagonal wooden canopy hung from above and gilded and painted. The apse was further disguised at low cost by hanging six long strips of brocade attached at the top to cartouches which matched the reredos.

During this incumbency Bishop Weston again came to the church, this time in August 1923, when he presided at pontifical Benediction. Father Bloxam had as his curate for a time Ronald Knox's brother Wilfred, who had also been at Bourne Street and was later to become well known as a writer and in particular as one of the central figures in the Oratory of the Good Shepherd in Cambridge. Bloxam's stay at Hoxton was, however, short: he resigned because of ill health in 1927 and died in April 1928.

On this occasion the Bishop insisted prior to replacing Bloxam that the new incumbent should revert to the vernacular. After some negotiation on this subject, the new vicar was confirmed as Revd D. A. Ross, who, like Bloxam, had a 'London, Brighton and South Coast' background: he had been curate at successively St Mellitus, Hendon, St Thomas, Hove, and then St Peter-le-Poer, Friern Barnet. Fynes-Clinton acted as bishop's chaplain at Father Ross' induction, thus showing mutual goodwill at last between Winnington-Ingram and the Papalists in his diocese.

Although the services thereafter were in English, the church continued to be uncompromising in tone. Father Joblin joined the staff in 1928, and in 1929 he became the English Secretary of the Confraternity of Unity when it was established in England, as already discussed. He and Revd R. J. H. Ellis were curates together and later

Revd J. Milburn, a well-known priest in Brighton and elsewhere in the post-Second World War period, was on the staff.[11] It would be right to say, however, that matters were quieter during the period from Father Ross arriving until the Second World War. He was not one of the 21 who actively defied the post-Prayer Book Revision ban on Benediction.

In 1940 the church was badly damaged during air raids. Father Ross was able to make temporary arrangements to continue services in the presbytery, and the back cover of *Reunion* carried a stylised picture of the Marian shrine at the church. The hope that it would be rebuilt after the war came to nothing and in 1948 the parish was merged with that of St Anne, Hemsworth Street. The area was being depopulated and in any event there were plenty of other churches in the neighbourhood, so in about 1954 the remains of St Saviour were demolished. Following the merger, and after a short interlude deputising for Father Hope Patten, who was suffering one of his bouts of illness, Father Ross went on to take on the parish of Holy Trinity, Leeds Road, Bradford, which was in a rather socially similar neighbourhood to Hoxton despite the geographical distance from it, and then in 1956 he replaced his former curate Father Joblin as chaplain to the Laleham nuns for a year before retiring.

There were of course other churches in London which developed a tradition of Papalism over the years,[12] and one which was much less notorious than St Saviour was St Alban, Margravine Road, Fulham, which was equally unobtrusive in the sense that it was away from any main roads and was in what was then a solidly working-class area. It has already been mentioned several times in this work as such a centre.[13]

St Alban was built by Sir Aston Webb and Ingress Bell in 1896. Betjeman described it thus (1968): 'Red brick Arts and Crafts Gothic full of altars, confessionals and statues, including an unusually big Holy

---

11 Father Milburn was at St Stephen, Grove Street, Liverpool (now demolished) in the post-war period, then at St Paul, Brighton. He was also Chaplain General of the Society of Mary. In both churches he introduced ultramontane practices and furnishings.

12 St Silas, Pentonville, near St Saviour, Hoxton, was another with local support: this church for a time held a noon mass in Latin for lapsed Romans every Sunday.

13 See Goodison: *St Alban, Fulham: The First One Hundred Years.*

Child of Prague wearing a golden crown. A well-used church with an Italian ethos.'[14]

The vicars of St Alban during its most ultra years were Revd J. E. Watson, who was later to be one of the 21, and Revd C. C. Higgs.

Father John Watson was an undergraduate at Sidney Sussex College Cambridge, which had a Catholic tradition for much of the twentieth century despite its Cromwellian legacy; he then went on to Ely Theological College. His first curacy was at Harrow Green, Essex (1896–9), followed by St Philip, Clerkenwell (1899–1907). He then moved to Great Addington, Northamptonshire (1907–13) before returning to London as curate of Christ Church, South Hackney, under Revd C. R. Deakin, the originator of the Anglo-Catholic Congresses (1913–16) and then of St Michael, Ladbroke Grove, under Prebendary Denison (1916–18). In the latter year he moved to become vicar of St Alban, and remained there until his death in 1934. He was succeeded by Father Charles Chester Higgs, who had been a curate at the church from January 1916, immediately after his ordination in 1915, until that time.

When Father Watson went to the church in 1918 he succeeded Revd G. G. Elliott, vicar since 1911, who moved to the exalted surroundings of St Bartholomew, Brighton. Father Elliott had instituted a series of initiatives to relieve poverty in what was then a very poor area of London, and the church remained well respected in the neighbourhood for many years thereafter. When Father Watson arrived he immediately changed the nature of the services by adopting overnight the full Roman system of liturgy and discipline. The local congregation was lost, and thereafter, although the affection for the church remained, very few in the immediate vicinity attended. All the services were in Latin, communion was always in one kind only, and confessional boxes were installed with grills in the Roman style.

Initially there were two curates at the church as well as the vicar, and Father Kewley has already been mentioned as serving there for a time. The church was placed under episcopal ban by Winnington-Ingram in 1923, and that resulted in withdrawal of the diocesan grants for curates: the vicar set up a Benediction Defence Fund to pay them, and the Catholic League and other organisations contributed to it. However, it

---

14 Betjeman: *Collins Pocket Guide to English Parish Churches: The South*, p. 270.

was financial pressure which led to Father Kewley being asked to leave in 1926.

St Alban continued with its entirely Roman practices after St Saviour had been made to use English. After most, though not all, the locals had effectively boycotted the new regime, Father Watson attracted an eclectic congregation from across London, and the church was left to go its own way. In 1927 there were about 200 in the congregation, although details are somewhat difficult to ascertain because one of Father Watson's idiosyncrasies was that, although he kept baptism and marriage registers, he refused to keep a register of services, saying that God knew who came to his sacraments. He also ceased all pastoral visiting, on the basis that people should come to church rather than the church to the people.

Father Watson was clearly not the easiest of people with whom to deal: he tolerated the Church Lads' Brigade, which flourished for many years, because from it were drawn most of the servers, but refused to permit any other organisations, such as Girl Guides. He restricted the choir to plainsong and many of them left to go to other churches.

The continued policy of Romanism at St Alban also meant that relations between Father Watson and Winnington-Ingram were extremely strained and the funds available to the parish were cut down in consequence. However, the ever-tolerant Bishop acceded to a petition from the parish to replace him with Father Higgs. This duly occurred, although there were Kensitite protests at the installation.[15]

After Watson's death Father Higgs had to manage on his own for some time, although he did have a curate for a while shortly before the war, but he continued with the same policy. In contrast to Father Watson, he was a much-loved figure in the neighbourhood, popular because of his willingness to appear in court to speak on behalf of the local villains. During the war he stood by his people during the bombing, and that again endeared him to them. The dilemma which he faced, however, was well seen when he agreed to use English for Benediction in order to assuage the Bishop: this was sufficient to permit Winnington-Ingram to restore the diocesan grants, but it antagonised some members of the congregation, who thought that Father Watson's legacy ought to

---

15 The Bishop was recorded in the local paper as saying at the induction that 'It does not follow that the visit of a Bishop means that he wholly approves of all that is going on in a church.'

be maintained. Father Higgs did in general follow his predecessor's policy, not least because he believed that Father Watson was haunting the vicarage and making sure that standards were upheld.[16]

The war dispersed much of the congregation which had been gathered, and in the post-1945 period numbers were sadly depleted. However, while the Church of England agonised over South India and other issues, Father Higgs continued as perhaps the only Anglican parish priest in London then to use the Latin mass for all his services. He spent 43 years at St Alban, a long and solitary ministry which only ended when he suffered a sustained bout of ill-health and moved in 1958 to become chaplain to the Benedictine nuns at Burford, where he was able to continue saying the Tridentine Mass, in accordance with their use. He died on 17 March 1969, exactly one week after Father Butler of Kettlebaston, another uncompromising adherent to the old ways.

Higgs was succeeded as parish priest in 1959 by an Australian, Revd K. V. Moore, who had previously been curate of St Thomas, Shepherd's Bush, another centre of Papalist teaching: he reintroduced the vernacular to St Alban after 40 years of Latin, but by then parish life was run down and his efforts to revive it were an uphill struggle. Also of course, the congregation which did remain was used to the former regime: the churchwardens both resigned in protest against the changes which were brought in. He was succeeded in 1967 by Revd G. Palmer, who remained in the parish for 30 years and again had to labour hard to rebuild the trust of the parishioners, which had been lost over the years.

Very different in its locale from either of the two churches so far discussed was the church of the Annunciation of Our Lady, Bryanston Street, Marble Arch, which is situated in a West End side-street very near to Oxford Street. The church itself has had an unusual history. It replaced the eighteenth-century Quebec Chapel, which stood on the same site, and was given parochial status and the title of The Annunciation as late as 1894. In 1909 Revd Bernard Shaw became vicar, and he was later commemorated by a brass in the new church, which was designed by Sir Walter Tapper and consecrated by Bishop Winnington-Ingram on 24 June 1914, a very late date for central London. Tapper built an enormously tall nave with a north aisle (but no corresponding south aisle), designed after the manner of Bodley. It was apparently

16 Information from Revd G. Palmer.

intended to add a long cloister to the church as well as an integral vicarage above a west gallery, but the outbreak of the First World War put an end to those plans. The furnishings which were added over the years, many in the baroque idiom, were chosen to enhance, rather than detract from, the existing architecture. As originally designed there was a screen with curved rood beam high above the congregation, and in due course the church acquired an immense reredos with triptych by Bewsey, which could be opened with almost mechanical precision by a mere touch from a server at the appropriate time on Holy Saturday. The Italianate candlesticks were of appropriate dimensions and the church was also provided with notable Stations of the Cross by John de Mars and sixteenth-century paintings from the Continent.

The church always had a tradition of Anglo-Catholicism, although it is little mentioned in contemporary sources between the wars. Father Bernard Shaw was succeeded as vicar in 1922 by Revd Pomfrett Waddington, who was in turn succeeded in 1937 by Father C. P. Shaw, who had been chairman of the 21 incumbents while vicar of St Mary Magdalene, Paddington. His stay at the church was very short, although he went on to other posts elsewhere. Father Shaw was succeeded by Revd D'Arcy Hutton, whose brief incumbency (1939–41) was ended by a scandal and who later went over to Rome. Archdeacon C. F. Fortescue was then handed the incumbency in order that the parish might be stabilised, and he stayed until 1947 when he was replaced by Revd Walter Gervase Bennett, who stayed until his death in 1976.

Father Bennett has already been mentioned in connection with the Annunciation group, which briefly brought the church to the forefront of ecclesiastical politics in the early 1950s. In fact however, particularly in later years, he stood aloof from most such controversies. He was the son of a Low Church vicar in the Cotswolds, and after Keble College, Oxford, and Ely Theological College was ordained deacon in 1933 and priest the following year. He came to The Annunciation after curacies at Grimsbury, Banbury (1933–5), St John the Baptist, Holland Road, Kensington (1935–41), St Mary, Swanley, Kent (1941–2), and St Thomas, Shepherd's Bush (1942–7).

Father Bennett was a great supporter of the Walsingham devotion and a Guardian of the Shrine, and at one time held high masses at the church on all feasts of Our Lady: the *Church Times*, in one of its more censorious moods, refused to carry advertisements for services on such un-Anglican festivals as Our Lady of Lourdes. The spirituality of the church was uncompromisingly Latin throughout his time, and the vicar had no truck with the cult of King Charles the Martyr, which was favoured by some other Papalists, as he took the view that a saint could only be a saint if so declared by the Vatican. The services were in English, and following Vatican II were modernised so as to bring them into conformity with the new decrees from Rome, although the spirit of the reforms was not exactly welcome: Father Bennett used to opine that liturgical reform was a cross he had to bear. Communion was generally given in one kind only even into the 1970s, and the celebrant wore a biretta long after they had fallen into desuetude elsewhere.

The Kensitites were predictably distressed by what occurred at The Annunciation, and in 1962 E. C. Last, the local organiser of the Protestant Truth Society, wrote an *Open Letter to the Bishop of London* in which he described (inaccurately) a service of High Mass and Absolutions of the Dead at the church, which he referred to as an 'extraordinary display of witchcraft'. Perhaps it was fortunate that Mr Last did not attend on Corpus Christi Day, which was always celebrated with great solemnity. Not only was every available candle placed on the altar, but also a number of reliquaries: Father Bennett also ensured that the rose petals which were strewn in front of the procession of the Host were suitably perfumed by adding essence to them in advance.

Last also drew attention to the practice which prevailed at this church, as at some others, of exhibiting a notice to the effect that the church was not in communion with Rome, so as to deter the unsuspecting. In later years a notice was displayed indicating that there were no Sunday evening masses at the church, but there was one at St James, Spanish Place, the nearby Roman church. It was also the custom at the church to pray for 'X, Our Pope, Y Our Bishop (of London)'; and for the benefit of visiting priests, there was a notice in the vestry informing him 'Nomen episcopi (Y) est', referring of course to the Anglican diocesan, but this was placed next to a picture of the Holy Father. Lest these examples give an impression of preciousness, it should be said that the services were in fact conducted with little fussiness and with much less elaboration than at some churches of more moderate churchmanship, and the furnishings, as Peter Anson remarked, were in the best possible taste. 'High Church' was a term of mild disapprobation to those of Father Bennett's inclination, and he was accustomed to refer to All Saints, Margaret

Street, and St Alban, Holborn, as 'those High Church places down the road'. Some continuity with earlier events was also demonstrated by the attendance at the church in post-war years of a redoubtable lady who had been brought up at St Saviour, Hoxton, and always wore a mantilla over her head at mass.

It was perhaps fitting that Father Bennett's death, on 16 October 1976, occurred while he was on a parish pilgrimage to Walsingham, a place with which he had been closely associated for so many years.[17]

17 The author attended this church from 1971 to 1973 and much of the information set out was gathered during that time.

9

ANGLICAN PAPALISM IN CORNWALL
Father Sandys Wason and
Father Bernard Walke

Cornwall was home during the early part of the twentieth century to two of the more extraordinary priests whom the Church of England has produced, Leighton Sandys Wason (1867–1950) and Nicolo Bernard Walke (1874–1941), both of whom were always known by their respective second Christian names. They were friends and allies for a period, and were each committed to a Papalist outlook, although both were individuals whom it was difficult to categorise. They, however, are well remembered long after their respective deaths, when their more conventional colleagues are forgotten.

Sandys Wason has been the subject of a recent full-length biography by Roy Tricker (1994), which has brought before a wider public not only his career in the Church but also his literary talents. On the other hand, whereas Bernard Walke wrote a certain amount about himself in his much-praised *Twenty Years at St Hilary* (1935), and his friend Frank Baker wrote of him in *I Follow But Myself* (1968) and *The Call of Cornwall* (1976) as well as in the introduction to the reissued edition of Walke's own book (1982), there is as yet no full biography of him, although there are a number of pamphlets, and considerable interest has been shown in his life and work.

Sandys Wason, like Hope Patten, appears to have accepted the Anglo-Catholic interpretation of Christianity as a given whole, and he was never tempted by the claims of Rome despite his treatment by the Anglican authorities. He was an undergraduate at Christ Church, Oxford, where he started a magazine entitled *The Spirit Lamp*, which was a parody of French symbolic poetry but was later taken over by Oscar Wilde and his coterie, and went on to Ely Theological College. He was ordained deacon on 23 December 1894 and served his title at Elmswell in Suffolk, which was then enjoying a brief period of relatively advanced Anglo-Catholicism. The Bishop, however, refused to ordain him as a priest, apparently because of his use of the rosary as a devotional aid, and in 1897 he moved, still as a deacon, to the very different surroundings of St Andrew, Plaistow, where he was priested on 25 September 1898. It was during this period that he made the acquaintance of the author Compton Mackenzie, who was later to use Wason as the model for his character Father Oliver Dorward in *Sylvia Scarlett* and in the Mark Lidderdale trilogy, *The Altar Steps*, *The Parson's Progress* and *The Heavenly Ladder*. Mackenzie refers to preserving Wason's 'glorious eccentricity', albeit inadequately, in those books.[1] In 1898 he met him again, and they walked over to Froyle in Hampshire where the squire, Sir Hubert Miller (also parodied in the novels), had furnished the village church in continental fashion. Mackenzie also credits Wason with having first coined the term 'spike' for an obsessive ritualist.[2]

In 1899 Wason became a curate at St Michael, Shoreditch, which was then under episcopal discipline because of its liturgical practices. In due course the vicar, Revd H. M. Middleton Evans, and one of his curates, Revd W. W. Hume, went over to Rome, while the other curates, Revd A. N. Vowler and Wason himself, remained within the Church of England. Although in many circumstances priests who were put under pressure by their bishop received sympathy from their colleagues, there was in this instance little comfort shown to Father Middleton Evans, who was widely thought at the time to have behaved unreasonably. In 1941 he was featured in a series in *The Pilot* entitled 'Why did they leave us?' in which Father Hole said that he should have persisted and disregarded parliamentary control. In 1903, after these secessions, the ban on the church was lifted.

Although Wason did not go over to Rome then or at any time later, there is no doubt that his attitudes were those of a thoroughgoing Papalist, and in addition that he had formed those attitudes earlier than had many others. Tricker says:

> He saw himself as a priest of the Catholic Church, of which the Church of England was a very small part, and to him the final

---

1 Mackenzie: *My Life and Times, Octave Two*, p. 202.
2 Ibid., p. 203.

authority for what went on in the Catholic Church must be the Pope and the Holy See . . . To him if you were an Anglican you were a Catholic and you held the Catholic Faith – undiluted and in all its fullness.[3]

Wason's eccentricity was that he seemed sometimes to fail to understand why everybody did not hold similar views. He himself always used the Latin breviary and whenever possible said the mass in that language. He is said to have had little physical presence in church and to have had a somewhat monotonous and expressionless voice. Unlike his friend Father Walke, he had very little charisma. He did, however, take his priestly office very seriously: there is an extraordinary photograph in Tricker's book showing Wason playing tennis, correctly dressed for that sport but still wearing his biretta on his head.

In 1905 Wason was appointed to the living of Cury with Gunwalloe, two villages near Helston in Cornwall with a total population of about 500. Neither church had much if any tradition of Anglo-Catholicism, and indeed most of the parishioners were actually Methodists. Wason did not allow that state of affairs to deflect him from the course which he thought proper. On the first Sunday of his incumbency he announced there would be daily mass at 8 a.m., and that on Sundays there would be Sung Mass at 11 and Devotions to the Blessed Sacrament at 6 p.m.

This sudden change was not to the liking of those who were accustomed to attend the parish churches, and their distaste for the new vicar was increased when he tended to favour the agricultural labourers against the farmers who were the majority of those who did come. However, Wason's literary contacts did flourish and he wrote a considerable quantity of nonsense verse, which was well regarded. Among his visitors at Cury were A. A. Milne, James Barrie, and Conan Doyle, who used the area for his story *The Devil's Foot* in which a death takes place in a house based on Wason's vicarage. Compton Mackenzie and his wife actually lived in the house for a year from 1907 as his lodgers. Mackenzie was amazed by the spectacularly disorganised way in which Wason lived, although he was very fond of him and assisted with the Sunday School. He wrote in his memoirs: 'By the time Faith [his wife]

---

3 Tricker: *Mr Wason . . . I Think*, p. 21.

and I arrived as paying guests at Cury Vicarage, dear Wason had managed to empty the church of any congregation it ever had by what in those days was called ritualism.'[4] The congregation was indeed small, although there were a few who became devoted to their eccentric priest.

Gunwalloe church, which is virtually on the beach, was by far the more attractive of the two buildings, and Wason further enhanced it by the provision of an altar by Comper in memory of his mother.

Although there were a few locals who supported Wason, there were many others who were appalled by his religious views, and they made vociferous complaints to the Bishop of Truro. In early 1910 Wason was told to use only the Book of Common Prayer (a volume which he regarded with ill-disguised contempt and was wont to refer to as the 'Book of Comic Prayer') and then on 27 June 1910 he was put under discipline and confined to his parish. He did not conform to his Bishop's requests, and indeed during the First World War moved from Devotions to Benediction of the Blessed Sacrament as the evening service. Latin was used both at Cury and at Gunwalloe. In fact, Wason's most measured response to the episcopal pressure was to write a book entitled *The Anathema Alphabet or Syllabus of Errors condemned by the English Bishops since 1840* for the Society of SS Peter and Paul, a pamphlet which ridiculed a number of the more pompous pronouncements of the episcopal Bench.

Wason's view, which he shared with most other Anglican Papalists, was that he did not recognise the system of ecclesiastical courts, because the ultimate appeal was to a secular body (the Judicial Committee of the Privy Council). When therefore he was brought to trial at Truro Cathedral on 25 April 1919 for his refusal to use the 1662 Book, he failed to appear. The consequence was that on 27 May 1919 he was sentenced to be deprived of his living, a penalty which he refused to accept throughout the remainder of his long life. He always subsequently regarded himself as the true parish priest of Cury cum Gunwalloe.

Wason was one of the few Anglo-Catholics on whom the full rigour of the law was actually directed, although at about the same time Revd Reginald Wynter of Taunton was also ejected. A mob of Cornish farmers emptied the church of its new fittings, and Wason retreated to the

---

4 Mackenzie: *My Life and Times, Octave Four*, p. 11.

vicarage, where he said mass until that too was invaded, and he was forced to flee to his friend Walke at St Hilary.

The events at Cury created a considerable stir. The English Church Union was reluctant to defend Wason because they refused publicly to defend the service of Benediction. However, a protest meeting was held in Caxton Hall to support him, at which Alban Baverstock, Conrad Noel, Ernest Kilburn, and the venerable Arthur Tooth spoke. Later his case was taken even further. On 26 February 1920 a delegation from the Federation of Catholic Priests, headed by Darwell Stone and Father Bull SSJE, met the Archbishops of Canterbury and York. Randall Davidson was unimpressed and was recorded as saying: 'Do you tell me there does not exist on earth any mode for dealing with such a man as Wason? You say the institution of legal procedure is unjust. Do you mean that the Bishop must retire and give up the matter when the Priest persists in defiance?'[5]

After his deprivation, Wason never held office in the Church of England, though he continued to regard himself as the parish priest of Cury and always said prayers for his people. For many years afterwards he was effectively an itinerant, staying with various priestly friends in different parts of England. In 1924 he was made Secretary of the SSC, but his organisational skills were very few and far between. He did inherit an aptly named firm of publishers, Cope & Fenwick (which had been established in 1906), which sold devotional literature from the back room of the Medici Society, as had the SSPP. In 1927 he published a novel entitled *Palafox* but that was not a commercial success. Finally, in 1942 he was officially licensed to assist Father Hargrave Thomas at Needham Market, thus returning after a long interval almost to Elmswell, where he had first been a curate. In 1946 he moved on to the rather different environs of the dockland church of St Peter, Limehouse, where he helped the vicar, Revd C. C. Hordern, another Anglican Papalist. Father Hordern had at one time been a curate at St Michael, Shoreditch, and was later for many years vicar of St John the Baptist, Holland Road, Kensington, before joining the Roman Catholic Church while almost on his deathbed. Despite that, his funeral was held at his former church, and he was buried in his Anglican biretta.

Wason died in 1950, possessing little by way of material goods and in

---

5 Bell: *Randall Davidson*, p. 1025.

the eyes of many a failure. His visual field was even more limited than that of Hope Patten, but he lacked the latter's force of personality and charisma, and he made the mistake of thinking that what he believed to be the proper presentation of Christianity was automatically accepted as such by those who had no prior understanding of what lay behind it. Walke wrote of Wason that he had a 'mannerism adopted to conceal, from all but his most intimate friends, a nature too shy and at the same time too intolerant of the commonplace to meet with the world's approval'.[6]

Walke was a very different man from Wason in many respects, although his ecclesiastical views were not dissimilar. He came from a Tractarian background: one of the first pioneers of the Catholic Revival in Cornwall was his grandfather, Revd William John Coope, of the church of King Charles the Martyr, Falmouth. Walke's father was also a priest in the same tradition, but his parish was in the New Forest. Walke, like Hope Patten, did not attend either school or university. His father educated him at home and his knowledge was random, but he developed a deep love of the countryside, which he retained all his life. He also escaped from the formalism of public school education of the time, which marked so many of his contemporaries.[7]

Bernard Walke followed the family tradition in proceeding to ordination, although he was in many ways not at all traditional in his outlook. He proceeded to Chichester Theological College, was made a deacon in 1900, and served his first curacy at St Michael, Walthamstow, the only time in which he exercised his ministry outside Cornwall (1900–2). He arrived there shortly after the departure of Alban Baverstock, who was also a curate in Walthamstow and was appointed to Hinton Martel in 1899. During that curacy Walke was ordained as priest. He then moved to successive curacies at St Ives (1902–5) and Polruan (1905–12), before becoming vicar of St Hilary, near Marazion, in 1913.

There is no doubt that Walke was an Anglican Papalist, although somewhat unconventional when seen against many of the supporters of that tendency. He himself wrote in his autobiography: '[I] was convinced that the Catholic Movement in the Church of England, which began in the rediscovery of the Church as a divine institution, could have

---

6 Walke: *Twenty Years at St Hilary* (1982 edn), p. 283.
7 Allchin: *A Good Man Who Could Never Be Dull*, p. 10.

no other end but a corporate union with the Apostolic See of Rome.'[8] He was also a signatory to the 1932 Centenary Manifesto, which was in quite unambiguous Papalist terms. Much, but not all, of his thinking was Latin in origin and, for example, he placed in one of the new stone altars at St Hilary 'stark and bare' relics of St Rosa of Lima 'the fair flower of the New World'.[9]

Walke's somewhat idiosyncratic approach to his ministry became clear even during his curacies. He disappeared for days on end with the fishing fleet, or explored the life of the local tin miners. Compton Mackenzie first met him in December 1907 when he was at Polruan, and Walke immediately made an impression on the writer, who referred to him as 'an outstanding personality'.[10] Later Mackenzie compared him to the legendary Anglo-Catholic priest Robert Dolling, saying: 'Bernard Walke had the same gift of love for the poor, the same burning devotion to the example of Jesus Christ.'[11]

In 1911 Walke married, which again put him outside the conventional tenets of Anglican Papalism. His wife, Annie Fearon, was an idiosyncratic priest's wife, but a fine artist. A work by her hangs today in St Mary, Bourne Street, and another in Truro Cathedral, and she was also instrumental in assisting with the redecoration of St Hilary church. More importantly perhaps, she introduced Walke to a circle of artists in the area, many of whom were members of what has become known as the Newlyn School. The Walkes had no children.

In 1913 Walke was appointed to the living of St Hilary, with which his name is always associated. The church in the village was rebuilt in 1853 by William White after a fire. The village straggles over several settlements and at that time the parishioners numbered some 600. There were five or six Nonconformist chapels in the parish, and Walke saw as one of his objectives to rescue the local people from the routine of 'Wesley guilds and tea drinking' into which they had relapsed, and to bring them back to the True Faith. He wrote that 'I was persuaded that the religious instinct of the Cornish people would never find satisfaction apart from the teaching and worship of the Catholic faith; as the last of

---

8 Walke: *Twenty Years at St Hilary*, p. 30.
9 Ibid., p. 123.
10 Mackenzie: *My Life and Times, Octave Four*, p. 21.
11 Ibid., p. 23.

the English people to forsake the old religion, they would be the first to return to the old ways.'[12]

A problem which was later to manifest itself was that the parish boundary ended about 200 yards from the church on one side, and that therefore the church was not in the centre of the area which it served. This, and the fact that Walke's appeal was to an eclectic congregation, meant that many of the regular attenders were not in fact parishioners in the technical sense.

There is no doubt that Walke was a man of considerable personal charisma, who disarmed by his personal holiness many who would otherwise have opposed him. During his first years in the parish he was indeed able to do what many others could not, namely to instruct the congregation in his vision of the Catholic faith, and to enthuse not only local agricultural labourers, but also his wife's artistic friends. A regular congregation of about 80 was built up, and it appears that he was well supported locally. He was a familiar figure in the lanes around in his donkey and cart: he devoted a chapter of his autobiography to donkeys, of whom he was particularly fond.

From the very start of his ministry in St Hilary, Walke was much concerned for the underprivileged, and in due course he started an orphanage in a former public house called 'The Jolly Tinners', which later was affiliated to the Holy Family Homes begun by Alban Baverstock, and later still moved to Walsingham. In the First World War he took an unpopular pacifist stance, which involved him in ministering to conscientious objectors in Dartmoor Prison. He also instituted the service of Benediction, as an act of reparation for the wrongs of war. At the end of the First World War he was much concerned with organising relief for Russia after famine followed the Revolution, and more particularly with an attempt to set up a lay order working for a just society, to be known as Brethren of the Common Table. The interesting point about that project was that he was perfectly prepared to work with other denominations, and was particularly interested in the Quakers, at a time when his fellow Anglican Papalists regarded Rome as the sole source of wisdom. He was also a leading light in an attempt to set up a Miners' Co-operative in the early 1920s, with the aim of reopening a mine, but after a promising beginning, in the end this too came to nothing.

---

12 Walke: *Twenty Years at St Hilary*, p. 30.

It is interesting, however, that while Walke was involved with these left-leaning enterprises, he regarded the Church as hierarchical: he, like many Anglo-Catholics, had no time at all for Parochial Church Councils, and never had one at St Hilary. On the other hand, he had no time either for the church courts which had condemned his friend Wason, and he therefore never applied for faculties for any of the many alterations he made to the furnishings of the church.

Walke's involvement with the artistic community meant that the additions to the fitments of the church which he made were not restricted to the more usual statues and crucifixes, although he did introduce those. He was anxious, as he said in his own *Guide* to the church, to make clear that not only was the new building constructed on the foundations of the old, and using the same stones, but 'it is the old Faith that is taught and practised within its walls that gives to the Church that sense of continuity with the past'.[13] He followed the fashion of the time in placing a large number of granite altars in the building, all of which were suitably decorated. A fourteenth-century French image of St Anne was placed under the chancel arch. Above the altar of the Chapel of the Sacred Heart was erected a fifteenth-century Flemish painting and in the chapel itself there was a seventeenth-century Spanish baroque statue of St Joseph. There were various other rather less conventional additions, such as a set of six Cornish witch-watching balls hung in the chancel,[14] and a model house which was a thanks offering to Our Lady by the parents of a boy who fell from the third storey of the original and was said to have been healed by her intercession.

The most striking impression in the church was given by the contemporary work. The vicar's wife painted an altarpiece showing St Joan of Arc, not commemorated here, as she was elsewhere, because of the spirit shown by the French in resisting the Germans, but rather because she 'suffered torture and death rather than deny the voices of her Saints and the direction of her conscience'.[15] Annie Walke also painted the Blessed Virgin and the Christ Child. Ernest Proctor (1886–1935), a leading member of the Newlyn School, painted the Visitation on the

---

13 Walke: *A Cornish Church* (1929), p. 2.
14 Perhaps intended as a local alternative to the ostrich eggs which the eccentric Revd E. J. G. Forse found in Burgos: see *Ceremonial Curiosities and Queer Sights in Foreign Churches*, p. 108.
15 Walke: *A Cornish Church*, p. 2.

Lady Chapel altar, the harrowing Entombment on the Altar of the Dead (a memorial to Walke's friend Gerard Collier, who had co-operated with him in his various industrial enterprises, and died young), the crucifix over the chancel arch, and the panels on the pulpit which depicted Cornish saints. Roger Fry (1866–1934) painted St Francis of Assisi for the altar dedicated to that saint. Phyllis Yglesias, who was of Spanish descent although she lived locally, painted the crucifix in the Lady Chapel which was placed in memory of Canon C. F. Rogers, who had been parish priest at St Mary, Penzance, and in retirement said his daily mass there. The most striking feature of the redecoration however was the panels on either side of the chancel. The stalls behind were coloured bright red and black, and the paintings depict further episodes in the life of the Cornish saints. They were carried out by Annie Walke, Ernest Proctor, his wife Dod Proctor, Gladys Hynes, Harold Knight (husband of the better-known Dame Laura Knight), and others. In the Lady Chapel was a series of paintings carried out in about 1925 by 12-year-old Joan Manning-Sanders, who had been encouraged to paint by Annie Walke. Her parents, George and Ruth Manning-Sanders, were writers and friends of Walke, who lived nearby at Sennen. It is unlikely that any other priest at that time would have permitted a child of that age to decorate his church.

These artistic endeavours were known only to relatively few. St Hilary became known to a wider public because Walke was also a talented play-wright. Not only that, but his friendship with BBC producer Filson Young led to the broadcasting of his striking and unconventional plays and led also to visits to St Hilary by Walter de la Mare and George Bernard Shaw. The impact of these early outside broadcasts was con-siderable, not only because at that time it was extremely unusual to hear Cornish or other regional accents on the radio, but also because at that date the performance of drama in church was regarded with some suspicion by many people. It was the Christmas play, 'Bethlehem', which made the greatest impact: it was broadcast every year from 1926 to 1934. The plays showed Walke's ability to reach out beyond the confines of the committed to the outside world. 'Bethlehem' was the best-known play, but there were a number of others, some of which were also broadcast. In 1939 Faber & Faber published three of his plays, 'The Upper Chamber', 'The Eve of All Souls', and 'The Stranger at St Hilary'.

There was, however, another aspect to the drama. The plays were as

17. Shrine of Our Lady, Church of the Annunciation, Bryanston Street, Marble Arch, 1960s. (*Michael Yelton Collection*)

18. Father Hope Patten in procession, 1952, to mark the 21st anniversary of the refounding of the Shrine of Our Lady of Walsingham. (*Shrine of Our Lady of Walsingham*)

19. (A) The Community of St Augustine in choir at the Walsingham shrine. (*Shrine of Our Lady of Walsingham*)

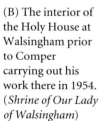 (B) The interior of the Holy House at Walsingham prior to Comper carrying out his work there in 1954. (*Shrine of Our Lady of Walsingham*)

20. Father Hope Patten in later years.
(*Shrine of Our Lady of Walsingham*)

21. Father Hope Patten a few seconds before his collapse and death, taken as he approached the Shrine Church. (*Shrine of Our Lady of Walsingham*)

22. Arnold Harris Mathew robed as an Archbishop. (*Rt Revd H. Weston-Smart Collection*)

ARNOLD HARRIS MATHEW
ARCHIEPISCOPUS

The Order

for the

Celebration of Low Mass

✠

according to the
Use of the Illustrious Church
of Salisbury

✠

rendered into English (and rubricated in detail, the directions taken from those in the printed editions of the Sarum Missal of several dates, from the Sarum Consuetudinary and Customary, and from "Alphabetum sacerdotum" and such other handbooks and tractates as were in common use by the clergy of England in the times before the Reformation).

by

J. E. BAZILLE-CORBIN, M.A.(Oxon), D.D. (*h'ou*)
Barrister-at-Law, *Grand Chancellor of the Order*
Rector of Runwell S. Mary, Essex. *of the Grand*
S. Stuart.

✠

7

23. Father Bazille-Corbin's Sarum Mass book: note the hand annotated addition of his title as Grand Chancellor of the Order of Stuart. (*Rt Revd H. Weston-Smart Collection*)

24. (A) The gravestone of Revd Herbert Ignatius Beale 'at a somewhat wayward angle' in the churchyard at Great Sutton, Essex. (*Michael Yelton*)

(B) The church of All Saints, Great Sutton, a stronghold of irregular Episcopal activity for many years. (*Michael Yelton*)

25. St John Fisher, as painted by Enid Chadwick on the screen at Kettlebaston, Suffolk, about 1952. (*Michael Yelton*)

(B) Shrine of Our Lady, Church of the Coronation of Our Lady, Kettlebaston. (*Michael Yelton*)

26. (A) Shrine of the Sacred Heart, Church of the Coronation of Our Lady, Kettlebaston. (*Michael Yelton*)

27. Benediction at St Stephen, Grove Street, Liverpool, given by Father John Milburn on the Eve of Corpus Christi Day. (*Richard McEwan Collection*)

28. Cleaning up the rose petals after Benediction at St Stephen, Grove Street, Liverpool. The wall mounted reliquary came from St Michael, Edinburgh. The lady with the carpet sweeper (Ursula Taylor) was such a devoted follower of her priest that she with others moved to Brighton when he became parish priest of St Paul in that place. (*Richard McEwan Collection*)

29. (A) High altar at St Michael, Hill Square, Edinburgh, after refurbishment with baroque embellishments. (*Richard McEwan Collection*)

(B) The same altar after installations of wall mounted reliquaries, later moved to St Stephen, Liverpool. (*Richard McEwan Collection*)

30. (A) Portable statue of Our Lady in St Paul, Oxford, in the time of Father Roger Wodehouse.
(*Richard McEwan Collection*)

(B) Shrine of Our Lady of Victories also in St Paul, Oxford.
(*Richard McEwan Collection*)

31. (A) High altar of St Michael's mission church, West Hoe, Plymouth, after refurbishment under the direction of Father Maurice Child, about 1912–14: one of the first examples of the Back to Baroque Movement. (*Richard McEwan Collection*)

(B) Altar of Our Lady in St Michael, Plymouth. (*Richard McEwan Collection*)

32. (A) The Spanish Mission style in the Church of England: St Francis of Assisi, Boxmoor, Hemel Hempstead, by Paul Waterhouse. (*Michael Yelton*)

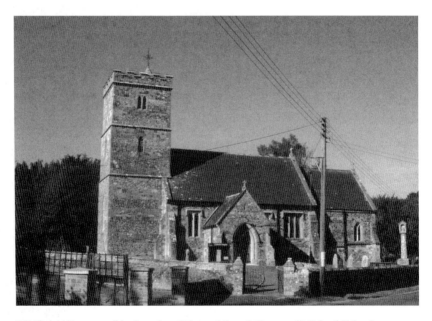

(B) Father Baverstock's church at Hinton Martel, Dorset. (*Michael Yelton*)

uncompromisingly Catholic in tone as was the whole of Walke's teaching, but what was expected in the context of St Hilary itself surprised some outsiders, particularly the ever-vigilant Protestant Societies, who were especially active in the early 1930s as Anglo-Catholicism looked to be taking over the Church of England. Their interest was awakened by the widespread publicity given to St Hilary by the BBC.

The Protestant opposition was led by J. A. Kensit, the well-known agitator and the then secretary of the Protestant Truth Society, but also needed some local assistance. That came in the form of a disgruntled parishioner, Miss A. M. King, who developed a deep antipathy for Walke which was not shared by most of the village: her antagonism may possibly be because she had been prevented from developing her self-appointed vocation as a parish worker. She was to be the instrument by which the outside groups were able to use the law in their favour. Kensit referred to the contents of the church, in a characteristic phrase, as 'a whole catalogue of Romish appurtenances'.[16]

The first step in the offensive launched against Walke and his people was an application to the Truro Consistory Court, which came before the Chancellor, Sir Philip Baker Wilbraham, in March 1932. Walke refused to appear, in accordance with his belief as to the authority of the court, and the Archdeacon of Cornwall was refused audience on the grounds that he had no *locus standi*. Walke justified his stance later: 'It was no hasty decision that led me to refuse to plead before or accept the judgment of [the Chancellor's] court on matters spiritual. As a citizen I regretted having to place myself in conflict with the law of the land, but as a Catholic priest I felt bound to defend to the best of my ability the rights of the Church.'[17]

Miss King made application for the removal of a large number of articles. Her counsel said to the Chancellor that 'this was a church where advanced services were held, and where the teaching and ceremonies pointed, not merely to the danger of abuse, but to the actual existence of images and to general conduct not authorized by law in the Church of England'.[18] In this, he was of course correct. Judgment was almost inevitably given for the removal of a large number of articles, namely

---

16 Kensit: *Contending for the Faith*, p. 130.
17 Walke: *Twenty Years at St Hilary*, p. 293.
18 *Church Times*, 19 February 1932.

the high altar tabernacle, two crucifixes (including one above that tabernacle), a baldachino over the high altar and a monstrance. No order was made in relation to the five stone altars then in the church, which included the high altar. The order provided that the vicar and churchwardens should remove the articles, or in default the petitioner could do so.

The *Church Times* commented that the episode 'made very pitiful reading ... An outside Protestant Society, with its bulging money-bags, has put into action antiquated and generally discredited law.'[19]

Walke's reaction was to preach a sermon in which he extolled the importance of spiritual over legal factors, saying: 'Any dishonour, therefore, done to the image of her who bore Him, and of St Joseph, who watched over his infancy, is an offence against the majesty of God.'[20]

Walke was of course a pacifist by deep conviction. However, it appears that he was not as naive as may sometimes have been thought. It seems clear that after the first decision in the Consistory Court he adopted the same tactic as had Father Fynes-Clinton some years before, namely removing from the church some condemned articles and replacing them with cheap substitutes. This conclusion appears not only from Walke's own words, but also from the later judgment of the Court of Arches, in which the Deputy Dean found quite clearly that:

> In fact, the articles which were removed from the church were not the original articles at all, but in the interval which decency and good order prescribes between the date of making of the order and its execution, [Walke] caused or permitted imitations or fakes to be made and put up in the place of the originals for the purpose of deceiving the persons by whom the order was executed. Accordingly, as a result of this carefully planned stratagem, when the licence of the Chancellor came to be executed, the originals had been removed to a place of safety, which was illegal, and the fakes had been put up in their place, which was dishonest.[21]

The fact that the items had been removed was not made clear at the time, for obvious reasons. However, the judgment did not prevent Walke

---

19 Ibid., 11 March 1932.
20 Ibid., 18 March 1932.
21 *Roffe-Silvester* v. *King* [1939] P 64 at p. 70.

moving forward with his scheme for the refurbishment: the Chancellor had condemned the high altar tabernacle, but after his judgment not only was that not removed but a further tabernacle was installed on the Sacred Heart altar.

On 10 August 1932 St Hilary made headline news in *The Times* and the front page in the *News Chronicle*, and received extensive coverage in the other daily papers. It is for the incident which was so described that the name of the village and of Walke is now best known, which is unfortunate.

On 9 August 1932 a group of about 40 to 50 led by Miss King, Kensit, and Revd Norman Chivers, minister of Christ Church, Ilfracombe (which was a parish of the ultra-evangelical Free Church of England), gained entrance to the church and imprisoned one of the church-wardens in the belfry. Walke was fetched by a young bell-ringer, went to the church, and was himself so imprisoned. The intruders removed the articles which they thought had been condemned by the Chancellor's judgment. The exact train of events is not easy to ascertain: they certainly appear to have used crowbars to take out the bracket on which the statue of St Joseph had previously stood, although the statue itself was certainly not there at the time. It, together with the images of Our Lady and of St Anne, had been removed and substituted. However, the high altar reredos by Ernest Proctor was removed, as were the stations of the cross and many lights. In his book Walke said that he tried to withdraw into himself while the desecration was taking place, although 'I might shut my eyes, but I still saw men standing on the holy altar, hacking at the reredos or carrying away the image of Our Lady, I could not close my ears to the sounds of hammering which now filled the church.'[22] He describes how he could not subsequently enter a mediaeval church without seeing the ghostly figures of those who cast out Mary at the time of the Reformation.

Walke was told by the leader of the group (presumably Kensit) that he could only remove the Blessed Sacrament, which was in the new tabernacle, not covered by the order since its introduction post-dated it, if he gave up the condemned monstrance. This he refused to do, but in due course he was allowed to remove the Sacrament, which he carried out through a group of his parishioners who had gathered to see what

---

22 Walke: *Twenty Years at St Hilary*, pp. 296–7.

was happening. As he passed between them, they knelt with candles in their hands.

That night, there was a service of reparation in the church, before which the Sacrament was carried back to its usual resting-place. Walke says in his book that restoration of the structure took place that week, and 'other images were substituted for those carried off'.[23] This appears to be somewhat disingenuous, as in fact the originals were returned to the church. The former font had been used as a holy water stoup, and although that was initially reported to have been badly damaged, in fact that turned out not to be the case. It was also said that certain items had been taken which were not covered by the judgment, including an icon, a cross over the stoup, and the Florentine bracket which was so difficult to remove. The reredos itself may not have been covered.

This incident stirred vigorous controversy on all sides. The Chancellor rather tactlessly declared that 'if these people acted strictly in accordance with the faculty, they were perfectly within their rights'. One of the raiding party, who seem to have been drawn mainly from Plymouth and only included Miss King among the locals, is said to have declared to Walke : 'We don't care what's in the faculty or not. We are going to clear the whole place out.'[24] However, it is clear that, with the possible exception of the reredos and some other items, they did in fact confine themselves largely to what was thought to have been condemned by the Chancellor.

The debate was conducted on a national scale. The then leader of the Labour Party, George Lansbury, was one of the few committed Anglo-Catholics in Parliament. He wrote an angry letter to *The Times*: 'on all sides I find the strongest expression of opinion that if the Church of England can only exercise jurisdiction through the use of what is in effect mob law, the sooner the Church is disestablished and removed from the jurisdiction of laws made by heretics, Jews, infidels and others, the better'.[25] The *Church Times* commented in an editorial: 'We trust that the vicar will leave his church exactly as Mr Kensit has left it, a monument of bigotry and of the Church's inability to protect itself.'[26] A correspondent to the same paper urged the need for immediate action,

---

23 Ibid., p. 299.
24 *Church Times*, 12 and 19 August 1932 and *The Times*, 10 August 1932.
25 *The Times*, 12 August 1932.
26 *Church Times*, 12 August 1932.

because: 'If nothing is done, the Kensit party will go through the country despoiling thousands of churches.'[27]

The need for reform of the ecclesiastical courts was yet again widely canvassed: Donald Hole, ever true to his principles, wrote in the *Church Times* that a new system should be established with a final appeal to the Pope, although he recognized that that was not possible at the time: 'Of course . . . in the present abnormal conditions, an appeal to Rome is impracticable.'[28]

It should not, however, be thought that the reaction to what occurred at St Hilary was all in similar vein. There were some who delighted in what occurred. Kensit was reported as saying: 'The parishioners for some years have been deprived of their rights and the PTS responded by advice and aid to their cry for assistance.'[29] W. P. Adams, the leader of the Cornish branch of the National Church League, was more outspoken: 'The issue before the country is this. Is *idolatry*, pure and simple and without disguise, to be permitted in the National Church? St Hilary Church reeks with the grossest God-dishonouring superstition.'[30] The most outrageous contribution on that side of the divide came from one H. C. Wanstall, who described himself as 'a solicitor by profession, a Protestant by conviction, and a Christian (I hope) by conversion and grace'. He claimed that 'Thousands of Protestants in the Church of England . . . must have gloated over Mr Kensit's action, as I did all the day the news came out. To us such an act is not sacrilege or desolation, but is the highest form of the worship of God, and is strictly in accordance with the example of Our Lord.'[31]

Perhaps the most sensible contribution came from an unexpected quarter. One bishop not known for his tact was H. Hensley Henson of Durham, but he wrote: 'Neither the disobedient incumbent nor the legalist bookseller (i.e. Kensit) holds a tenable position. Catholic principles cannot coincide with the parochial individualism of the one, nor can legal government tolerate the pseudo-parochial activities of the other.'[32] Another letter to *The Times* from a layman continued the same

---

27 Letter from C. J. Bex to the *Church Times*, 19 August 1932.
28 *Church Times*, 2 September 1932.
29 *The Times*, 15 August 1932.
30 *The Record*, 26 August 1932.
31 Letter from H. C. Wanstall to the *Church Times*, 26 August 1932.
32 Letter to *The Times*, 22 August 1932.

line of thought: 'To the majority of English Churchmen, who abhor the methods of Mr Kensit, [Walke's] policy seems to have nothing in common with Catholicism, but to be more akin to Congregationalism, minus the rights of congregations which that system secures.'[33]

A diocesan act of reparation for the sacrilege was held in the cathedral. There is no doubt that Bishop Frere was sympathetic to Walke, but he was not of course able to interfere with the decision of the Chancellor. By the Sunday after the raid, the church at St Hilary was back in order and the miserere was sung as a further act of reparation. On 15 August 1932, less than a week after the church had been invaded, 20 priests and about 200 people took part in the procession for the Assumption of Our Lady.

Although matters appeared to have settled down, there was some local agitation. The civil Parish Council, which was composed mainly of Nonconformists, passed a resolution calling for Walke's removal. Kensit held a meeting at which he harangued the Bishop of Truro. The strain began to tell on Walke, and he was diagnosed as suffering from tuberculosis. He had to enter a sanatorium, where he wrote his book, and by December 1932 services at St Hilary were being taken by local clergy, particularly Canon Carr of Penzance. In that month there were widespread disturbances in church, with the mass being interrupted by 60 or 70 protestors singing 'Onward Christian Soldiers' and 'There Is a Fountain Filled with Blood'. On one occasion, they sang the National Anthem after the service. However, these tactics were countered by local sympathisers, who rallied round and filled the church. On 21 December 1932 Frere sent a letter to the parishioners to encourage them in the difficult times through which they were living: 'Be patient, therefore, under this trial; and pray that God may over-rule it for your strengthening in faith and loyalty, and may use your witness for the setting forth of His glory.'[34]

In January 1933 the support being shown to Father Walke from other supporters of Anglo-Catholicism was vividly demonstrated by the arrival in the parish to take some services of Father Whitby from Bourne Street. In the longer term, Revd E. A. Gill took charge while Walke continued to convalesce, and it was reported that 200 took part in the Corpus Christi procession in June 1933.

---

33 Letter from J. S. Bezzant to *The Times*, 30 August 1932.
34 *Church Times*, 23 December 1932.

In the meantime, although it was reported in early 1933 that the crucifix was still missing, a large number of ornaments was recovered by lorry from Miss King's house, which suggests that by that time she well appreciated that some of what had been removed in the raid were not items which the Chancellor had ordered to be taken out. There was, however, no further extra-legal activity.

Legal proceedings, however, continued. A summons was taken out by the police against Miss King and others for disturbing divine service, contrary to s2 of the Ecclesiastical Courts Jurisdiction Act 1860. The Justices, the Chairman of whom was one Colonel C. H. Paynter, Diocesan Vice-President of the National Church League, dismissed the charge, apparently on the grounds that the service which Canon Carr had been holding at the time of the disturbance was not divine service within the meaning of the legislation, because it contained deviations and alterations not authorised by the Book of Common Prayer. The prosecution appealed to the King's Bench Divisional Court, where Mr Justice Lawrence would have none of that argument. He allowed the appeal, saying:

> We are of opinion that it cannot have been intended that an Act providing for summary conviction for brawling should depend for its application upon the difficult questions which have arisen upon the ceremonial law of the Church of England. The Act was designed to protect the clergyman from disturbance in the performance of his duties and to preserve order, decency and reverence in the church during the performance of those duties; it has no reference to whether he performs them properly.[35]

The next step was that a man giving a Hertfordshire address applied for a summons against Father Gill for throwing water over him, which referred to the Asperges at the commencement of the Sunday mass. The application was refused: the tactic was not new and had been used in the past by John Kensit, the better known father of the J. A. Kensit concerned here.

In May 1934 Walke returned to the parish. Miss King submitted a petition under the Clergy Discipline Act 1840 to the Archbishop of

---

35 *Matthews* v. *King and Others* [1934] 1 KB 505 at p. 516.

Canterbury and the Bishop of Truro, but in general a period of respite followed. Revd L. V. Jolly, vicar of Towednack and a leading light in the campaign to revive the use of the ancient Cornish language, wrote in *Cornwall Labour News* that 'those who will not rejoice [at Walke's return] are generally of a joyless anti-Socialist type, given to much legality, and, by the look of them, but little to pudding and laughter'.[36] At Easter 1935 there was even a broadcast of one of Walke's plays, which led to a protest by an organisation called the Laymen of England League. In mid-1935 *Twenty Years at St Hilary* was published to general acclaim. The *Church Times* was laudatory: 'Not since Robert Dolling's recollections of Portsmouth or Mother Kate's of St Saviour's Priory has there come from one who has spent himself in serving others a book of such rare and modest attractiveness.'[37]

There were, however, some warning signs. In early 1935 Frere resigned: his successor, Dr J. W. Hunkin, was regarded by Anglo-Catholics with a considerable degree of suspicion. By November there were rumours, reported in the press, of a new Protestant offensive.

The real storms did not start breaking over the parish until Walke announced in May 1936 that his continued ill-health obliged him to resign the living. Revd E. B. Clarabut, formerly of Blisland, and once Walke's vicar at Walthamstow, took charge of the parish until the resignation took effect, which it did on 27 August 1936. Walke and his wife retired to Mevagissey, high above the harbour, his constitution gravely weakened by the tuberculosis. A national appeal was made for a retirement present for him.

The living of St Hilary was in the hands of the Dean and Chapter of Truro. They nominated Revd C. G. Roffe-Silvester of St Agnes, also in Cornwall, a choice which caused the *Church Times* considerable pleasure. They had already praised his vigour in his previous parish, and declared unequivocally that 'he is an Anglo-Catholic', which he was, although not perhaps in the same mould as Walke.[38]

On 25 September 1936 an application was made to the High Court for an injunction to prevent the Bishop instituting Father Roffe-Silvester. The grounds for the application were that the vacancy had not been notified to the Parochial Church Council, as was required by the

---

36 *Church Times*, 15 June 1934.
37 Ibid., 5 July 1935.
38 Ibid., 28 August 1936.

Benefices (Exercise of Rights of Presentation) Act 1931: Walke of course had never had a PCC, but counsel argued that one existed for legal purposes, since the vicar and the two churchwardens were *ex officio* members. This over-subtle argument was rejected and Mr Justice Lewis granted the injunction, so St Hilary once again featured in the Law Reports.[39] In the same year which that Act passed into law the historian of the SSC had written, with reference to Parochial Church Councils: 'The Catholic Church being a monarchical kingdom with a Sacred Hierarchy, and not a democratic body run on Parliamentary principles, was one in which laymen could have no share in the governing voice.'[40] Walke's attitude was not therefore by any means unusual among those of his cast of mind.

The next conflict was in relation to the composition of the Parish Electoral Roll. Miss King claimed that many Protestants had been driven over to Methodism, but her objections on this occasion were less successful than those of her opponents. In all, the Lay Electoral Commission removed 149 names, 118 of which were at the instance of the anti-King faction. In February 1937 the first meeting of the parish took place, and passed off in good humour, but Miss King was subsequently chosen as Diocesan Conference representative, and the Protestants won 11 places on the Council, the Catholics eight.

Roffe-Silvester was then reappointed, and although a further writ was then served, Hunkin performed the ceremony of induction without interruption in May 1937. In his sermon he referred to Walke with appreciation as 'an unusual man of unusual gifts and charm' but went on to make an appeal for moderation. He made it clear that, despite his regard for Walke's personal qualities, he could not condone his practices: 'Unfortunately this sacred building has been treated as a kind of proprietary chapel loosely attached to Western Christendom. The incumbent has been a law unto himself. There have been wide departures from the Book of Common Prayer.'[41] The last sentence was nothing if not a masterly understatement.

The writ was withdrawn, and Roffe-Silvester was therefore indisputably the vicar of the parish, but there can scarcely have been a more difficult position to fill. He attempted to do his best to satisfy everyone,

39 *King v. Bishop of Truro* [1937] P 36.
40 Embry: *The Catholic Movement and the Society of the Holy Cross*, p. 376.
41 *Church Times*, 25 May 1937.

and introduced Matins as well as continuing the sung mass on Sunday mornings: he also abandoned the practice of extra-liturgical devotions to the Blessed Sacrament. It was reported in 1938 that the attendance at Matins was about 12, at the sung mass about 100. It is of considerable interest also that in October 1937 a correspondent informed the *Church Times* that all the ornaments which had been the subject of the first hearing in the Chancellor's court were still in church, which confirms that they had in fact largely been removed prior to the raid and then reinstated.[42]

Unfortunately, the situation thus reached, which seems to have been a tribute to the new vicar in almost impossible circumstances, was not acceptable to Miss King and her associates. In early 1938 there was more trouble over the electoral roll, and then a further application was made to the Consistory Court for the removal of the ornaments previously complained of, together with the stone altars, and other items, including a new granite shrine which had been erected since the disturbances and which bore the words 'Holy Mother of God, pray for us and for those who came to the aid of this church in 1933.' At the Easter vestry the vicar was asked to resign.

The Chancellor of the Diocese of Truro was by this time Sir Montagu Graham-Harrison, who reserved judgment in late March 1938 and delivered his ruling in June. He commented on the shocking behaviour of some protestors, one of whom had apparently said, 'I will only pray for a good Protestant', but went on to declare illegal six stone altars, two aumbries (*sic*: this in fact referred to the tabernacles), the old font used as a stoup, a confessional box, two sanctuary lamps, four candlesticks, a sanctus bell, and a thurible, but not the pictures. He also ordered the removal of the witch-watching balls and the model house. The Chancellor, however, issued confirmatory faculties to Roffe-Silvester in relation to a number of other items, on the basis that once Walke was no longer parish priest they were unlikely to be used for superstitious purposes.[43]

This ruling thrust St Hilary back to the centre of debate over furnishings. Roffe-Silvester's representative asked for information about stone altars elsewhere, and a correspondent declared: 'It is time that someone

---

42 Ibid., 1 October 1937.
43 Ibid., 24 June 1938.

should speak for the inarticulate peasant worshippers of St Hilary. Bernard Walke taught them to worship God . . .'[44]

Roffe-Silvester did not have the conscientious objections to the Chancellor's court which Walke had displayed. He had appeared before him, and now appealed to the Court of Arches, the Dean of which was then the same Baker Wilbraham as had tried the 1932 St Hilary case. He therefore stood down in favour of his deputy, W. N. Stable, KC, later to be a famously bucolic High Court Judge, whose judgment forms the third occasion on which St Hilary had featured in the Law Reports. Miss King did not cross-appeal against the grant of the confirmatory faculties.

The Deputy Dean was less than complimentary to Walke, saying at one point in his judgment that: 'It seems doubtful whether Mr Walke held any services in the church out of the Book of Common Prayer or which bore any real resemblance to those services.'[45] He showed on the other hand considerable sympathy for Miss King, at least so far as her motives were concerned. Part of the judgment reads:

> For a matter of close on a quarter of a century her rights, not only in matters connected with the ornaments and decorations of her parish church, but also in the services which she was entitled by law to have celebrated there, were consistently ignored, and when she obtained redress for some of the injury she had sustained, that redress was rendered nugatory by further acts of lawlessness on the part of her parish priest . . . Her principal motive is, I think, the very proper one of rescuing the law from the contempt into which it has fallen and establishing the rights of Church people, including the right to have those rights determined in accordance with the law and not the caprice or whim of any particular individual.[46]

The Deputy Dean held that the Chancellor was correct in law in holding that a stone high altar was illegal, and ordered that it be removed. He was, however, prepared to hold that the five stone side altars were not necessarily illegal, since once a wooden table had been provided in a church all other altars were decorative. He confirmed the faculty for removal of the tabernacles and the crucifix above the high altar

---

44 Letter from M.W. Rogers to the *Church Times*, 28 October 1938.
45 *Roffe-Silvester v. King* [1939] P 64 at p. 68.
46 Ibid., at p. 72.

tabernacle which had been condemned in 1932, but permitted the confessional box to remain.

The result of that judgment was that Roffe-Silvester felt that he could no longer continue; he resigned and was replaced by Revd J. C. Lasham of St John, Penzance, who was told by his bishop in August 1939 to use the Prayer Book, for it was 'in that Book that the Church speaks'.[47] Weekday services ceased, there was only one celebration of Holy Communion on Sunday, at 8 a.m., and the Blessed Sacrament was no longer reserved. Roffe-Silvester said that the bishop had instructed him to empty the tabernacle when he left, but he had refused to do so.[48]

St Hilary faded from national consciousness as international affairs supervened. Meanwhile, in Mevagissey, Walke was losing his battle against the disease which was ravaging him. A few months before his death on 25 June 1941 he was received into the Roman Catholic Church: it is not now clear what precipitated this move, although it seems that his wife had already taken the same step. She lived on until 1965, increasingly made reclusive by deafness and in poor health for many years.

One consequence of the Deputy Dean's ruling was that, since he had concluded that the Chancellor had come to the erroneous conclusion that the stone side altars were necessarily illegal, he remitted to him consideration of whether they should be removed or whether confirmatory faculties should be granted for them.

It appears that the litigation did not finally end until 1946, but that the side altars were indeed removed, presumably as a result of an order of the Chancellor.

Colin Stephenson wrote in 1970 that 'today the church stands with the stone altars hacked out but the reredoses still in place, while the shrines are untended. It has not only a negative and desolate air but an active feeling of evil, so that to visit the church is a painful experience.'[49] In fact, matters were soon to change. In the 1970s Revd R. J. S. Mackenzie founded the Friends of St Hilary and a start was made in the restoration of the interior. The Lady Chapel altar was rescued after 50 years in the churchyard, and reinstated. The Sacred Heart altar has also been restored. A new nave altar was dedicated in 1978 in memory of Father Walke, and a tablet erected to his memory. The paintings were

47 *Church Times*, 11 August 1939.
48 Ibid., 24 November 1939.
49 Stephenson: *Walsingham Way*, p. 209.

cleaned and renovated in 1996–8 and the statues of St Anne and St Joseph are still in the church. The desolation described by Canon Stephenson has been entirely dispelled.

It is perfectly apparent from the memories of many who met Walke that he was a man with real charisma, who impressed himself on a wide variety of people as a thoughtful and holy man. It was a real indictment of the Church of England that a man like that should be marginalised and his work attacked. He was certainly one who was able to reach out from his Anglican Papalism to see a wider vision of the Church and of humanity than were many of his contemporaries.

10

EPISCOPI VAGANTES AND THE REORDINATION OF ANGLICAN CLERGY

There are few subjects more shrouded in mystery and about which clear information, even at this length of time, is more difficult to garner than that of the reordination of Anglican priests by irregular bishops. It is, however, an important issue because it throws considerable light on the attitude of certain Anglican clergymen, particularly those who were anxious for reunion with Rome, to the validity of their own orders.

Revd H. R. T. Brandreth, in his seminal work *Episcopi Vagantes and the Anglican Communion* (1947, second edition 1961), attempted to define the meaning of the term *episcopus vagans*. He came to the following conclusion so far as modern times are concerned:

> Today a man is placed in this category who has, or claims to have, received irregular or clandestine consecration; or, having been consecrated regularly and canonically, has been excommunicated by, or otherwise cut off from, the Church which consecrates him, functions as a Bishop and is not in communion with any historic metropolitical See.[1]

Anson wrote further and at more length on the subject in his *Bishops at Large* (1964) and there has more recently been an explosion in the numbers of such bishops, especially in the United States of America.

The importance of these bishops to those Anglican clergy who did not wish to go over to Rome, or who would have been prevented from exercising their priestly vocation had they done so by reason of their marriage or some other impediment, was that they appeared to offer a guarantee that the priest in question was validly ordained. It was also

---

1 Brandreth: *Episcopi Vagantes*, pp. 1–2.

thought that the conferring of indisputably valid orders on Anglican priests would obviate the problem caused by the Papal Bull of 1896 and pave the way for reunion without the necessity for reordination. On the other hand, if there were indeed many priests who were surreptitiously and irregularly reordained by *episcopi vagantes*, that would indicate that the charges of disloyalty which were frequently made against Anglo-Catholics in general and Anglican Papalists in particular had some foundation in fact.

The starting-point for this episode was undoubtedly the consecration of three prominent members of the Association for the Promotion of the Unity of Christendom, founded in 1857, an organisation which has already been briefly discussed. After its condemnation in Rome, the association continued as a relatively small pressure group within the Church of England. One of its best known members was Revd Dr F. G. Lee (1832–1902), who was vicar of All Saints, Lambeth, from 1867 to 1899. His church, demolished to make way for an extension of Waterloo Station, was very near indeed to Lambeth Palace, a fact sometimes commented on adversely by those opposed to the incumbent.

In 1877 Lee and an associate, Revd T. W. Mossman, a country clergyman from Lincolnshire, were clandestinely consecrated as bishops. Another of his group, Dr J. T. Seccombe, a layman from Norfolk, had almost certainly been so consecrated before that time. A very large number of different accounts have been given of the circumstances in which these consecrations took place, none of which appears entirely satisfactory. Brandreth's version was doubted by Father J. H. Creran SJ in his review of the first edition of his book, and Anson proffers other explanations. Lee was extremely secretive about this and other matters and destroyed many of his papers before his death. [2]

In any event, in 1877 the three issued a manifesto of the Order of Corporate Reunion, which put forward a public proposal for the re-ordination of the Anglican clergy with a view to their orders being accepted as valid by all other churches. Lee was expelled from the English Church Union when this became known, and although he continued as vicar of All Saints it is not clear how often, if at all, he and the other two bishops exercised their episcopal functions. It may well be that they

---

2 The Vatican, contrary to assertions which have been made in the past, claims to have no relevant documents in relation to this matter.

secretly reordained some Anglican priests, but no records appear to have survived. It is also not clear whether or not they consecrated any other bishop to continue their succession, although one R. C. Jackson, who lived on well beyond the First World War, may have been an OCR bishop, as might J. C. Whitebrook, who lived until 1961 and wrote a learned book on *The Consecration of Archbishop Parker* in 1945. Whitebrook is also thought to have been the author of a well-informed anonymous article entitled 'A Chapter of Secret History' published in the *Church Times* on 28 April 1922.

Lee lost a great deal of influence once the fact of his consecration became known. He seceded to Rome shortly before his death and took many secrets to his grave. Mossman was received into the Roman Church on his deathbed, but Seccombe appears to have reverted to middle-of-the-road Anglicanism after his excursion into the more exotic side streets of the OCR.

In 1905 another shadowy organisation made its presence felt. The Society for the Restoration of Apostolic Unity issued a pastoral letter from three unnamed prelates who claimed to be the Archbishop of Whitby, the Bishop of Lindisfarne, and the Bishop of Dorchester. It made little progress and soon disappeared from view again. Its pastoral indicated that it had been founded in 1903, and its message was that it would 'remedy all defects and . . . heal all infirmities' (presumably by reordination). The authors asserted that they had 'received or derived' their consecrations from a 'Bishop of the Holy Catholic Apostolic Roman Church'.[3]

The next, and in many ways the most important, figure in the story is Arnold Harris Mathew. He was born Arnold Harris Matthews in 1852 and although he prepared at one stage for the Anglican ministry in the Scottish Episcopal Church, he changed his allegiance and in 1877 was ordained into the Roman priesthood at Glasgow. By 1886 he was a parish priest in Trowbridge, and Father Creran says that a letter published in the local paper to the effect that '[Lee] is undoubtedly a bishop, which is more than can be said of his neighbour at Lambeth Palace' was written by Mathew under a nom de plume.[4] If that is right, then it shows his early interest in matters which were to occupy him

---

3 First Pastoral of the Society for the Restoration of Apostolic Unity, pp. 5–6.
4 Creran in *The Month*, June 1953.

afterwards. He subsequently asserted that Lee had been consecrated by the Archbishop of Milan.

At some point in about 1889 Mathew left the Roman priesthood 'for rationalist reasons' (or alternatively because he had discovered that his predecessor had been a homosexual) and became for a time a Unitarian. He then approached the Church of England and had a period from about 1891 onwards as unofficial curate of the fashionable Anglican church of Holy Trinity, Sloane Street, at which point he was calling himself Revd Count Povoleri; he was fond of titles and after the death of his father in 1894 was frequently to refer to himself as the *de jure* Earl of Landaff. In 1892 he married: his wife was a relative of Gladstone. The Holy Trinity episode ended when the former vicar of the church was in turn found to be a homosexual and had to leave England hurriedly. Mathew was very prudish about such matters and feared guilt by association: he resigned, following this by a period of lay life, during which he tried to set up a zoo in Brighton, and designed part of that in London. He then devoted himself to writing several of the scholarly works on ecclesiastical history which he produced over the years. By this time at least he was using the form 'Mathew' for his surname.

In 1907 Mathew approached the Anglican authorities and again offered himself for ministry, but was refused. Later that year he was approached by a renegade Roman priest named Richard O'Halloran, who had an oratory in Ealing, and who asserted to him that there were many dissident members of the Roman Catholic Church who wished to affiliate themselves to the Old Catholic Church, which had no presence in this country. O'Halloran himself had applied in 1902 to be consecrated a bishop by the Old Catholics and been refused. Mathew then announced that he wished to throw in his lot with the Old Catholics and invited the Archbishop of Canterbury to agree to intercommunion with that body prior to his consecration.

There seems little doubt that both Mathew and the Dutch Old Catholic bishops were misled by O'Halloran into thinking that there were significant numbers of potential members of the Old Catholic Church in England. There may also have been some Anglicans who saw his consecration as affording an escape route to them from the Established Church in the event that there were new disciplinary measures in the light of the Royal Commission report. However, the problem with Mathew, which recurs frequently over the next few years, is to decide whether he was merely naive and easily influenced or actually dishonest in his dealings.

The Bishop of Salisbury, John Wordsworth, who had extensive personal contacts with the Old Catholics, actually caused the post-ponement of Mathew's consecration when he pointed out that he was married: the conservative Dutch Old Catholics did not abandon priestly celibacy until 1922, unlike their counterparts in Germany and Switzer-land, and they wished to be assured that he had not left the Roman Communion in order to marry. A contemporary letter from Utrecht to Salisbury makes it clear that the Old Catholics thought there was a potential congregation for Mathew in England, and refers to him as 'very reliable and a considerable man of high repute'.[5] The first part of that description could not have been further from the mark, as events were to prove.

However, the consecration went ahead in due course and there is no doubt that Mathew was validly and publicly made a bishop at the Cathedral of St Gertrude, Utrecht, on 28 April 1908. The Old Catholic Archbishop of Utrecht subsequently confirmed to the Bishop of Salis-bury that he wanted a regionary or missionary bishop in England for disaffected Roman Catholics.

Mathew soon found out that there was in fact no such body of potential members of the Old Catholic Church. However, he busied himself with an extensive correspondence, writing to all the Anglican bishops that he accepted that Anglican orders were valid, and then on 1 October 1908 to the Archbishop of Canterbury complaining of Spencer Jones advocating Romanism in the Church of England.[6] In 1909 he was trying to obtain the use of the semi-underground church of the Resurrection, Brighton, the least successful of the Wagner founda-tions in that town, which was even then about to be declared redundant. He also became a vice-president of the Society of St Willibrord, which fostered good relations between the churches of Utrecht and Canterbury.

It may not be without significance that one of those who saw through Mathew was the ever-present Fynes-Clinton, who wrote to the Arch-bishop of Canterbury on 15 February 1910 warning against Mathew,

---

5 Letter from Bishop van Thiel to Bishop Wordsworth in uncatalogued Brittain papers in Lambeth Palace Library.
6 Davidson papers, Lambeth Palace Library, 332D.

and was also in touch with his contacts in Russia telling them to have nothing to do with him.[7]

One of Mathew's problems was that he was unable to accept the reality of the situation when it became apparent, namely that he was a bishop without a flock. He insisted on attempting to increase the numbers of clergy and bishops for his minute congregations.

In order to set out the position in relation to the reordination of Anglican clergy, it may be helpful to set out first Mathew's career after his consecration.

On 9 February 1909 Mathew ordained as a priest W. Noel Lambert, who was then the minister of an independent Congregational Chapel in River Street, Islington, and the following year he ordained a German, C. W. Bollman, also as a priest. Lambert's chapel then became Mathew's Old Catholic Pro-Cathedral and the following year Lambert was appointed as Dean.

Although it had become clear that there was no large body of Roman Catholics who wished to leave their church and throw in their lot with Mathew, there were odd individuals, two of whom were A. W. Howarth and H. I. Beale, both of whom were Roman priests who had fallen out with their diocesan bishop in Nottingham. At that time Beale was running an extra-episcopal mission in Gunnersbury, Chiswick. Mathew consecrated both of them as Old Catholic bishops on 13 June 1910 at Corby (now Corby Glen), Lincolnshire, following which they were excommunicated by the Roman authorities.

In December 1910, not long after those consecrations, Mathew broke completely with Utrecht and declared the autonomy of his own church. He was thereafter regarded with distaste by the Dutch Old Catholics, who thought he had hoodwinked them into ordaining him. He in turn thought, incorrectly, that the Old Catholic Church was becoming more Protestant in its thinking. He explained his thinking in a *Declaration of Autonomy and Independence* dated 29 December 1910. He also resigned from the Society of St Willibrord, partly at least because of yet another sexual scandal, this time concerning the secretary, Revd G. E. Barber, who had intrigued against Mathew and then killed himself to avoid the exposure of his personal preferences.

Mathew pressed on with his expansionist policy and decided to make

---

7 Ibid.

bishops of four of his clergy. On 7 January 1911 he consecrated as bishops F. H. Bacon, F. C. C. Egerton, C. F. Hinton, and W. E. Scott Hall. The latter has a footnote in literary history, since he later ran a boarding house in West London for a time at which T. S. Eliot lodged, before the author found a more congenial home in the clergy house of St Stephen, Gloucester Road. Hinton, Egerton, and Scott Hall were of little importance in what followed, but Bacon was central to the events which later occurred. The day after this consecration, the new bishops elected Mathew as Archbishop of London.

These were not the last consecrations which Mathew carried out. On 29 June 1913 he raised to the episcopate an Austrian known as Prince de Landas Berghes et de Rache, who soon left to go to America. On 28 October 1914 he made Revd F. S. Willoughby a bishop. This latter consecration does show Mathew's naivety and the way in which it was possible to take advantage of him.[8] Willoughby had been for his time an advanced Anglo-Catholic, although married. He had been parish priest of Hooton Pagnell, Yorkshire, where he had set up St Chad's Hostel as a training college for the priesthood: in due course this became St Chad's College, a constituent part of the University of Durham. In 1906 Willoughby moved to St John the Baptist, Stockton-on-Tees, where he continued to propagate his views with some success. In 1914 he was invited by the Bishop to resign not only his living but also his orders, in order to avoid allegations of homosexuality as well as financial irregularities. The details are now obscure and were never properly investigated at the time, but it seems likely that there was force in what was alleged. It also seems clear that Willoughby did not tell Mathew the truth about the circumstances of his departure from Stockton, and left the impression that he had been forced to resign because of his ritualist views, although these matters would have become clear before the consecration had Mathew made some elementary enquiries: as it was, the allegations resurfaced very shortly afterwards, and Mathew, as already demonstrated, was over-sensitive to allegations of sexual irregularity. Mathew's general reputation had already been severely damaged by a pre-war libel action which he brought against *The Times* in 1913, in which he was exposed as something of a charlatan, and his elevation of

---

8 For information on Willoughby see Kitchenham: 'Frederick Samuel Willoughby', *passim.*

Willoughby confirmed the view that his judgement was seriously at fault. The new bishop was later expelled from Mathew's organisation and after a period as a Liberal Catholic ended his life in the Roman Communion. Some of Mathew's defenders have asserted that the Willoughby episode demonstrates Davidson's capacity for double-dealing, in that he did not pass on the information about Willoughby to Mathew, although made aware of it: that seems to be a somewhat convoluted exculpation for what was another elementary error of common sense by Mathew.[9]

In late 1915 Mathew announced that he intended to return to Rome, but this did not occur and he soon reverted to independence. His relations with the Roman authorities were always very difficult because he had not only given up the priesthood to become a Unitarian, but had subsequently married and then had raised two Roman priests to the episcopate.

On 14 April 1916 Mathew made J. C. T. A. Williams (who took the forenames Bernard Mary in religion) a bishop, and on 2 July 1916 he elevated James McFall to the episcopate as Bishop for Ireland. Williams was made Mathew's perpetual coadjutor with right of succession. Surviving letters from Williams to Brandreth, written in the 1940s when the latter was researching his book, make it clear that Williams was far more measured in his tone than many of his associates, and it may be that the information he gave was as reliable as any in this murky area.[10] He also left memoranda of value, although he burnt many documents before his death. Williams was a fervent Jacobite and Legitimist who refused to acknowledge the validity of any Act of Parliament passed after 1688.

Problems emanating from the Mathew movement affected the Church of England in two different respects. One concerned those ordained by Mathew who wished to become Anglican priests: it was necessary to consider whether or not they needed to be reordained or conditionally reordained before they could so act. The other, more obscure question was the extent to which clandestine reordination of existing Anglican priests by Mathew and his bishops took place.

It is clear from the surviving correspondence that Mathew caused

---

9 See for example J. Pinnington in *Glastonbury Bulletin*, October 1984.
10 See a file of papers compiled by Brandreth, in Lambeth Palace Library, MS 2178.

Archbishop Davidson a great deal of trouble, and further that Davidson was very patient with him. It is also clear that no proper strategy was worked out to deal with the very real problems which were represented by the Mathew succession, until the matter was debated at the 1920 Lambeth Conference.

A clear example of the odd attitudes shown by some of Mathew's associates can be seen in the case of Beale.[11] There was no question in his case but that he was a validly ordained priest, and further no question that the Anglican establishment would not allow him to function in their Communion as a bishop.

Shortly after his consecration by Mathew, Beale approached the Church of England with a view to exercising his ministry. He was sent to the Gladstone Library at Hawarden for a period of study and reflection, but by 1911 was again signing himself as 'bishop', usually followed by the initials SPCF, standing for Society for Propagating the Catholic Faith. He then again asked for employment in the Church of England, but by 1915 was reported to have reverted to Rome. In 1916 he again asked for a licence to officiate and his request was supported by Revd A. Hay, vicar of South Mymms, Hertfordshire, who was closely associated with Mathew towards the end of the latter's life. The request was granted, and Beale was appointed as a curate at St Saviour, Poplar, where he worked from 1916 to 1919. He then went to be chaplain to the Duxhurst Farm Colony (1919–21), but by 1920 he was again asking whether he could resume 'episcopal work'. In 1921–3 he was in the United States, and was then granted permission to officiate in the Diocese of London from 1924.

In 1925 Beale was appointed to the living of the small village church of All Saints, Great Sutton, Essex, an area which is still very rural despite being only a few miles from the crowds thronging the shops and seafront of Southend-on-Sea. The holder of the advowson was none other than Lambert, by then within the Church of England. In the churchyard is a tombstone with a small crucifix on it, recording the resting-place of Herbert Ignatius Beale, vicar of the parish from 1925 to 1927 and giving his date of death as 26 October 1927. No more details are apparent and the tombstone has subsided over the years so now it is at a somewhat wayward angle, which may be thought to have some symbolic meaning

---

11 The papers relating to Beale are in the Davidson papers file 333D.

to the passer-by who knows the history of the man commemorated. Williams reported that he had asked Beale how the latter could stay in the Church of England when he clearly did not believe in its position, and received the cynical reply that a man must live somehow. He also says that a last-ditch attempt was made by the Roman Catholic Church to persuade Beale to return to it just before his death, but that this was not successful.[12]

It is not clear whether or not the few parishioners living in the marshes around Sutton knew of their vicar's past, nor indeed of the background of his successor, Revd Dr T. R. Coatbridge Williams, who held the living from 1929 to 1947. Coatbridge Williams had been ordained as priest by McFall on 4 October 1918 and in 1921 was raised by him to the rank of Canon. In 1926 or 1927 he was reordained as a priest in the Diocese of Chelmsford in the Church of England, and was then presented to the living of Great Sutton by Lambert. The final twist to the story is that in 1933 McFall consecrated Coatbridge Williams as a bishop, although the latter continued to exercise an ordinary parochial ministry in the Church of England for many years. He left Essex for Leicestershire in 1947.

Lambert was an even more curious case. Bishop Winnington-Ingram, with his usual ability to see the best in a man and to overlook the difficulties associated with him, decided in January 1911 that Lambert should be encouraged in his desire to become an Anglican priest. Davidson was fairly clearly critical of this decision, but felt he could not overrule it. Other critics of it included Fynes-Clinton and Langford-James, both of whom made their views known.

The Bishop of London arranged for Lambert to act as a parish worker at St James, Islington. However, in early 1912, a year after he had been accepted, Lambert again turned his back on Canterbury, but later that year came back again. He then did some further study and in 1913 was appointed by Winnington-Ingram as curate of St Saviour, Poplar (where he was to be succeeded by Beale), where he performed priestly functions without being reordained.

The unfavourable picture of Lambert that emerges from these vacillations is partially corrected by that of the young Joseph Williamson, who was then a boy in Poplar, and later wrote with great feeling of the

---

12 In the Brandreth papers, Lambeth Palace Library, MS 2178.

struggles which he faced in seeking ordination from a working-class background. He says that Lambert befriended and encouraged him when others would not do so and speaks warmly of him personally both then and later, without mentioning the unusual features of his life.[13]

In 1916 Lambert was appointed vicar of St Gabriel, Chrisp Street, Poplar (sometimes called St Gabriel, South Bromley), a poor back-street church buried in the far reaches of the East End. It was to be for the next few years a unique institution in the Church of England, since of the staff over that period at least two and probably in addition two more, including Lambert himself, were *episcopi vagantes*. In 1935 Lambert moved on to St Mary, Norwood, Hayes, also in the Diocese of London, which was his last appointment. He had not lost all his ties to Anglo-Catholicism, as in the late 1930s he was Warden of the Benedictine Community of SS Mary and Scholastica in Suffolk, which had previously been under the jurisdiction of Williams. He died in 1954 and it was written just before then that he did not give out any information about his past.[14] His son was also ordained and acted as his father's curate at Poplar and then at Norwood for periods: it is interesting that the son was forenamed Bernard Mathew (*sic*), the latter no doubt after the bishop. He then succeeded his father as parish priest of Norwood.

As well as Lambert, Winnington-Ingram also allowed Bollman to function as an Anglican priest without reordination, and he was permitted to minister at St Mary, Charing Cross Road, but was then interned during the war as an enemy alien.

The second bishop to be on the staff of St Gabriel was Francis Herbert Bacon, who had been born in Ontario, Canada, in 1857. His role in reordaining existing priests will be set out later, but on 2 May 1913 he wrote to Davidson that he wished to retire from his episcopate into the Anglican Communion and resign all his connections with his previous organisations, and indeed announced this course publicly in *The Guardian*.[15] He then went to the United States for a few years, purportedly because his brother was worried that the family stained-glass company was losing business because of his activities. He reappeared in England in 1917 and renewed his request from an address near

13 Williamson: *Father Joe, passim.*
14 By Williams in the Brandreth papers, Lambeth Palace Library, MS 2178.
15 Davidson papers, Lambeth Palace Library, 332D.

Newmarket.[16] In the meantime, he had consecrated at least one bishop across the Atlantic. In due course, Winnington-Ingram accepted his entreaty.

The Lambeth Conference of 1920 considered the whole question of the validity of the orders of those ordained by Mathew and resolved as follows:

> The circumstances of Bishop Mathew's consecration are so uncertain, and his subsequent isolation is so complete, that, without casting any sort of reflection on the validity of Old Catholic Orders, or discussing the theological question of abstract 'validity', we feel that as a matter of practice, in the event of persons ordained by him or his successors desiring to come over to the Anglican Church and exercise their ministry in communion with it, the only proper course would be for them (if in all respects suitable) to be ordained *sub conditione*.[17]

This statement was disingenuous, since the circumstances of Mathew's consecration were in fact perfectly clear, but it at least set down a policy to be followed. That policy put Winnington-Ingram in a difficult position, since he had already licensed Lambert and Bollman without them being reordained. Bacon had not been licensed at that time. The Bishop asked Lambert to submit himself to conditional reordination, but Lambert initially refused. However, on 21 December 1920 Winnington-Ingram did conditionally reordain both Lambert and Bacon.[18] At about the same time at least two others were likewise reordained *sub conditione*, namely A. T. B. Haines, who had been priested by Willoughby in 1915 and who later went across the Atlantic, where in due course he was himself consecrated as a bishop in a way outside the mainstream of church life, and J. Arnold Carter, who had been ordained priest by Mathew on 23 March 1913, and was almost certainly later ordained as a bishop by him. Another person absorbed into the Church of England in a similar way was Revd E. H. O. Cooper, who later held a parish in the Scottish Episcopal Church.

Extraordinarily, the Bishop of London sent both Bacon and Carter to be Lambert's curates at St Gabriel, Poplar. Bacon agitated thereafter to

---

16 Ibid.
17 Quoted in Brandreth, *Episcopi Vagantes*, p. 5.
18 Davidson papers, Lambeth Palace Library, 332D.

be allocated the mission district of St Francis in Southend, but this was refused and he remained at St Gabriel, unpaid, involving himself particularly in assisting young men of the area to emigrate to the Empire. In 1927 however, at the age of 70, he was appointed to the living of another East End church, All Saints, Buxton Street, Mile End (now demolished), at which he was entitled to a stipend. He appears to have had some private means, but he did have an invalid wife to look after. His ecclesiastical career ended shortly thereafter in extraordinary circumstances.

On 14 February 1928 Bacon appeared before the Recorder of London (Sir Ernest Wild KC) sitting at the Central Criminal Court in the Old Bailey.[19] He was charged with a 30-year-old woman, Annie Bolton, on an indictment alleging conspiracy to supply abortifacients. The prosecutor was the well-known Sir Travers Humphreys, whose last case as a barrister it was: he was elevated to the High Court Bench on the final day of the trial. Bacon was defended by the well-known KC Sir Henry Curtis-Bennett, with L. A. Byrne, later a High Court Judge, as his junior. Both defendants initially pleaded not guilty, but after giving evidence on 16 February Miss Bolton changed her plea to guilty. Bacon gave evidence in his own defence, but on 20 February, after a retirement of only ten minutes, the jury convicted him. He was sentenced to 15 months imprisonment, Miss Bolton to six months.

The Recorder in sentencing Bacon referred to him as a Jekyll and Hyde character. It became clear in the course of the trial that for about ten years (i.e. from the time he had returned to England) he had had an interest in a firm of chemists called Powell Manufacturing Company Ltd, which had originally been trading from Pimlico, but in 1927 had moved to Replingham Road, Southfields. Miss Bolton gave evidence that Bacon was known at the firm as Harold Baron LL.D. Bacon accepted that he had used that name in the past, and asserted that he had been given a Doctorate of Law in Canada in 1909. The business advertised its wares under the trade name of Dr Hannah Brown, who was a fictitious person. It is clear that the jury rejected Bacon's denial that he knew of the real business of the company, and his assertion that it sold only laxatives. Nothing appears to have been said in court about his association with Mathew or his episcopal status. The

---

19 See *The Times*, 15, 16, 17, 18, and 21 February 1928.

episode demonstrates yet again the lack of judgement of Winnington-Ingram.

Bacon served his sentence, and died on 10 April 1932. There is nothing to indicate that he was involved further in ecclesiastical affairs after his release.

Carter moved on from St Gabriel in 1922 to St Alban, Teddington, and then in 1925 became parish priest of Hampton Poyle, near Oxford, moving in 1927 to Lillington, near Leamington Spa: after the Second World War he took on a parish in the Diocese of Hereford.

Although the placing together of two such ecclesiastical stormy petrels as Lambert and Bacon was, to say the least, unusual, they were joined at St Gabriel from 1924 to 1926 by a curate with an even more varied past. Henry Bernard Ventham, a much older man, had been involved with Lee's Order of Corporate Reunion and Nugée's Order of St Augustine, and had been a novice both with Father Ignatius at Llanthony and with the Benedictines before they moved to Caldey. Ventham had at one point attempted to start an Old Catholic Benedictine Community in co-operation with O'Halloran, but this venture was short-lived. In addition to those involvements with the fringes of Anglo-Catholicism, he had been ordained as a bishop in 1903 by one H. M. Marsh-Edwards, who was in the succession of J. R. Vilatte, and he himself was almost certainly the Bishop of Dorchester in the 1905 Society for the Restoration of Apostolic Unity. Vilatte's own orders are subject to some doubt and Marsh-Edwards had been deprived of his living as an Anglican priest for sexual offences. Later still Ventham had been conditionally reordained as a priest by Mathew. In 1922 he rejoined the Church of England, and not only was accepted, but was ordained as deacon and then priest in 1924 and immediately sent to St Gabriel as the junior curate.

In 1926 Ventham became vicar of South Creake, Norfolk, which is very near to Walsingham. He died there in 1944 after an incumbency of a curious nature. Anson says of him: 'He regarded the Established Church of England with a cynical indifference, doubtful if many of its clergy had valid orders. The parish of South Creake in his eyes was a sort of ecclesiastical peculiar, of an East Anglian petite église of which he was the primate.'[20] He did, however, carry out extensive restoration work to

---

20 Anson: *Bishops at Large*, p. 273.

the beautiful parish church, so his odd life on the edges of the Church of England provided one lasting legacy. Local people recall that from time to time young men stayed in a cottage in the village, and were supposed to be reading for ordination, whether regularly or irregularly. Ventham's successor at South Creake, Revd M. Smith, took the view that he used to ordain up to the subdiaconate and then leave those so ordained to proceed to Anglican orders if they so desired.[21] Certainly one such young man was Revd H. Moxon, later vicar of All Saints, Lincoln, and then of Cowbit, near Spalding, who for many years kept the anniversary of Ventham's death by praying at his grave. Ventham had refused the ministrations of Father Hope Patten on his deathbed and apparently died without sacraments, although it is thought Father Moxon, who was curate at nearby Burnham Deepdale from 1943 to 1950, may have been present at his demise.

It is now necessary to turn back to look, against that background, at the evidence relating to reordination by Mathew and his colleagues and to see how it fits in to those facts.

Bacon first made contact with the Archbishop of Canterbury in 1912, when he told him of the ordination of the six bishops referred to above, including himself, and said that in addition there were 14 who had been ordained as priests for the Old Catholic Church. On 9 October 1912 Bacon went to see him. Davidson recorded that he was a 'frank and outspoken little man' and that he thought that he was telling the truth. He told Davidson that Mathew had conditionally reordained 67 Anglican priests, all of whom were beneficed clergymen of the Church of England. In a subsequent letter dated 24 October 1912, however, he referred to subordinate clergy in the Church of England 'seeking regularisation' at his (i.e. Bacon's) own hand.[22] Shortly after that he told Davidson that he himself was retiring from the OCR and into the Anglican Communion, as already mentioned.

It is not clear whether or not the Anglican authorities were aware at that time of an advertisement which had been placed in *The Torch*, one of Mathew's short-lived periodicals, on 19 June 1912. In it was announced the revival of the Order of Corporate Reunion. It asserted that reunion with Rome could come about by a Uniate church, which

---

21 Information from Canon B. J. Findlay.
22 Davidson Papers, Lambeth Palace Library, 328D.

might include married clergy, but required 'placing beyond question the validity of the orders of the clerical members'. Although the advertisement said that Mathew would reordain Anglican priests, and made it clear that payment would not be sought, in fact the address given was that of Bacon at 33 Esmond Road, Bedford Park, where he had a private oratory. It also suggested that Mathew had been approached by certain Anglicans intent on reviving the Order, rather than the other way about.

In 1914 Mathew wrote a series of letters to Hay which have been preserved and which show clearly that he was propagating the OCR at that time with considerable vigour.[23] On 12 May 1914 he wrote: 'for people like *yourself* we have never had anything but the warmest & deepest sympathy and it has been to me a great and [illegible] pleasure to give undoubted and unquestionable orders to those who have applied for them and I am always prepared and [illegible] to do so, as are my colleagues . . . a great many are inquiring about the OCR'. His writing is very difficult to decipher but the purport is clear.

On 14 June 1914 he wrote again: 'With regard to the OCR & conditional ordination – I have ordained *five* Anglicans in that way, but I believe 260 others have been ordained by one or other of the Bishops.' Three days later he said: 'I am prepared to give the benefit and grace of an unquestioned ordination . . . we have 265 clergy now working within the Church of England.' He also referred disparagingly to Lambert, who had just been appointed curate of St Saviour, Poplar, saying, 'He knows *a good deal* hence has been petted by Lord London [i.e. Winnington-Ingram] in order to keep him quiet.'

On 8 October 1914 Mathew wrote to Hay again, setting out explicitly the policy of keeping those who joined the Order in their benefices. He also made clear that secrecy was required: 'We ordain *conditionally* and so far only *privately* and no names are published or revealed outside the OCR.'

Mathew issued a pastoral letter on 1 November 1914 again allying himself to the revived OCR. He also published a book in the same year entitled *The Catholic Church of England, its Constitution, Faith, Episcopal Succession, etc.*, in which he inserted regulations to be observed by clerical members of the OCR, including daily celebration of the mass and the use of the Roman Missal in Latin or English, or, if that was not

---

23 Brittain papers, Lambeth Palace Library.

possible for a public celebration, an approved liturgical book: this was not the SSPP *Anglican Missal*, as Anson suggests, as that was not published until 1921. By this time he was planning a huge new cathedral for London, a replica of the Votivkirche in Vienna, to hold his non-existent congregations.

At about the same time Willoughby also issued a circular offering reordination and mentioning the Seminary of St Willibrord, which seems never to have functioned.

In 1915 Mathew contacted Winnington-Ingram and offered to re-ordain and reconsecrate him, which was not an offer met with any enthusiasm. He is said, however, in May 1915 to have asserted that he had conditionally reordained about 300 Anglican priests.

It was shortly after that point that he decided to resubmit himself to Rome, before yet again changing his mind, as already described.

On 15 April 1916, the day after he had consecrated Williams, Mathew met Davidson face to face in Canterbury. There is in the Lambeth Palace Library a contemporaneous pencil note of this meeting, probably taken by Davidson's chaplain.[24] Mathew told Davidson at that interview that he had *not* reordained hundreds of Anglicans: he said Bacon might have done so, but he had not. He asserted that he had only reordained three or four, and then only where there had been some difficulty with their baptism or the like.

The same theme was continued in a letter which Mathew wrote to his friend Hay on 14 July 1916, which was sent on by the latter to Davidson on 12 December 1916.[25] In it, Mathew said that the OCR had been revived by Anglicans, not by him, and that he had simply been asked to help. He said, though, that the 1912 appeal was not his document and he had had nothing to do with it. He said that he had been approached by four people in all, two of whom had suspected some defect in their baptism and two others who were now in the Antipodes, and had reordained them, but that there were no more. All this of course was contrary to the tone of his correspondence with Hay in 1914 and this letter may have been intended to be sent on to Lambeth Palace. Mathew was obsessed by the issue of defective baptism, and took the view that Davidson himself had never been baptised, so all consecrations carried out by him were invalid.

24 Davidson papers, Lambeth Palace Library, 328D.
25 Ibid., 331D.

Only one name of those said to have been so reordained emerges in all the preserved correspondence with Davidson in the Lambeth Palace Archives, and that was only mentioned because the priest concerned had not only gone over to Rome, but had made the matter public. This was Revd B. H. A. F. Berlyn, who had been a curate at St Alban, Fulham, from 1909 until shortly before the arrival of Father Watson in 1915. The church in his time there was not as Papalist as it later became, but on the other hand was still in the forefront of Anglo-Catholicism in London.[26]

Another man who contacted Mathew (although there is no evidence that he was reordained) was Revd H. T. C. Steenbuch, who had been regularly ordained in 1902 and then worked in Korea before becoming curate of St Peter Walworth from 1912 to 1916 and then of Christ Church, Southwark, for the next three years. Steenbuch's undated letter asked whether the OCR could be revived, and said he had been in contact with Hay and Lambert.[27]

Mathew moved during the war from Kent, where he had lived for some years, to South Mymms. His was an unhappy marriage and his wife had left him; for a time he was almost destitute.

Mathew was very friendly with Father Hay, and it is possible that he reordained him: it has been suggested that he also raised him to the episcopate, but the evidence for that is unclear. It is only fair also to say that Hay categorically denied, in a letter to the Archbishop of Canterbury, that he had been reordained. In 1919 Hay let Mathew take services in the parish church, with which Winnington-Ingram was content, but on this occasion he was overruled in firm terms by Archbishop Davidson, who by this time was strongly opposed to Mathew having any official position. Interestingly Lambert, who might have been better advised to keep his head down, also interceded on Mathew's behalf.[28]

It will be remembered that by this time Lambert, who had been closely associated with Mathew for some years, was at St Saviour and then St Gabriel, Poplar. Brandreth asserts that 'probably on 22nd August 1917' Mathew consecrated both Lambert and Carter as bishops. He goes on to say, however, that some mystery attaches to these consecrations as

26 Ibid.
27 Brittain papers, Lambeth Palace Library.
28 Davidson papers, Lambeth Palace Library, 331D.

they are not contained in Mathew's own Register (which he had seen) or in the copy made for Williams (which he had also seen). He goes on 'there is, however, adequate proof that these persons claimed the episcopate'.[29] Anson says that a letter which he had seen 'makes it fairly certain that Noel Lambert . . . was an OCR bishop'.[30]

It may now be possible to throw some more light on this episode. Hay left certain papers, including letters from Mathew which have already been mentioned, to the custody of his friend Dr F. Brittain, a Fellow of Jesus College, Cambridge who had a strong interest in irregular bishops and academic frauds of various sorts. Among the papers is a cyclostyled list of ordinations carried out by Mathew, which does not contain the names of any who were already Anglican priests. It does, however, record the ordinations to the priesthood both of Lambert and of Carter. By both of their names an unknown hand has added, in pencil, the date 15/16 December 1919, which, judging by the way the list was compiled in relation to other people, seems to indicate consecration to the episcopate. That date, if it be correct, may also explain the absence of any reference to this in Mathew's own Register, because by that time he was only a few days from death and may not have written up the record.[31] Brittain himself wrote much later, on 23 January 1962, that he knew that Carter and Lambert were in episcopal orders.[32] His statement to that effect was quite unequivocal.

Also in the Brittain papers are two letters from one signing himself Robert E. Wood, dated respectively 10 November and 6 December 1919. In the first, written on the paper of the British Expeditionary Force section dealing with Chinese labourers in France, the writer asks to be reordained before going to do missionary work in China. In the second, he says 'I do feel myself reinstated as a priest, and to say mass once more is wonderful.' The clear inference is that between those two dates Mathew reordained him.[33] This tantalising information was obliquely referred to by Anson,[34] but its effect is diminished by the non-appearance of a priest of that name in the contemporary *Crockford*. He

29 Brandreth: *Episcopi Vagantes*, p. 37.
30 Anson: *Bishops at Large*, p. 89.
31 Brittain papers, Lambeth Palace Library.
32 See a file of papers compiled by Anson in Lambeth Palace Library, MS 4233.
33 Brittain papers, Lambeth Palace Library.
34 Anson: *Bishops at Large*, p. 214.

may of course have used an assumed name, or he may simply have failed to send in his particulars to the directory. Brandreth though, in private letters in 1959, says that Mathew's own Register set out the consecration of Wood as Regionary OCR Bishop for China.[35]

It can therefore be suggested as a strong hypothesis that towards the very end of his life Mathew consecrated Wood, Lambert, and Carter, but recorded only the first in his Register. The timescale would also indicate why the names of none of these three were contained in the copy held by Williams, which had no doubt been supplied some time before. The last consecration known to Williams was that of McFall.[36]

Mathew died at South Mymms on 20 December 1919 and is buried in the churchyard there. The only person with him when he died was one F. E. Wright, whom he was to ordain as priest the following morning. Williams records that he was later asked to carry out the ordination, and refused, but that Bacon ordained Wright in due course.[37]

It will be remembered that Williams had been appointed by Mathew as his successor. However, between 17 January and 1 October 1920 Bacon acted as Williams' coadjutor: word of something of this had reached Lambeth Palace, where it was reported to the Archbishop by an anonymous correspondent that Hay and Lambert had elected Bacon to succeed Mathew. On 17 May 1920 Winnington-Ingram's chaplain wrote to Davidson to say that Lambert had told his bishop that he had been approached to succeed Mathew, but had refused.[38] Williams records that Lambert was appointed as President of the OCR at this point, with Hay as Vice-President.[39]

The Archbishop was also apprised of a letter written by Bacon to Lambert on 31 May 1920, in which he said that he personally had ordained *sub conditione* 264 Anglican clergy. Davidson took this sufficiently seriously to cause enquiries to be made of Bishop Shedden of Nassau, who was in the country for the Lambeth Conference, and whom he regarded as 'an extremist'. Shedden saw Davidson on 10 June 1920

35 Letter from Brandreth in the archives of the British Orthodox Church, dated 12 August 1959.

36 As appears from a memorandum by Williams headed 'A list of bishops consecrated by Archbishop Mathew' in the archives of the British Orthodox Church.

37 Brandreth papers, Lambeth Palace Library.

38 Davidson papers, Lambeth Palace Library, 332D.

39 Brandreth papers, Lambeth Palace Library.

and then wrote on 16 June, on both occasions saying the whole story was nonsense. He also reported Father Langford-James as saying that he had never met anyone who had been so reordained. He did, however, report further that Mathew had told him (Langford-James) that he had reordained one or two people, and that Bacon had reordained 200 or more. It also appears, both from these archives and from a further story recounted by Anson, that Langford-James himself had been offered reordination and the episcopate had been hinted at, but he had declined the offer. Langford-James described Mathew as 'a first class liar'.[40]

On 17 August 1920 Davidson received a letter from one W. G. Warwick, who was then in Truro, strongly praising Mathew.[41] This is made the more interesting by the fact that Warwick is recorded in the cyclostyled list referred to earlier as having been made a subdeacon by Mathew on 2 April 1919, and also by the assertion by Anson that Warwick had been ordained priest by Bacon on 14 August 1920. He had earlier been referred to in a letter quoted by the author and written by Bacon in February 1920 in these terms:

> The Archbishop of Canterbury and Bishops know nothing about the OCR but are always trying to find out, but now that poor old A. H. M[athew] is no more they will find out still less. I would strongly advise W[arwick] not to receive the priesthood with any idea that it will help him in the *Ecclesia Anglicana*, for it will not. It will make him an undoubted priest and this should be worth much, but it would be better for him to seek ordination in the Anglican Church as a simple candidate (not mentioning the OCR) and look upon the Ceremony as a Ratification of his Baptismal Vows, or something of that sort.[42]

Warwick was indeed ordained in the Church of England in 1923–4, although Davidson declared in October 1921 that he was unsuitable for ordination,[43] and had a long career in various ministries until his death in 1955. While vicar of St George, Bloomsbury, he is said to have kept a

---

40 Davidson papers, Lambeth Palace Library, 332D and see Anson: *Bishops at Large*, pp. 88–9, footnotes.
41 Davidson papers, Lambeth Palace Library, 331D.
42 Anson: *Bishops at Large*, p. 88.
43 Davidson papers, Lambeth Palace Library, 335D.

mistress and allowed her husband to run a travel agents from the vicarage.

Equally interesting was the attitude of Lambert to Mathew's death. In its immediate aftermath he wrote a most intemperate letter to Davidson in which he referred to himself as one 'whose difficulties have been set at rest by Bishop Mathew'. On 1 January 1920 he wrote to the effect that he had Mathew's Register of ordinations and said he would arrange a meeting with Davidson. He wrote, 'I fancy your Grace hardly realizes the extent of the OCR.' When it was proposed later that year that he be reordained by Winnington-Ingram, Lambert wrote on 17 August 1920 that 'hundreds' had been ordained by Mathew and that the records were in his hands.[44]

On 8 December 1920 Lambert again asserted that he had the Register in his possession. It was seriously considered that proceedings should be taken against him, but on 9 December 1920 Williams wrote to Davidson asking him to hold off from proceedings.[45] It was 12 days after this that Winnington-Ingram saw fit to conditionally reordain Bacon and Lambert and then to send Bacon and Carter to act as Lambert's curates.

Brandreth had had sight both of the Register which was in Lambert's hands after Mathew's death and of the copy held by Williams. He says that Mathew's Register was 'removed at his death by an unauthorized but interested party, and was for many years kept secretly by . . . Lambert'.[46] His retention of the Register was in fact anything but secret, as has been demonstrated. Williams said that Hay was initially responsible for removing the Register, which makes sense since he was so close to the cottage where Mathew died.[47] Williams later arranged that all his own papers should be destroyed, which may have included his copy of the Register: he did, however, leave a memorandum on the consecrations of which he knew.

Mar Georgius (H. de Willmott Newman), another irregular bishop, wrote in his memoir of Mathew that the Register was removed 'within a few hours' of Mathew's death by those anxious to erase their names from it.[48] Brandreth and Anson both also say that there were signs of erasures

---

44 Ibid., 331D

45 Ibid., 335D.

46 Brandreth: *Episcopi Vagantes*, p. 37, footnote.

47 Brandreth papers, Lambeth Palace Library.

48 Newman (Mar Georgius): *In the Shadow of Utrecht.*

in the Register, and these were carried out by those who wished to disguise their reordination. In fact, if the hypothesis set out above is right, and Lambert and Carter had just been consecrated as bishops by Mathew, they had a very strong motive to get hold of the Register in case the fact of the clandestine episcopal consecrations became known. In fact of course, the Register did not reveal the consecrations, and so the fact that Lambert had it did not need to be kept secret.

It may be thought that history has been too kind to Arnold Harris Mathew. Brandreth wrote, 'Bishop Mathew was personally devout, sincere, and virtuous, with a genuine simplicity of character . . .'[49] It does not appear that either Brandreth or Anson were aware of his specific assertions to both Davidson and Hay in 1916 that he had only reordained three or four Anglican priests. Those assertions are demonstrably false, because the Registers appear to have contained far more names – hence the need to doctor them after Mathew's death.

It is absolutely clear that Mathew suffered an extreme form of ecclesiastical *folie de grandeur*, in which he regarded himself as the equal to the Archbishops of Canterbury, York, and Westminster. However, it seems clear also that he was a barefaced liar on the central question as to how many men he had reordained.

The evidence that Bacon was involved in reordaining Anglican priests is even stronger, because he admitted it in the letter mentioned above. What is bizarre in his case is that he was accepted for the Anglican priesthood, and then promoted to his own parish, when the suspicion against him was so strong. The fact that he was placed with both Lambert and Ventham was an act of gross folly by Winnington-Ingram. Of course it also subsequently became clear that Bacon not only was dishonest and immoral, but had been leading a double life for many years.

Lambert's career was equally strange. The evidence from his own pen in 1920 should have debarred him from office, but instead he was moved from his East End church (where the work was without doubt hard) to a much more congenial post in Middlesex.

Anson refers to a number of letters which he had seen, one of which has already been quoted, and says: 'Judging from the letters preserved, this clandestine, cloak-and-dagger way of obtaining guaranteed "valid" orders by what were called "bedroom ordinations" went on for several

---

49 Brandreth: *Episcopi Vagantes*, p. 19.

years.'[50] In Pusey House is a correction of that passage in Anson's own hand, in which he has crossed out 'several' and written 'about ten'.[51]

There can be little doubt that clandestine ordinations took place during the 1910–30 period among those Anglican clergy who were dubious of their own position. It seems very likely that Bacon continued to reordain priests after his move to St Gabriel, which Anson describes with reference to his time there as 'notorious as a hot-bed of underground episcopal activities'.[52] Williams on the other hand, after taking over the residue of Mathew's own organisation, refused to reordain any more Anglicans. It is also difficult to know whether these reordinations continued after Bacon's fall from grace.

Ventham certainly was known in later years for his consecration of the holy oils in his church at South Creake, but little more has come to light of his activities. Lambert's influence seems to have declined after his move to Norwood.

Carter on the face of it was living a quiet life in the country, but Anson was contacted very much later by an apparently reliable source, Revd H. H. Bloomfield, who had read his book, and recalled as a young man before the Second World War having seen Carter's episcopal regalia at Lillington. He also thought that there was a picture showing not only Carter but also Warwick in pontificals.[53] Carter certainly gave the outward impression of being committed to Anglican Papalism: in 1940 Lillington was one of the parishes supporting the Holy Hour for reunion with Rome and at his death on 14 December 1967 he was recorded as being a member of the Catholic League. There is a certain irony in an undated letter he wrote to Father Silas Harris (internally dateable as from 1935) in which he says: 'Unless we can form a Uniate church and feel that although we are in the Church of England we are independent of the strange ways of our brother clergy, I can see little hope.'[54]

It is very difficult to estimate the total numbers involved in this matter, but it appears that there must have been far more than the 100 or so suggested by Anson.

It does seem clear, however, that clandestine reordinations then

---

50 Anson: *Bishops at Large*, p. 89.
51 Rea papers, Pusey House.
52 Anson: *Bishops at Large*, p. 89, footnote.
53 Anson papers, Lambeth Palace Library, MS 4233.
54 Harris papers in Pusey House.

became less frequent. It was said that the Revd W. J. J. Cornelius, parish priest of the now demolished church of All Saints, North Peckham, was reordained with some others by Bishop J. C. Sibley in 1928, and seems clear that in 1940 Revd S. E. P. Needham, vicar of Farthinghoe, Northamptonshire, was consecrated as Mar Theodorus, Bishop of Mercia, by Bishop J. B. Banks. Needham continued in his living.

H. J. M. Heard (Mar Jacobus II), who had been consecrated in the Ferratte rather than the Mathew Succession, claimed to be the Ruling Prelate of the OCR, and in 1944 an attempt was made to unite the various successions in the person of Newman, who took the title Mar Georgius. In 1945 he claimed to have succeeded Heard as Ruling Prelate of the OCR.

It appears that between 1945 and 1959, Mar Georgius was willing to 'validate' the orders of Anglican clergy, but in the latter year, without forewarning, he issued a pastoral letter abandoning the practice. However, it appears that he had only in fact reordained two men in the Anglican priesthood, Revd A. G. Brodie, and Father Bazille-Corbin, whose name has already been mentioned in Chapter 7, both in 1948.[55]

Brodie was curate of St Nicholas, Charlwood, Surrey, and in charge of the daughter church of St Michael, Lowfield Heath, from 1947 to 1953 and was a man of private means and high ideals. His reordination was made open at his request and published in Mar Georgius' *Orthodox Catholic Review*: this led to a request for him to see first the bishop of his diocese (Southwark) and then Archbishop Fisher himself. The latter explained that his own policy was to take no action about ordinations *sub conditione* unless a large number were involved, and then he would pass legislation to expel all those concerned from the Anglican priesthood, but in any event this legislation would not be retrospective. Brodie was made vicar of St Peter, Brockley, in 1953, after these matters became public, and continued as an Anglican priest until his death in 1961.

John Edward Bazille-Corbin came from a Guernsey family and was called to the Bar before training for the priesthood. He was a Jacobite and the founder of the Monarchist League, with a brilliant mind and no common touch. He was ordained in 1921 and became vicar of Runwell St Mary, not far from Great Sutton, in 1923, but soon abandoned parish

---

55 See S. Newman-Norton: 'Mar Georgius and the Reordination of Anglican Clergymen', *Glastonbury Bulletin*, March 1981.

visiting and other such activities. He was not only a High Tory but also a great devotee of Sarum rites, unusually for such an extreme Anglo-Catholic. In 1946 he was reordained priest by Banks and in 1948 consecrated by Newman, taking the title 'Mar Marcus Valerius, titular Bishop of Selsey and Rector-Provincial for Canterbury in the OCR'. In 1958 he was raised to the status of Archbishop *ad personam*. He was then showered with various bogus decorations by such as the pretenders to the Kingdom of the Two Sicilies. In the meantime, he used an English version of the Sarum rite in his church and ran his parish until his retirement in 1961. His new status became known to the Bishop of Chelmsford in 1954 after Bazille-Corbin was named in *The Pilot* by Revd F. H. Amphlett Micklewright, who wrote a series of articles on Mathew and his successors, and some painful correspondence followed, the upshot of which being that the vicar of Runwell promised not to reordain any Anglican priests.

In 1958 a pamphlet was issued by one Mar Adrianus, who claimed to have revived the OCR yet again. The circumstances of that are obscure.

Even apart from the Mathew succession, there were other *episcopi vagantes*, some of whom have been mentioned, the best known of whom perhaps being Bishop U. V. Herford (1866–1938), who was on friendly terms with Mathew for some period. He was particularly concerned with the ordination of those Nonconformists who were anxious to move towards Catholic worship, the best known of whom was W. E. Orchard, a former Congregationalist, whose King's Weigh House in London was transformed into a quasi-Roman place of worship: he then went over to Rome in 1932. Herford ordained Orchard and others to assist him, and reordained Revd W. Rowland Jones, an Anglo-Catholic priest who began and ended his life as a Methodist, an odyssey he describes in his autobiography *Diary of a Misfit Priest* (1960). Winnington-Ingram encouraged Jones to join the staff of the King's Weigh House, but Orchard insisted that he be reordained by Herford, a ceremony performed in the latter's house at Oxford with his wife knitting in the background and complaining at the length of the ceremony as she had to get to the baker.[56] It is less than likely that Herford reordained other Anglican clergy, as Jones appears to have been a special case.

It is also clear that many of those who became involved in this

---

56 Jones: *Diary of a Misfit Priest*, p. 97.

ecclesiastical underworld were personally of doubtful morals. An Anglican priest in the Diocese of Chelmsford, Revd V. A. Palmer Hayman, was consecrated by Heard as a bishop of the so-called Free Catholic Church in 1930. He had been in charge of the mission church of St Alban, Leyton,[57] and the ceremony took place there in the presence of the congregation. He envisaged an organisation which would provide a refuge for persecuted Anglo-Catholics, and he ordained one G. D. Figg, who was said to have ministered unofficially thereafter in various Anglican churches. However, Hayman not only then became Chaplain to the British Union of Fascists, as a result of which he was interned during the Second World War, but later was sent to prison for fraud on more than one occasion.

In the 1950s there was a short-lived organisation within the Scottish Episcopal Church known as the Order of St Michael the Archangel, which was associated with the church of St Michael, Hill Square, Edinburgh, which has already been mentioned. It seems unlikely that the vicar of the time (Revd C. H. Scott, formerly at St Michael, Folkestone) did not know of these matters. Father Scott was vicar of St Michael, Edinburgh, from 1952 to 1964: the church was closed the following year and adapted for secular use, and the parish was joined with that of All Saints, Tollcross.

One Robert Millar (whose circumstances and identity are unclear) claimed to be a member of the OSM and to have been consecrated to the episcopate in 1941: he asserted that he was Regionary Bishop of Oxford. A surviving document shows that on 21 March 1953 Millar consecrated one 'Georgius Bell' to the episcopate in St Michael and another that on 29 September 1954 Bell ordained as a priest John Ross. Bell has been plausibly identified as George Bell, an engine driver who was prominent in various ritualistic fraternities and was also a part-time verger at St Luke, Edinburgh.[58]

Ross was also a layman in 1954, and was married at St Michael the following year. He then acted as a priest outside the Episcopal Church for some years, before being ordained into it in 1971, and said that in 1969 he destroyed the archives of the small and short-lived Order. In 1989 he joined the Celtic Orthodox Church and in 2003 he died.

---

57 Anson refers to this as St Alban, Leytonstone, but in fact it was in Leslie Road, Leyton. It was closed shortly after the irregular consecration took place.
58 Documents in the possession of the British Orthodox Church.

Ross indicated in the 1960s that the OSM had been intended as a revival of the OCR, and that there was a sister branch in England. However, even if they were, it does not appear from the surviving fragments of evidence from Scotland that there was any widespread reordination of priests: the whole episode seems to have been rather low-level.

There have from time to time been rumours that a number of leading priests, particularly Fynes-Clinton, were secretly in episcopal orders. In his case those rumours are contradicted by those who knew him well and are also out of accord both with his Papalism and with a genuine regard on his part, strange as it may seem, for the Church of England. It appears to be a canard which should be discounted wholly. Further such rumours have surfaced about other Papalists, even Bennett, which again appear to have no foundation. The sort of organisation which appeared in Scotland, and may have existed in England, was of a different nature from that envisaged by Lee and Mathew.

There can be little doubt that those who sought reordination in the clandestine way described came from those who were dubious about their own orders. There were a number of Papalists who made it clear that they accepted all the papal claims save as to the validity of Anglican orders, which raises the suspicion that it was among them that reordinations took place, so that their last worry was put to rest. On the other hand, even apart from the witness of those who knew them, the written evidence strongly suggests that not only Fynes-Clinton but also Langford-James, the two co-founders of the Catholic League, were in no way involved in these underground activities.

It was a matter of some irony given the history of Mathew and his relations with Utrecht that after the signing of the Bonn Accord of 1932 between the Church of England and the Old Catholic Church, bishops of the latter body participated in consecrations of Anglican bishops.[59] The fears of those who subscribed to a merely mechanistic view of the transmission of orders were therefore in due course largely assuaged, as the validity of Old Catholic orders was widely acknowledged. In a curious way therefore that which Mathew and Bacon sought to offer to Anglican priests came about in any event, although indirectly and gradually.

---

59 Hughes: *Stewards of the Lord*, pp. 340–1, has a table showing the involvement of Old Catholics in the consecration of Anglican bishops.

There is no doubt, however, that the episode in general is a serious blot on the reputation of many priests. A priest who was secretly re-ordained and therefore regarded his ordination by an Anglican bishop as either of no validity or of dubious validity forfeited the right to be considered as a member of the Church of England and played straight into the hands of those who accused Anglo-Catholics of treachery.

The most peculiar feature of the Mathew/Bacon affair was the attitude of the episcopate. It is perhaps not surprising bearing in mind his generally lax disciplinary standards that Winnington-Ingram was so ready to accept men with so many question-marks over them. It is even more surprising that Davidson was as accommodating as he was. The acceptance of Bacon as a priest was little short of scandalous when one bears in mind that he had admitted reordaining clergy, and the placing of him under Lambert, instead of as part of a team in a parish with an experienced vicar, was asking for trouble.

11

THE ARCHITECTURE AND FURNISHINGS OF ANGLICAN PAPALISM

One of the most obvious concomitants of the Oxford Movement was the belief that Gothic was the only style of architecture for Christian worship. That view began to be challenged only towards the end of the nineteenth century, with the neo-classicism of Father Nugée's Priory in Walworth, and more decisively with John Dando Sedding's Church of the Holy Redeemer, Clerkenwell (1887–8), which looks to the casual passer-by as if it was transplanted from Italy: it may only be coincidental that it was erected in one of the centres of Italian settlement in London.

Even at the beginning of the twentieth century, Gothic reigned supreme in Anglo-Catholic circles. At Caldey, the most advanced out-post of the forward movement in the first decade of that century, Carlyle turned to Eden for the reredos in the abbey church. However, over the next 20 years (1910–30) there was to be a sea change in the way in which the more ultramontane Anglicans regarded the architectural styles.

That change in taste was strongly promoted by, and probably origi-nated from, the Society of St Peter and St Paul, which although less Papalist in fact than its adherents liked to pretend, was an important catalyst. The Society came about as a result of a meeting in Bruges in the summer of 1910 between Samuel Gurney, Ronald Knox and Maurice Child.

Knox was one of the many lost leaders of Anglo-Catholicism. The son of the ultra-Protestant Bishop E. A. Knox of Manchester, one of the fiercest opponents of Prayer Book Revision from the Evangelical side, he was regarded as among the cleverest undergraduates of his generation. His sparkling wit and gift for the striking phrase was put at the disposal of the nascent Papalist party in the Church of England from his ordina-tion as deacon in 1911 until his decision in 1917 to secede to Rome, a decision he never regretted, although to many it appeared that his great gifts were underused in his new home. His biographer, Evelyn Waugh, later wrote that Knox's view of the Church of England prior to his departure was: 'She was a true branch of the Latin Church of the West, which through an accident of history had been partly severed from the trunk. She was feloniously held in bondage by the state. She was justly entitled to all the privileges that had been hers in 1500 and to all the developments of the Council of Trent. It was her manifest destiny in God's own good time to return rejoicing to her proper obedience.'[1] As with many of Ronald Knox's pronouncements, the slightly overblown language does not conceal the force of what he was saying.

Knox had known Samuel Gurney both at Eton and as a fellow under-graduate at Oxford. They decided to visit Belgium, a country which was regarded with considerable interest at that time by Catholic-minded Anglicans because the country had largely escaped the anti-clericalism which had affected France, and was regarded as particularly devout, as well as being easily accessible. Gurney was a scion of a Norfolk banking family and had considerable private means, which he was prepared to devote to promoting Anglo-Catholicism. In later life, perhaps surprisingly, he became much influenced by Moral Re-Armament.

It was in Bruges that Knox and Gurney met Maurice Child, often described as the *enfant terrible* of Anglo-Catholicism. Child was ordained deacon in 1909 and priest in 1910: he was slightly older than the other two travellers. He too had private means, which like many aspects of his life were somewhat mysterious. It was thought that he inherited money, but certainly it enabled him to keep a flat in the West End even when serving as curate elsewhere.

Bruges had a profound effect on all three of the young Anglican enthusiasts, and from that meeting came the SSPP. The importance of the Society was that it propagated the view that the Gothic style stood for moderation and the English Use, whereas those supporting reunion with Rome should follow the continental example and adopt the baroque as its fashion. Knox wrote later:

[Roman] Catholics will not easily realize the extent to which in the Church of England the mediaevalist movement has been captured and exploited by a comparative moderate party. Broadly speaking,

1 Waugh: *The Life of Ronald Knox*, p. 109.

'Gothic' and 'Renaissance' accessories symbolize a difference not of taste, but of view; the 'Gothic' belongs to the 'loyal' Churchman who takes his stand on the practice of the early Church and fulminates against 'Roman' innovations.[2]

That change came about in the years from 1911 when the SSPP was founded to 1920 when the first Anglo-Catholic Congress was held and baroque was beginning to hold sway among the advanced wing of the Church of England.

When the Bruges meeting took place, Child was a curate at St Andrew, Haverstock Hill, Hampstead, although in fact he operated at the far more liturgically forward daughter church of St Silas, Kentish Town, and he then moved to St James the Less, Plymouth, in 1912. The two years which Child spent in the West Country saw the introduction into the mission church of St Michael, West Hoe, of two baroque altars said to have been designed to follow Central or South American proto-types: they were almost certainly the first products of the SSPP thinking, although Father Scott is said to have installed a baroque altar at St Saviour, Sunbury, about ten years earlier. The church which he served was later replaced by a permanent building with new furnishings. Unfortunately the Plymouth altars too seem to have disappeared with-out trace although photographs exist of them: the church was closed in the 1930s and became a factory, but was reopened in 1948 after bombing had destroyed the parish church. It then became a daughter church of St Andrew before being declared redundant again in about 1995 and is now used by the Orthodox. In those pre-First World War summers Child and his fellow curate Revd W. G. V. C. Baker entertained Knox and Gurney in Plymouth and there was a great deal of plotting and fun-making. Father Vincent Baker had been a curate with Child in Hampstead, and went with him to Devon, but, unlike him, later went over to Rome and joined the Oratory.

Many of the leaders of the SSPP were connected with St Mary, Bourne Street, and the vicar, Revd J. C. Howell, was a strong supporter. His successor, Father Whitby, had had his first mass card printed by the SSPP very shortly after its foundation and while he was still a curate at St Columba, Haggerston, and he continued after his appointment to

---

2 Knox: *A Spiritual Aeneid*, p. 62.

have the interior of the Bourne Street church remodelled to draw attention away from the rather plain Gothic architecture and towards the more exotic baroque furnishings.

There is no doubt that Child was a brilliant propagandist. He used the intellectual ability of Knox, who became Chaplain of Trinity College, Oxford, and of Revd N. P. Williams, of Exeter College, and his own sarcastic pen to poke fun at the pompous and unsmiling aspects of the episcopate.

However, while the SSPP enthusiastically supported the introduction of the baroque style for furnishings into the Gothic churches in which most Anglo-Catholic services were held, it is important not to equate the Society too closely with Anglican Papalism. There was, as already discussed, a strong tendency among some Anglo-Catholics to disguise the words of the Book of Common Prayer with baroque vestments, music and furnishings. There was no church where that tendency was more apparent than St Mary, Bourne Street, under Father Whitby. The letter which he wrote refusing to join the Confraternity of Unity because of his promise at ordination to use the Book of Common Prayer is very revealing.[3] The casual visitor to Bourne Street saw what appeared to be a Roman service, although the language used for the audible parts was English. There was an element of *trompe l'oeil* about the SSPP, although there is no doubt that its wider effect on the Papalist movement was considerable.

The progress towards adoption of baroque was temporarily halted by the First World War, although Prebendary Denison imported a continental altar in Counter-Reformation style to his church of St Michael, Ladbroke Grove.

In 1917 Father Roger Wodehouse, another strong supporter of the SSPP and well connected through his aristocratic relations, transformed the high altar of the small church of St Thomas the Martyr, Oxford, of which he was then the curate. The ethos was that of the eighteenth-century Continent, and he commissioned for the sanctuary a reproduction of an Italian painting of which the original was in the Vatican.

In the period immediately after the First World War, the move to refurnish Anglican churches in accordance with European precedents gathered pace. The best-known exponent of this form of somewhat

_____

3 In the unsorted Rea papers at Pusey House.

artificial neo-baroque was the artist and stained-glass painter Martin Travers (1886–1948).[4] Travers was distinguished in a number of fields, and is often wrongly associated only with the baroque fittings of the period 1910–40. He appears to have had no strong religious convictions, certainly after the First World War, and his stained-glass in particular was commissioned by many churches of different varieties of liturgical practice.

Travers carried out work at St Mary, Bourne Street, which provided a precedent for other places, and a major refurbishment for Father Fynes-Clinton at St Magnus the Martyr; his rather less comprehensive work at St Saviour, Hoxton, has already been discussed. He also installed new altars at St Saviour, St Albans, SS Peter and Paul, Kettering, St Mary Magdalene, Paddington, and The Annunciation, Brighton, among other places, all of which were classic examples of the so-called Back to Baroque Movement.

The well-known Travers work at Bourne Street involved alterations to the altar and reredos: the latter had only been installed in 1909 and was designed in a neo-Wren style by S. Gambier Parry. Travers provided a sarcophagus-shaped altar in gilded wood, on which there was a large domed tabernacle, a wooden gradine, and six very large wooden baroque candlesticks. The reredos was altered with skill and subtlety so that Gambier Parry's arch and strapwork cresting were retained, but the background in the centre of the arch was cut out to allow blinds to be inserted, which could then be raised to cover the crucifix if necessary. Travers also designed a shrine of Our Lady Queen of Peace, but his plans for a more radical transformation of the interior with many other shrines was never carried through, and when an extension to the fabric was required in late 1924 the parish chose a scheme by H. S. Goodhart-Rendel.

It was Goodhart-Rendel who further modified the reredos into the form in which it is found today. In about 1934 he added volutes at the side and above a cartouche of the Coronation of Our Lady. The total effect of the work so carried out by Gambier Parry, Travers and Goodhart-Rendel was much admired and imitated by those who were more Papalist than the clergy at Bourne Street.

It is generally agreed that the work carried out by Travers for Fynes-

---

4 See Warrener and Yelton: *Martin Travers (1886–1948): An Appreciation, passim.*

Clinton at St Magnus the Martyr was one of his most effective schemes. Of course the problems which he faced at a Wren city church were very different from those which he had faced at a small stock-brick Gothic building such as St Mary, Bourne Street. However, there was more finance available at St Magnus, and also the work was designed as a whole and so carried out between 1924 and 1928.

The refurbishment of St Magnus was intended to reflect the views of the rector. Travers remodelled the church so as to give the illusion that the Reformation had never occurred and the parish had remained under Vatican jurisdiction throughout. Once again, the continuity with the past which was regarded as so important by the Papalists was stressed. However, unlike in many other places, the work was carried out under the faculty jurisdiction. Many Papalists ignored the legal system of the Church of England completely, an approach which sometimes carried within it the seeds of further problems, as at St Hilary. There were for example no faculties for the work either at Bourne Street or at Hoxton.

Travers modified the high altar reredos of St Magnus, restoring most of the upper storey, part of which had been removed in the nineteenth century. Above the reredos he added a painted and gilded rood, and at the foot he lettered and decorated the panels. Two old door frames were used to construct side chapels and placed at an angle across the north-east and south-east corners of the church. One, the Lady Chapel, was dedicated to the rector's parents in 1925, and the other held a statue of Christ the King.

Originally, a baroque aumbry was used for Reservation of the Blessed Sacrament, but later a tabernacle was installed on the altar and the aumbry was used to house a relic of the True Cross.

The remodelling went far beyond the rebuilding of the reredos. Two new columns were inserted in the nave to make the lines regular, and the pulpit was opened up and provided with a soundboard and crucifix. A new altar with console tables was installed and the communion rails moved outwards to extend the size of the sanctuary. The interior was made to look more European by the removal of the old box pews and the installation of new pews with cut-down ends. Travers also designed many other ornaments and accessories for the church, including a Benediction throne, and a statue of St Magnus of Orkney. In 1931 he added one of the first statues of Our Lady of Walsingham to be erected after the revival of the devotion.

Fynes-Clinton was a demanding but gifted client for Travers, and the combination of their two talents produced a most effective ensemble, which was a great improvement on the interior of the church before the work began.

In 1926 Travers was called in by Father Wodehouse, who by then had moved to become parish priest of St Paul, Walton Street, Oxford, a small neo-classical building which he wished to transform into a replica of a French church: the exterior already looked continental, and he wanted the interior to match. Although Travers' scheme was not adopted because of lack of funds, Wodehouse obtained a large tabernacle from Belgium which had an ingenious feature: by turning a key in the appropriate place, the tabernacle turned itself round and the back was designed as a throne for Benediction. Other such genuine continental furnishings were introduced and the general effect was entirely alien to mainstream Anglicanism: that of course was exactly what was intended.

Nothing shows the transformation in taste among Anglican Papalists more clearly than the new furnishings introduced to Nashdom, the Lutyens house at Burnham, Buckinghamshire, to which the Benedictine Community moved from Pershore in 1926. While the furnishings of the Caldey Abbey had been in Gothic style, there was no question when the move to Burnham took place but that baroque should be the preferred style for the fittings. In fact, it well suited the luxuriance of the house.

The former 'Noble Salon' in the house found a new use as the Community's chapel, for which Travers provided a sarcophagus-shaped altar with two matching console tables and a canopy. The candlesticks were three-sided and were coloured red, gold, and black respectively so that they could be turned around according to the use for which they were required. Travers also designed a baroque reredos for an original Italian altar for the Chapter Room, which was donated by Father Whitby. The furnishings complemented the liturgy and the entire atmosphere of course was entirely Italian.

As the 1920s went on, the Back to Baroque Movement itself was modified. It became what is sometimes called the Anglo-Catholic Congress style, the apotheosis of which, to quote the late Sir John Betjeman in his *Collins Pocket Guide to English Parish Churches*, is the reredos designed by Travers for St Augustine, Queen's Gate, in 1928.[5]

---

5 Betjeman: *Collins Pocket Guide to English Parish Churches: The South*, p. 272.

The Butterfield church in South Kensington was a great centre for the Congresses, both because of its proximity to the Albert Hall and because its parish priest, Father Deakin, had had the original idea which led to the gatherings.

In 1926 Travers designed a Calvary memorial to the departed of the parish, complete with baroque candlesticks, which was installed in the nave of the polychromatic church. The existing iron screen was removed and the church whitewashed. Although the whitening became controversial in later years, it did provide a suitable backdrop to the exotic furnishings which were introduced.

The enormous reredos, reminiscent of those found in South America, then arrived. The scheme finally used was the third which had been prepared for the church, and was in fact a modification of an earlier design for the equally ultramontane church of Holy Trinity, Reading, but not used there.

The effect given was extremely theatrical. The wood was covered with silver foil and then varnished with gold, and although on close examination it can be seen that the reredos is quite flat, the *trompe l'oeil* effects produced make it appear much more three-dimensional. In front of it, a large tabernacle and six Italian baroque candlesticks were installed on the altar and thereafter alterations to the pulpit, new communion rails, and a double-sided wooden frontal for the high altar. Travers then designed Stations of the Cross for the church, again finished in silver foil varnished in yellow and over-coloured with umber. In 1932 Travers designed a backing to the shrine of Our Lady and then in 1938 he provided a lady chapel altar and triptych.

It is interesting to stand back for a moment and look at the way in which this large Victorian Gothic church was, by these internal changes, not only made to look completely different from the vision of the architect, but also altered in atmosphere. The intention of the Papalists in their refurnishings was to make the churches in question look as if they were not, and never had been, Anglican. That was easier in the case of a Wren church such as St Magnus the Martyr, where the total impression given at the end of the refitting was of congruity, than in the case of a Victorian building such as St Augustine, where the additions have a somewhat artificial air.

It would be wrong to suggest that Travers was the only architect or designer who produced work for the Back to Baroque Movement. There were a number of others, particularly Wilfred Lawson, who founded Faith Craft in 1923, but few were able to produce work of the distinction of Travers. Articles were also bought from the Art and Book Shop outside Westminster Cathedral, and from continental sources. Maurice Child was particularly adept at acquiring items from Europe, for example from convents which were closing or amalgamating. Child himself, however, turned to Travers when, in 1935, he was given a parish of his own (Cranford, then in Middlesex) for the first time. In the following years he refurnished the interior of the small mediaeval brick church of St Dunstan in one of the last examples of the Back to Baroque tendency. His friend Gurney similarly employed Travers to refit another small mediaeval church, St Swithun, Compton Beauchamp, then in Berkshire, after he set himself up as the village squire in about 1924.

There were other places where the money was not available to carry out extensive renovations. The priests in those parishes tended simply to add large numbers of cheap statues to the interior, with associated pricket stands and sometimes drapes and canopies around and above. St Alban, Fulham, was such a church, as were St Alphege, Southwark, and St Michael, Islington. Altars also multiplied, so that in some churches there was an altar in almost every available space, and this was particularly marked in monasteries, so that each priest could say a private mass each day.

The ethos however, even when complete refurbishment was not attempted, was still baroque and un-English. Churches such as St Bartholomew, St Michael, and St Martin in Brighton and St Andrew at nearby Worthing all had alterations which were designed to make them look less Anglican. Even the Scottish Episcopal Church was not immune from this tide, and Anson referred to St Michael, Edinburgh as 'a lonely Northern outpost of the most Tridentine variety of Anglo-Catholicism',[6] complete as it was with neo-baroque furnishings in what was in fact a former Free Church of Scotland building. [7]

Although Cranford in many ways marked the last flowering of the Back to Baroque Movement, it continued in the north of England for

---

6 Anson: *The Call of the Cloister*, p. 413.
7 This church is long since closed, but a number of furnishings were taken to All Saints, Tollcross, Edinburgh. Some reliquaries were used by Father Milburn in St Stephen, Liverpool, and the altar rails are in St Paul, Brighton, Father Milburn's last church.

rather longer: in many places the advance of the Anglo-Catholic Movement north of the Trent had been slower than further south and it ran behind churches in London and the south-east. A recent history of St Hilda, Cross Green, Leeds, which had a Catholic tradition from the 1870s when it was built, describes how even so it retained Prayer Book services with Sarum ceremonial and lengthy psalms until after the Second World War, when Roman rites were eventually adopted.[8]

Another interesting example is the church of St Augustine, Tonge Moor, Bolton, designed by R. Knill Freeman, where Travers' former pupil Douglas Purnell carried out work after the death of his master. Purnell designed the reredos and altar in the church in the 1950s but in a style reminiscent of 30 years previously. He also carried out work to St Aidan (a daughter church of St Augustine) and St Stephen, Lever Bridge, both in Bolton, St Catherine, Burnley, and St Peter, Blackburn. Anglo-Catholicism also flourished in Liverpool during the 1950s, and work was carried out to the interior of St Stephen, Grove Street, St John the Baptist, Tuebrook, and other churches.

The tendency to refurnish churches with the intention of making them look as if they were Belgian, French or Italian reached its culmination in the Holy House at Walsingham, which has already been discussed. The Walsingham Shrine was unusual in that it was a new construction, rather than a refurnishment of an existing building. It was also interesting that Hope Patten chose not to employ Travers to design the building. One of the main benefactors of the shrine was Sir William Milner, who was a partner in the architectural practice of Milner & Craze, who were given the contract. The only work Travers carried out at Walsingham was a small memorial to the mother of Father Eyden, the headmaster of Quainton Hall School. It may also be that Hope Patten wanted to use only architects committed to his own way of thinking.

Shortly before Hope Patten's death, he turned to the very elderly Comper to redesign the Holy House itself. Comper had begun his career as a faithful reproducer of mediaeval precedent, and his work had for that reason been associated with the proponents of the English Use. Although he never abandoned the richly decorated furnishings of that period, he later espoused 'beauty by inclusion', drawing from precedents

---

8 See Savage: *The Story of St Hilda's, Cross Green, Leeds, passim.*

of all periods and areas. He was a committed Anglo-Catholic, which appealed to Hope Patten, and his simplification of the furnishings of the Holy House is generally thought to have been a success.

Comper has, extraordinarily, never been the subject of a full study, but although there were some dark undercurrents in his life, with a half-hidden interest in the naked young male, his work is often light and joyful in tone. It was, however, extremely expensive to commission, as Comper was notoriously mercenary, especially in his later years, and was also very exacting in his choice of materials. In those respects he differed from Travers, who was uninterested in money and used cheap materials such as papier mâché where necessary to keep down the cost.

Some Papalists may have taken the view that Comper was irretrievably compromised by his espousal of the English altar, although Travers was quite prepared to design such altars where they were required. However, others were quite ready to turn to Comper to redecorate the interior of their churches, provided of course that the finance was available. The strong tide towards the baroque was not universal. One of the exceptions to that tide was Father Corbould in his church at All Saints, Carshalton, where he employed Comper to install richly decorated and gilded fittings, including an organ case and rood, in Gothic style. Comper, who lived in Sydenham, attended the church for a time thereafter. Corbould was much criticised for the amount which was spent on the interior of the church at a time when his congregation was declining.

Although Corbould employed Comper for the work which he required at the parish church of All Saints, Travers had earlier been instructed to construct the mission church of the Good Shepherd in Carshalton Beeches (1929–30), which replaced the temporary building at which Hope Patten had ministered during his time there. There were severe constraints on the money available to build this and other new churches in the suburbs at that time, but the Good Shepherd is interesting as it was one of the very few new buildings of the era designed with Anglican Papalism in mind. Travers and his associate Grant freely interpreted the baroque of South America to construct the building, although a failure fully to appreciate the climatic conditions of Surrey meant that the church has always had severe damp problems. There were baroque stencils on the moulded pre-cast plaster ceiling, and a very large rood hung above the altar. The simple reredos and altar originally stood within riddel posts but with six baroque candlesticks and a crucifix. It was anomalous that riddel posts and indeed an aumbry, as opposed to a tabernacle, were provided, but they probably represent the furthest that the Southwark Diocesan Advisory Committee was prepared to go at that time, and the money was being provided through the Bishop's scheme for 25 New Churches. However, there was a window of Our Lady Queen of Heaven, and in the porch Travers designed windows for the Bishop, showing his arms, and also for Father Corbould. The latter used play on words, depicting a rook ('caw') and cricket bails flying ('bowled'). Although substantial work has been done to the church since that time, particularly after a fire in 1967, and it is now a parish in its own right with a different churchmanship from that of Corbould, the building remains interesting.

There were few other such uses of the Spanish colonial style, although Paul Waterhouse, son of the better-known Victorian architect, used that source of inspiration to build the Convent of the Incarnation for the Community of the Sisters of the Love of God in Oxford, and also the church of St Francis of Assisi in Boxmoor, Hemel Hempstead.

Another example of an inter-war church which was indistinguishable inside or outside from its Roman equivalent is also dedicated to St Francis of Assisi, in Dalgarno Way, North Kensington, originally a daughter church of St Michael, Ladbroke Grove.

As well as the installation of fittings in the baroque style, it became *de rigueur* for Papalists to wear Roman-style vestments. Chasubles were stiff and of the fiddle-back style, sometimes imported from the Continent; the more voluminous Gothic mass vestments were never worn. Cottas were short, but were generously edged with lace, and albs were often lace from the chest downwards. Outdoor clothes were also in the Vatican style, with cassocks buttoned right down the front or with cape attached (a soutane). No self-respecting priest was without his party badge, the biretta, which was worn in almost all formal photographs of Anglo-Catholic clergy of the time.

The best illustration of the effect for which Anglican Papalists were striving at this time can be seen in the two volumes illustrated by Travers and published by the SSPP as *Pictures of the English Liturgy*; the title itself was almost certainly another example of Child's sardonic humour, since the rituals pictured were far from English in derivation. Volume 2, *Low Mass*, was published in 1916 and volume 1, *High Mass*, followed in 1922.

In 1916 the Alcuin Club, a society devoted to the study of the Prayer

Book and composed of strong supporters of the English Use, themselves published a book entitled *Illustrations of the Liturgy* by C. O. Skilbeck, to which Dr Percy Dearmer, the *bête noire* of the adherents of the Western Use, contributed an introduction styled 'The Present Opportunity'.

Pictures of the English Liturgy, volume 2, was a reply to that, and the introduction was entitled 'The Lost Opportunity'. The author was anonymous, but was probably Maurice Child, and he wrote: 'The proposed revival (of the Sarum use) has failed, as any movement is bound to fail which begins and ends in studies, and private chapels, and the moderate shrines of the well-to-do. The History of the attempted revival of the "English Use" is the story of a lost opportunity . . . Today the Sarum use barely survives, the Western use spreads widely but with increasing deformities . . .'[9]

There was a considerable gap before the appearance of what was confusingly called volume 1, with its pictures of High Mass. Again, it is likely that Child wrote the introduction, which sets out the proposition that the ceremonial of the mass should be 'the simplest form prescribed by the only authority which legislates on such matters, namely the Congregation of Rites in Rome. And that, not so much because it is "Roman", as because it is the simplest, most convenient, most easily studied, and (to modern minds) most intelligible method of rendering Divine Service. Moreover it is the form adopted (and perhaps adapted) in the vast majority of Anglo-Catholic Churches.'[10]

All the drawings in this volume, now rare and collectable, show priests in biretta and Roman-style vestments, servers in short cottas, altars with at least six baroque candlesticks and a crucifix, and sometimes reliquaries. In one, a high mass of Exposition is depicted with a crowned monstrance behind the altar. On the only plate where the congregation is shown, one woman has a mantilla on her head.

The changes which began to affect both Roman and Anglican worship after 1950 largely passed by Anglican Papalists at first. Whereas some, such as Fynes-Clinton, were willing to adopt lunchtime masses when the fasting rules were relaxed, others were disorientated. It was in fact the fasting rules which had influenced the whole pattern of worship in Roman and therefore Anglo-Catholic churches. As early as 1928

---

9 *Pictures of the English Liturgy*, Vol. 2, introduction.
10 *Pictures of the English Liturgy*, Vol. 1, introduction.

Dearmer saw this, when he wrote in *The Truth about Fasting*: 'Once . . . we cease to be trammelled by ideas about fasting, the difficulties which so continually baffle the clergy and offend the laity about the Sunday morning services completely disappear.'[11] The emphasis on eucharistic adoration, including especially the great controversies over Benediction which had caused so many problems during the inter-war period, ceased to have the same importance once evening communion became possible.

Further, the energy which had driven Anglo-Catholicism between the wars seemed to have expended itself, and increasingly the lead in innovation within the Church of England was taken by the proponents of the Parish Communion. It now seems clear that although that movement ran in parallel with the Liturgical Movement within the Roman Church, the two streams of development were separate and not derived one from the other.

There is no doubt that the Parish Communion movement had its roots in Anglo-Catholicism, but it did not spring from the Papalists described elsewhere in this book. They were concerned only to follow what was prescribed in Rome, and the Liturgical Movement on the Continent was alien to everything that they had been teaching for so many years. They largely shut their eyes to what was occurring in the religious communities in Belgium and elsewhere.

The real progenitor of the Parish Communion movement, Father Gabriel Hebert of the Society of the Sacred Mission, wrote in the community's newsletter as early as 1929 that: 'It is one of the failures of the wonderful Anglican revival of recent years that it has not succeeded in restoring the communion of the people as an integral part of the chief mass on a Sunday.' He went on to call the non-communicating high mass which was strongly favoured by all Anglican Papalists a 'mutilated rite'.[12] In 1935 he published *Liturgy and Society,* the central thesis of which was that the fellowship of the whole body of the Church would emerge: this again was wholly contrary to the sacerdotal and hierarchical view of the Church taken by Anglican Papalists. In 1937 Hebert published a book of essays entitled *The Parish Communion,* and in 1939 Revd H. de Candole, later Bishop of Knaresborough and a steadfast

---

11 P. Dearmer: *The Truth About Fasting* (Rivingtons, 1928), p. 5.
12 G. Hebert, in *SSM Quarterly*, Vol. 19, No. 109, p. 46.

advocate of the new liturgical forms, was invited to address a Synod of the Society of the Holy Cross on the subject. He recorded that there was strong opposition, although there could be no real disapproval as the Pope had encouraged the parallel Liturgical Movement. Those present deplored the emphasis on the communion of the people when they were teaching the sacrifice of the mass, and they were also concerned about the fasting rules.[13]

During the 1950s therefore Anglican Papalists found themselves under pressure both from within the Church of England, as the moderate, diluted Catholicism represented by the Parish Communion movement gained strength, and from the relaxation on fasting rules in the Roman Church which began in 1953. That pressure of course grew enormously once the Second Vatican Council turned around much of what had been regarded as cast in stone.

The effect of these changes and of the increasing amalgamation of livings was that the various shades of Anglo-Catholicism, of which Anglican Papalism was one, became less variable. There is no little irony in the fact that a sacrament house of Roman origin has been erected in Southwark Cathedral, from which much condemnation of such structures once emanated, but perhaps as much in the triumph in so many places of the very balloon-like chasubles of which Ronald Knox was so scornful.

There are few less fashionable areas at present than the Back to Baroque Movement, although there are signs of a revival in interest. There is little doubt, however, that it has run its course as a development in church furnishings and architecture.

---

13 Jagger: *Bishop Henry de Candole: His Life and Times.*

12

ANGLICAN PAPALISM
A Retrospect

The Papalist tradition within the Church of England was, it can be concluded, rather more important and influential over the period from 1900 to the Second Vatican Council than would be thought from the minimal attention given to it by most general ecclesiastical historians of the era. As earlier noted, it scarcely raises even a footnote in any but the most esoteric studies: the best introduction to thought among the Papalists, apart from their own writings, is contained in Father Curtis' book on Couturier, in which it is a side issue, albeit an important one for the purposes of that work.

The landscape of relations between Rome and Canterbury has changed so much since 1960 that it is difficult to think back into the mind of those on the Anglican side who were concerned to bring them together. It is, however, possible to see one clear truth, which is that the Anglican Papalists failed to foresee the enormous changes which were about to emerge from Rome. In that, they were of course not alone: in fact almost no-one did comprehend what was about to happen. A possible analogy in the political sphere is the inability of the West to foresee the collapse of the Soviet empire, and the difficulty faced by many politicians brought up in a Cold War atmosphere to adjust to the new reality. It is perhaps symbolic that in 1935 Spencer Jones wrote in *The Pilot* on the dogma of unchangeability.

The particular difficulty which the Anglican Papalists faced was that they had sought to steer the Anglican ship on a course which would lead it along the same course as the barque of St Peter. Once that barque began to deviate from what had appeared to be a sure and steady passage, inexorable in its direction, the compasses began to sway from side to side and the Papalists did not know which route to steer. Many were inclined, especially initially, to preserve as much as possible of the old ways, thus creating an even more sharply defined divide between themselves and the rest of the Church of England than had been the case before.

Thus the very last edition of *Reunion*, published in 1965, contained a bitter editorial denunciation of the new ways: 'The seeds of the liturgical revolution now progressing were sown by the clever propaganda of a handful of zealots whose eventual success, in England at any rate, was assured by the supine neglect, for generations, to instruct the faithful in the use of the Missal.'[1]

The Catholic League on the other hand at first took the ultra-defensive course and failed to look up at what was happening elsewhere, and then in 1974 and thereafter was forced by certain members, particularly Revd Raymond Avent, then the Assistant Priest Director, to examine its ethos critically. The League transformed itself from a largely pietistic, backward-looking group to one with a more educative function, and in due course even opened its doors to Roman Catholics and others interested in unity, while at the same time taking up the reforms of the Second Vatican Council.

The irony of course, on which comment has already been passed, is that for a time it looked as though that which the Papalists most wanted was at any rate possible. Union with a Roman church which used the vernacular, had enthusiastically embraced the Liturgical Movement and now promoted the distribution of communion in both kinds at the mass, appeared a far more desirable objective to the average Anglican than it did in its previous guise. The very domination of the ideas of the Liturgical Movement in both churches, complained of in *Reunion*, has meant that the liturgy employed in the Roman Church is now far more akin to that used in middle-of-the-road Anglican parishes than was ever the case before.

However, a lack of will, and even more of imagination, appeared to affect the Church of England, and as the years went by the door appeared to close more firmly in its face. The unilateral decision to proceed with the ordination of women – unilateral in the sense that it was taken in the absence of any such decision by the Roman Catholic or Orthodox Churches – was the most destructive single step to any hopes of reunion, as opposed to co-operation and friendship. It was of course taken in the

---

1 *Reunion*, Vol. 6, No. 62 (1965).

full knowledge that it would be so destructive, and in the cases of some of those who supported it enthusiastically, no doubt in the hope that it would be so. The full effects are yet to be seen, although it does appear that one unexpected consequence has been a rallying together of Anglo-Catholics opposed to the ordination of women under the umbrella of Forward in Faith, when some might have thought that a mortal blow had been struck to the successors of the Oxford Movement. However, a change of great moment has been that Anglo-Catholics find it much more difficult to argue that the Church of England as a whole, whether or not it appreciates it, is actually part of the wider Western tradition. There has been an internal schism which the proponents of women priests thought would be of short duration, but does not appear at the time of writing to be so. Women bishops may precipitate more defections to Rome, but also a further move towards a separate body which could become a Uniate Church.

It would be idle, however, to pretend that Anglican Papalism now plays any great part in the life of the Church of England. Its most prominent period was that set out in this book.

The aim of the Papalists was an internal transformation of the Church of England from below so that it adopted the liturgical and disciplinary standards of the Roman Church. That transformation had very limited success in the parishes, but rather more in the religious communities. It has been said that it did not assist ecumenical relations at all: one of the problems though came from the need to transform from the parish upwards. The Anglican Establishment absorbed and adapted Anglo-Catholicism so that men such as Lang and Ramsey, both of whom had accepted the movement to different degrees, were accepted as archbishops, but there was no will in the higher echelons of the Church to move towards union with Rome or even the acceptance of the Pope's authority under a Uniate Anglican Church.

Even so, it must be recognized that successive Archbishops of Canterbury had to preserve the unity of the Anglican Communion. Some Anglican Papalists on the other hand faced up realistically to the fact that their aims were capable of achievement only if the Church of England itself was split in the process. Father Langford-James in *The Bridge Church* saw the positive benefits of separation from Modernists and Protestants, thus setting the Catholic-minded section of the Church of England free to join with Rome. Plowden-Wardlaw in his proposal for a

Uniate Anglican Church set out the benefits thus: 'Uniate status will recreate an English vernacular church, and close the breach of 400 years, and shut out none except modernists, irreconcilable protestants, and those obsessed by the state connection . . .'[2] However, he then accepted that those he had excluded probably comprised three-quarters of the Church of England as it then was. His escape from that position was to conclude that the majority which he had just identified were not really Anglicans at all: 'the Church of England consists in reality of orthodox Anglo-Catholics to whom the other parties are historical addenda, recognized only as a matter of charity, good will and temporary necessity; so that in essence orthodox Anglo-Catholics are the whole Church of England'.[3]

This extreme form of casuistry did not assist the Papalist cause over-much. It was difficult enough for those who simply regarded themselves as 'advanced' Anglo-Catholics to justify defiance of the bishops, whose authority they were seeking to establish by setting before their parishioners the importance of the apostolic succession.

It was easier in the case of, for example, Father Rosenthal in Birmingham, as he was a personally charismatic man and devoted priest, and enormous pressure was placed on him by Bishop Barnes, who was conversely unpopular among many and also was acting in a way which most bishops regarded as improper. There was a great deal of sympathy for Rosenthal, as there was for Bernard Walke, particularly among those who had come across him.

Father Kilburn was regarded even by his opponents as a good and holy man, and was much respected among his flock for his hard work and identification with their needs. The parish magazine of St Saviour, Hoxton, carried the message that there was a priest available in cases of emergency at any time of the day or night, making it absolutely clear that the clergy were prepared to devote themselves to their people. The *Anglo-Catholic Annuals*, published between 1935 and 1940, carried lists of churches where the sacraments were available 24 hours a day, whereas today most churchgoers are prevented even from visiting the tabernacle by locks on church doors.

There was much less sympathy for those who appeared deliberately to

---

2 Plowden-Wardlaw: *Catholic Reunion*, p. 10.
3 Ibid., p. 13.

provoke the local bishop, especially where they had little local support. There is no doubt that the effect of an immediate change to Roman discipline and liturgy in some churches was to empty them, particularly where the priest concerned lacked the appeal of a Walke or Kilburn, and also where the church concerned was in the country, where there was less chance of attracting the sort of eclectic congregation found in London.

Anglican Papalists found the question of obedience to their bishops even more difficult, because of course the central plank of their thinking was that the teaching of the Western Church (i.e. the Pope) was a higher authority and should be followed in preference to the regulations imposed locally by Anglican bishops.

The issue of authority was one of the many ambiguities in Anglo-Catholic thought which were explored by Dr W. S. F. Pickering in his book *Anglo-Catholicism: A Study in Religious Ambiguity* (1989). Wilkinson, in his history of the Community of the Resurrection (1992) was extremely critical of this dilemma, saying that at the 'heart [of Anglo-Catholicism] was a canker, a defective morality born of equivocation and self-deception about authority'.[4]

It is this equivocation which gives such importance to the issue of the secret reordination of Anglican priests, an issue which has too frequently been avoided or skirted around by commentators unwilling to face up to some of the unwelcome facts, which appear to show both episcopal and archiepiscopal incompetence and on the other hand hypocrisy on the part of certain priests. The matter has to be faced squarely, and that episode does not reflect well on any of those involved.

Wilkinson further makes the point, which he couples with the canker just set out, that there was also within Anglo-Catholicism of the relevant period 'an unwillingness (understandable at that time) to acknowledge that homosexual attitudes dominated certain key areas of the movement . . .'[5] That again was a, usually unspoken, criticism of Anglo-Catholics from the outside. Later, when attitudes to homosexuality changed and many priests openly acknowledged that which had long been suspected, the criticism continued and all those who set out their principled objections to the ordination of women were tarred with the brush of misogyny.

---

4 Wilkinson: *The Community of the Resurrection*, p. 185.
5 Ibid.

It is even more difficult to discover whether homosexuality played a covert part in the groups concerned with Anglican Papalism than it is to ascertain the truth in relation to the reordination of priests by *episcopi vagantes*. There is little doubt that some who were enthusiastic promoters of union with the Holy See would on the other hand have been less willing to accept the discipline which came from Rome: the overt defence of a homosexual way of life which has been propagated by some Anglican priests in the last 30 years would not have been tolerated by the Vatican. On the other hand, there is nothing to suggest that homosexuality was the driving or binding force underlying the Papalist Movement, even if some of its followers were inclined in that direction.

These are weighty criticisms of the Papalist Movement, which must be taken seriously. On the other hand, its positive aspects and its achievements must also be recognised.

It has been the concentration on official communiqués, as opposed to the study of unofficial contacts, which has led some commentators to ignore completely the efforts of the Papalist party. In fact, as has been seen, there were from time to time pilgrimages to Rome by the various devotional organisations, as a result of which the Vatican authorities were made aware of the growth of Catholic devotions within the Church of England. These occurred at a time when there were very few formal or informal meetings of substance between the respective church authorities.

It was said that when Archbishop Fisher met Pope John XXIII the Pontiff had a lack of objective information about Anglicans and 'was disproportionately concerned with the revival of the Walsingham pilgrimage in the Church of England as evidence of a return to Catholicism'.[6] Fisher of course had no time for or sympathy with the Shrine of Our Lady of Walsingham, so was unable to see that it might be used as a basis for mutual coming together and joint endeavour. The same authors who put forward that criticism, Bernard and Margaret Pawsey, in their interesting study of *Rome and Canterbury through Four Centuries* (1974 and 1981) are particularly damning of the Papalists in almost the only reference to them in their book. They said: 'there was a disastrous tendency to use the Church of Rome in its most garish Latin, and therefore un-English, manifestations, as a model . . . In certain cases

---

6 Pawsey and Pawsey: *Rome and Canterbury through Four Centuries*, p. 317.

it was impossible to tell whether a particular church was in communion with Rome or Canterbury. This regrettable development of one wing of the Oxford Movement again undoubtedly hindered the progress of understanding with Rome, the very thing it was hoped to promote.'[7]

It may be that that tendency did not assist the Church of England in its relations with the Roman Catholic Church in England, but there is nothing to substantiate the proposition that it hampered the wider ecumenical picture. Father Curtis saw that in his work on Couturier, who has led to a wider understanding of the Church of England through the Papalists. Curtis is far more charitable than the Pawseys, saying:

> We are beginning to see that Anglican Papalists have been unfairly judged. Abbé Couturier saw this clearly . . . The true Anglican Papalists . . . are a small group with a long lineage in our Church and many are of the salt of the earth. Their particular standpoint many of them have recognized as involving a call to a life of reparation. Contrary to average opinion this small group is notable for its intellectual power as well as for its holiness.[8]

He then makes the point that the two books written by Anglicans which had most influence among continental Roman Catholics in the first half of the twentieth century were Spencer Jones' *England and the Holy See* and Gregory Dix's *Shape of the Liturgy*: the latter of course was equally important in England among his own communion. Both those works emanated right from the centre of the Papalist Movement, with Jones' work its founding testament, and even that Tendency's fiercest detractors have paid tribute to the importance of the work done by Dix.

It is also apparent from the archives that Fynes-Clinton was a more important figure than his detractors would have. His opponents looked only at his propensity for founding more and more organisations, many of which in the event had only a short life, without appreciating his enormously wide international contacts with both Eastern and Western churches, as well as his generally sensible counsel given to all who asked for it and some who did not. He was quite forthright from the outset in his condemnation of A. H. Mathew and his associates, where others were less unequivocal.

---

7 Ibid., p. 131.
8 Curtis: *Paul Couturier and Unity in Christ*, p. 163.

The Church Unity Octave has been superceded by the Week of Prayer for Christian Unity, and in that process its message has been somewhat obscured. Its importance however is more than historical. Spencer Jones and the early adherents of Anglican Papalism saw that if there was to be *unity* between the churches, as opposed to joint enterprises and co-operation on social matters, that could only come about by adherence in one way or the other to the central authority of the Papacy. The failure to accept that as the unequivocal starting-point for discussions on Christian reunion was the single most damaging omission on the part of Anglicans during the twentieth century.

In 1904 Father Jones wrote in Father Wattson's journal *The Lamp*:

The terminus ad quem of the Oxford Movement, by logical and divine necessity, seems to us to be the return of the Anglican Church to the supreme authority of the Holy See. To it we must come if we desire to possess a sanctuary once more.[9]

Almost one hundred years after those words were written, the logic which underlay them seems to be unnoticed in the thinking of the Anglican Communion, perhaps indeed less noticed than 30 years ago.

---

9 Quoted in Whitton: *The Necessity for Catholic Reunion*, p. 103.

BIBLIOGRAPHY

Ackroyd, P.: *T. S. Eliot* (Sphere Books, 1989)

Allchin, D.: *A Good Man Who Could Never Be Dull* (Three Peaks Press, 2000)

Almedinghen, E. M.: *Dom Bernard Clements: A Portrait* (John Lane, 1945)

Anglo-Catholic Annuals, 1935–40

Anon. ('Isidor'): *Aspects of Catholic Unity* (1938)

Anon. ('Vindex'): *General Disorder or the Establishment at the Cross Roads* (Coelian Press, 1938)

Anon. ('Vindex'): *Death and Bondage, or the Liberty of Bureaucracy* (Coelian Press, *c.*1944)

Anon. ('Vindex'): *An Open Letter to a Bishop* (Coelian Press, *c.*1944)

Anon. ('Vindex'): *Stunt Religion* (Coelian Press, *c.*1944)

Anon. ('Vindex'): *Why the Movement Does Not Move* (Coelian Press, *c.*1947)

Anon. ('Watchman'): *The Bishops and the Prayer Book* (Church Literature Association, 1937)

Anon.: *Report of the Conference on Benediction at St Saviour, Hoxton, 14th March 1918* (Talbot & Co., 1918)

Anson, P. F.: *The Benedictines of Caldey* (Burns, Oates & Washbourne, 1940)

Anson, P. F.: *Harbour Head: Maritime Memories* (Catholic Book Club, 1944)

Anson, P. F.: *A Roving Recluse: More Memoirs* (Mercier Press, 1946)

Anson, P. F.: *Abbot Extraordinary: A Memoir of Aelred Carlyle, Monk and Missionary, 1874–1955* (Faith Press, 1958)

Anson, P. F.: *The Hermit of Cat Island: The Life of Fra Jerome Hawes* (Burns & Oates, 1958)

Anson, P. F.: *Bishops at Large* (Faber & Faber, 1964)

Anson, P. F.: *Fashions in Church Furnishings 1840–1940* (Studio Vista, 1965)

Anson, P. F.: *The Call of the Cloister* (SPCK, 4th edn, 1967)

Anson, P. F.: *Building up the Waste Places* (Faith Press, 1973)

Bailey, S.: *A Tactful God: Gregory Dix, Priest, Monk and Scholar* (Gracewing, 1995)

Baker, F.: *I Follow But Myself* (Peter Davies, 1968)

Baker, F.: *The Call of Cornwall* (Robert Hale, 1976)

Barlow, B.: *A Brother Knocking at the Door: The Malines Conversations, 1921–5* (Canterbury Press, 1996)

Barnes, J.: *Ahead of His Age: Bishop Barnes of Birmingham* (Collins, 1979)

Baverstock, A. H.: *The English Agricultural Labourer* (Fifield, 1912)

Baverstock, A. H.: *The Priest as Confessor* (Cope & Fenwick, 1914)

Baverstock, A. H.: *Priesthood in Liturgy and Life* (Faith Press, 1917)

Baverstock, A. H.: *Benediction and the Bishops* (Cope & Fenwick, 1919)

Baverstock, A. H. and Hole, D.: *The Truth about the Prayer Book* (Williams & Norgate, 1935)

Baverstock, A. H.: *The Conspiracy to Unchurch the Church of England* (Coelian Press, 1945)

Bell, G. K. A.: *Randall Davidson, Archbishop of Canterbury* (Oxford University Press, 3rd edn, 1952)

Belton, F. G.: *Ommanney of Sheffield: Memoirs of George Campbell Ommanney, Vicar of St Matthew's Sheffield 1882–1936* (Centenary Press, 1936)

Betjeman, J.: *Collins Pocket Guide to English Parish Churches* (Collins, 2 vols, 1968)

Brandreth, H. R. T.: *Unity and Reunion: A Bibliography* (Adam & Charles Black, 2nd edn, 1948)

Brandreth, H. R. T.: *Dr Lee of Lambeth: A Chapter in Parenthesis in the History of the Oxford Movement* (SPCK, 1951)

Brandreth, H. R. T.: *Episcopi Vagantes and the Anglican Church* (SPCK, 2nd edn, 1961)

Brill, K. (ed.): *John Groser, East London Priest* (Mowbray, 1971)

Briscoe, J. F. (ed.): *V. S. S. Coles: Letters, Papers, Addresses, Hymns and Verses, with a Memoir* (Mowbray, 1930)

Burne, K. E.: *The Life and Letters of Father Andrew SDC* (Mowbray, 1948)

Calder-Marshall, A.: *The Enthusiast* (Faber & Faber, 1962)

Carpenter, E.: *Archbishop Fisher: His Life and Times* (Canterbury Press, 1991)

Carpenter, H.: *Robert Runcie, the Reluctant Archbishop* (Hodder & Stoughton, 1996)

Carpenter, S. C.: *Winnington-Ingram* (Hodder & Stoughton, 1949)

Catholic League: *Adoration of the Blessed Sacrament Reserved* (Catholic League, no date)

Catholic League: *An Explanation of the Profession of Faith of the Council of Trent* (Catholic League, no date)

Catholic League: *New Tracts for Our Times by a Committee of Anglican Priests: Tract V: The Calamity of the New Prayer Book* (Catholic League, no date)

Chadwick, O.: *Michael Ramsey: A Life* (Clarendon Press, 1990)

Chapman, M. D.: *The Fantasy of Reunion: The Rise and Fall of the Association for the Promotion of the Unity of Christendom* (Anglo-Catholic History Society, 2003)

Clarke, W. K. L.: *The Prayer Book of 1928 Reconsidered* (SPCK, 1943)

Clutterbuck, I.: *Marginal Catholics* (Gracewing, 1993)

Cobb, P. G. (ed.): *Walsingham* (White Tree Books, 1990)

Comper, J. N.: *Practical Considerations on the Gothic or English Altars and Certain Dependent Rubrics of the Book of Common Prayer* (St Paul's Ecclesiological Society, no date)

Creran, J. H.: 'Black Market in Episcopal Orders', *The Month*, June 1953.

Croft-Cooke, R.: *The Altar in the Loft* (Putnam, 1960)

Cross, F. L.: *Darwell Stone: Churchman and Counsellor* (Dacre Press, 1943)

Curtis, G.: *William of Glasshampton: Friar, Monk, Solitary 1862–1937* (SPCK, 1947)

Curtis, G.: *Paul Couturier and Unity in Christ* (SCM Press, 1964)

Dalby, M.: *Anglican Missals and their Canons: 1549, Interim Rite and Roman* (Grove Books, 1998)

Dark, S.: *Mackay of All Saints* (Centenary Press, 1936)

De-La-Noy, M.: *The Church of England: A Portrait* (Simon & Schuster, 1993)

Denison, H. P.: *Seventy Two Years' Church Recollections* (Robert Scott, 1925)

Dix, G. (ed.): *Open Letter of Superiors of Religious Communities to the Archbishop of Canterbury* (Dacre Press, 1943)

Dix, G.: *The Question of Anglican Orders* (Dacre Press, 1944)

Dix, G.: *The Shape of the Liturgy* (Dacre Press, 1945)

Donovan, M.: *After the Tractarians* (Philip Allan, 1933)

Doolan, B.: *The First Fifty Years: A History of the Catholic League from 1913 to 1966* (Crux Press, 1966)

Dunlop, C.: *What is the English Use?* (Mowbray, 1923)

Dunstan, P.: *This Poor Sort: A History of the European Province of the Society of St Francis* (Darton, Longman & Todd, 1997)

Eeles, F. C.: *Prayer Book Revision and Christian Reunion* (Cambridge University Press, 1923)

Eliot, T. S.: *Reunion by Destruction* (Council for the Defence of Church Principles, 1943)

Embry, J.: *The Catholic Movement and the Society of the Holy Cross* (Faith Press, 1931)

Farmer, R. J.: *The Catholic League 1913–1988* (Catholic League, 1988)

Farmer, R. J.: *Father Alban Baverstock SSC: An Exploration of his Life* (Catholic League, 1997)

Farrer, M.: *St Saviour's Hoxton: An Extraordinary Story* (Anglo-Catholic History Society, 2002)

Felicity, Mary, SPB: *Mother Millicent* (Society of the Precious Blood, 1968)

Fitzgerald, P.: *The Knox Brothers* (Harvill HarperCollins, 1977)

Forse, E. J. G.: *Ceremonial Curiosities and Queer Sights in Foreign Churches* (Faith Press, 1938)

Fox, A.: *Dean Inge* (John Murray, 1960)

Fynes-Clinton, H. J. and Corbould, W. R.: *What Are We to Say?* (Council for Promoting Christian Union, 1933)

Galloway, P. and Rawll, C.: *Good and Faithful Servants: All Saints Margaret Street and its Incumbents* (Churchman Publishing, 1988)

Gille, A. J. A. ('Father Jerome'): *A Catholic Plea for Reunion* (Williams & Norgate, 1934)

Goodison, E. (ed.): *St Alban, Fulham: The First One Hundred Years* (parish, 1997)

Gray, D.: *Earth and Altar: The Evolution of the Parish Communion in the Church of England to 1945* (Canterbury Press for the Alcuin Club, 1986)

Groves, R.: *Conrad Noel and the Thaxted Movement: An Adventure in Christian Socialism* (Merlin Press, 1967)

Gurney, S.: *Isabel Mrs Gurney afterwards The Lady Talbot de Malahide 1851–1932* (Jarrold & Simpkin Marshall, 1935)

Halifax, Viscount: *A Call to Reunion* (Mowbray, 1922)

Halifax, Viscount: *Further Considerations on Behalf of Reunion* (Mowbray, 1923)

Halifax, Viscount: *Reunion and the Roman Primacy* (Mowbray, 1925)

Halifax, Viscount: *Catholic Reunion* (Mowbray, 1926)

Halifax, Viscount: *Notes on the Conversations at Malines* (Mowbray, 1928)

Halifax, Viscount: *The Conversations at Malines: Original Documents* (Philip Allan, 1930)

Halifax, Viscount: *The Good Estate of the Catholic Church* (Longmans, 1930)

Halliday, R.: 'Father Clive Luget and the Visions of Middleton', *Ecclesiology Today*, May 2003.

Harris, S. M.: *What do the Celtic Churches Say?* (Council for Promoting Catholic Union, 1933)

Harris, S. M.: *The First Ten Years: The Witness of the Early Tractarians* (Council for Promoting Christian Union, 1934)

Harris, S. M.: *Reservation of the Blessed Sacrament* (Society for Catholic Reunion, 1936)

Hastings, A.: *A History of English Christianity 1920–1990* (SCM Press, 1991)

Hastings, A.: *Robert Runcie* (Mowbray, 1991)

Headlam, A. C.: 'A Defence of the New Prayer Book', *Church Quarterly Review* 208.7 (1927)

Hebert, A. G.: *Liturgy and Society* (Faber & Faber, 1935)

Hebert, A. G.: *The Parish Communion* (SPCK, 1937)

Henson, H. H.: *Retrospect of an Unimportant Life* (Oxford University Press, 1946)

Heppenstall, R.: *The Intellectual Part* (Barrie & Rockliff, 1963)

Hole, D.: *Anglican Papalists* (later reissued as *The Church of England and the Pope*) (Society for Promoting Christian Union, 1942)

Hole, D.: *The Church and 'The Church of England'* (The Church Shop and Talbot & Co., no date)

Hughes, A.: *The Rivers of the Flood* (Faith Press, 1973)

Hughes, J. J.: *Stewards of the Lord: A Reappraisal of Anglican Orders* (Sheed & Ward, 1970).

Hylson-Smith, K.: *High Churchmanship in the Church of England* (T. & T. Clark, 1993)

Inge, W. R.: *Vale* (Longmans Green, 1934)

Ingram, K.: *Basil Jellicoe* (Centenary Press, 1936)

Iremonger, F. A.: *William Temple, Archbishop of Canterbury, his Life and Letters* (Oxford University Press, 1948)

Jackson, V.: *Christian Unity* (Society for Promoting Catholic Union, 1942)

Jagger, P. J.: *Bishop Henry de Candole: His Life and Times 1895–1971* (Faith Press, 1975)

Jagger, P. J.: *A History of the Parish and People Movement* (Faith Press, 1978)

Jagger, P. J.: *The Alcuin Club and its Publications 1897–1987: An Annotated Bibliography* (Hymns Ancient & Modern Ltd, 1986)

Jalland, T. G.: *The Bible, the Church and South India* (Dacre Press, 1944)

Jasper, R. C. D: *Walter Howard Frere: His Correspondence on Liturgical Revision and Construction* (SPCK, 1954)

Jasper, R. C. D.: *George Bell, Bishop of Chichester* (Oxford University Press, 1967)

Joblin, B. E.: *Reverence* (Coelian Press, 1945)

Johnson, V. C.: *One Lord, One Faith* (Sheed & Ward, 1929)

Jones, A. E: *From Mediaeval Manor to London Suburb: An Obituary of Carshalton* (author, 1976)

Jones, S. J.: *England and the Holy See: An Essay Towards Reunion* (Longmans Green, 1902)

Jones, S. J.: *Rome and Reunion* (Longmans Green, 1904)

Jones, S. J.: *Benito Mussolini: An Introduction to the Study of Fascism* (Hunter & Longhurst, 1928)

Jones, S. J.: *Catholic Reunion* (Basil Blackwell for the Confraternity of Unity, 1930)

Jones, S. J.: *What do the Tractarians Say?* (Council for Promoting Catholic Union, 1933)

248

BIBLIOGRAPHY

Jones, S. J.: *What does the XVI Century Say?* (Council for Promoting Catholic Union, 1933)

Jones, S. J.: *L'Eglise d'Angleterre at la Saint-Siege: Propos sur la Reunion* (Paris, c.1941)

Jones, S. J.: *The Counter-Reformation in the Church of England* (Skeffington, undated)

Jones, S. J. and Wattson, L. T.: *Prince of the Apostles* (?New York, 1904)

Jones, W. R.: *Diary of a Misfit Priest* (George Allen & Unwin, 1960)

Jublilee Book of the Benedictines of Nashdom 1914–1964 (Faith Press, 1964)

Keast, H.: *Our Lady in England* (Society of Mary, 1985)

Kemp, E. W.: *N. P. Williams: A Memoir and Some Sermons* (SPCK, 1954)

Kensit, J. A.: *What I Saw in Rome* (Protestant Truth Society, 1924)

Kensit, J. A.: *Undiluted Romanism: A Call for Action* (Protestant Truth Society, 1929)

Kensit, J. C.: *Contending for the Faith: Part II: The Work Continuing from John Kensit's Death* (Wickliffe Press, 1939)

Kitchenham, P. P. G.: 'Frederick Samuel Willoughby 1862–1928, Anglo-Catholic Champion and Old Catholic Bishop' (unpublished article)

Knox, R. A.: *A Spiritual Aeneid* (Burns Oates, 1958 edn)

Knox, R. A. H.: *The Church in Bondage* (Society of SS Peter and Paul, 1914)

Kollar, R.: *Abbot Aelred Carlyle, Caldey Island and the Anglo-Catholic Revival in England* (Peter Lang, 1995)

Langford-James, R. L.: *The Bridge Church* (privately published, 1930)

Langford-James, R. L.: *The Peril of Isolation* (Society for Promoting Catholic Union, 1937)

Last, E. C.: *Open Letter to the Bishop of London* (Protestant Truth Society, 1962)

Leech, K. and Williams, R. (eds): *Essays Catholic and Radical* (Bowerdean Press, 1983)

Lloyd, R.: *The Church of England 1900–65* (SCM Press, 1966)

Lockhart, J. G.: *Charles Lindley Viscount Halifax, Part One: 1839–1885* (Geoffrey Bles, Centenary Press, 1935)

Lockhart, J. G.: *Charles Lindley Viscount Halifax, Part Two: 1885–1934* (Geoffrey Bles, Centenary Press, 1936)

Lockhart, J. G.: *Cosmo Gordon Lang* (Hodder & Stoughton, 1949)

Lunn, B. and Haselock, J.: *Henry Joy Fynes-Clinton, 1876–1959* (Church Literature Association, 1983)

Mackenzie, C.: *The Altar Steps* (Cassell, 1922)

Mackenzie, C.: *The Parson's Progress* (Cassell, 1923)

Mackenzie, C.: *The Heavenly Ladder* (Cassell, 1924)

Mackenzie, C.: *My Life and Times Octave Two 1891–1900* (Chatto & Windus, 1963)

Mackenzie, C.: *My Life and Times Octave Three 1900–1907* (Chatto & Windus, 1964)

Mackenzie, C.: *My Life and Times Octave Four 1907–1915* (Chatto & Windus, 1965)

Mackenzie, C.: *My Life and Times Octave Five 1915–1923* (Chatto & Windus, 1966)

Mackenzie, C.: *My Life and Times Octave Six 1923–1930* (Chatto & Windus, 1965)

Matthews, W. R.: *Memories and Meanings* (Hodder & Stoughton, 1969)

Maughan, H. H.: *Some Brighton Churches* (Faith Press, 1922)

Maughan, H. H.: *Seven Churches* (Coelian Press, 1948)

Maughan, H. H.: *Wagner of Brighton* (Coelian Press, 1949)

Maughan, H. H.: *Anglican Circus* (Coelian Press, 1953)

McGrath, A. E. (ed.): *The SPCK Book of Anglican Theologians* (SPCK, 1998)

Merritt, E. D.: *The Erratically Drafted Memoirs of Edmund Douglas Merritt* (Arthur's Press, 1951)

Monahan, W. B. ('The Voice from Worcester'): *Loyalty to the Church of England* (author, undated)

Monahan, W. B. ('The Voice from Worcester'): *Rome the Goal of the Oxford Movement* (author, undated)

Morse-Boycott, D: *Lead Kindly Light: Studies of the Saints and Heroes of the Oxford Movement* (Centenary Press, 1932)

Morse-Boycott, D.: *A Tapestry of Toil* (Faith Press, 1970)

Morton Howard, J. G.: *Epistola ad Romanos* (Council for Promoting Christian Union, *c.*1933)

Morton Howard, J. G.: *What Did the Church of England Say?* (Council for Promoting Catholic Union, 1933)

Morton Howard, J. G.: *What Does the Anglo Saxon Church Say?* (Council for Promoting Catholic Union, 1933)

Mosley, N.: *The Life of Raymond Raynes* (Faith Press, 1961)

Moss, C. B.: *The Old Catholic Movement: Its Origin and History* (SPCK, 1948 and 1964)

Murray, D. L.: *Reservation: Its Purpose and Method* (Mowbray, 1923)

Newman, H. de W. (Mar Georgius): *A Chapter of Secret History* (Patriarchal Press, *c.*1960, partly reprinted from the *Church Times*, 28 April 1922)

Newman, H. de W. (Mar Georgius): *In the Shadow of Utrecht* (author, 1954)

Noel, C.: *Jesus the Heretic* (J. M. Dent & Sons, 1939)

Noel, C.: *An Autobiography* (J. M. Dent & Sons, 1945)

Pawsey, B. and M.: *Rome and Canterbury through Four Centuries* (Mowbray, 1981)

Pawson, G.: *The Nonconformist Witness* (Coelian Press, c.1946)

Peart-Binns, J. S.: *Blunt* (Mountain Press, 1969)

Peart-Binns, J. S.: *Maurice B. Reckitt* (Bowerdean Press and Marshall Pickering, 1988)

Penhale, F.: *The Anglican Church Today: Catholics in Crisis* (Mowbray, 1986)

Perchenet, A.: *The Revival of the Religious Life and Christian Unity* (Mowbray, 1969)

Phillips, C. S. (ed.): *Walter Howard Frere, Bishop of Truro: A Memoir* (Faber & Faber, 1947)

Pickering, W. S. F.: *Anglo-Catholicism: A Study in Religious Ambiguity* (Routledge, 1989)

Pictures of the English Liturgy, vol. 1: *High Mass* (Society of SS Peter and Paul, 1922)

Pictures of the English Liturgy, vol. 2: *Low Mass* (Society of SS Peter and Paul, 1916)

Plowden-Wardlaw, J. T. ('Clement Humilis'): *The Oxford Movement Centenary (Supplementary) Missal* (Knott, 1933)

Plowden-Wardlaw, J. T. ('Father Clement'): *Catholic Reunion: An Anglican Plea for a Uniate Patriarchate and for an Anglican Ultramontanism* (Basil Blackwell, 1935)

Price, N. (ed.): *Streets of Heaven: 125 Years in the Parish of St Mary, Bourne Street* (parish, 1999)

Putterill, J.: *Thaxted Quest for Social Justice* (Precision Press, 1977)

Rea, D.: *The Church of South India and the Church* (Confraternity of Unity, 1957)

Reckitt, M. B.: *P. E. T. Widdrington: A Study in Vocation and Versatility* (SPCK, 1961)

Report of the Anglo-Catholic Congress, 1923 (Society of SS Peter and Paul, 1923)

Report of the Anglo-Catholic Congress: London 1927 (Society of SS Peter and Paul, 1927)

Report of the Anglo-Catholic Congress: London 1930 (Church Literature Association, 1930)

Report of the First Anglo-Catholic Congress (SPCK, 1920)

Report of the Oxford Movement Centenary Congress, July 1933 (Church Literature Association, 1933)

Report of the Sixth Anglo-Catholic Congress, July 1948 (Dacre Press, 1948)

Riley, A. (ed.): *Prayer Book Revision: The Irreducible Minimum of the Hickleton Conference* (Mowbray, 1911)

Ross Williamson, H.: *The Great Prayer: Concerning the Canon of the Mass* (Collins, 1955)

Ross Williamson, H.: *The Walled Garden: An Autobiography* (Michael Joseph, 1956)

Rowell, G.: *The Vision Glorious: Themes and Personalities of the Catholic Revival in Anglicanism* (Oxford University Press, 1983)

Rowell, G. (ed.): *Tradition Renewed: The Oxford Movement Conference Papers* (Darton, Longman & Todd, 1986)

Russell, A.: *Community of the Holy Cross, Hayward's Heath, 1857–1957* (Community, 1957)

Russell, G. E.: *Rosenthal* (Centenary Press, 1939)

Russell, H. P.: *From Hussar to Priest: A Memoir of Charles Rose Chase* (Kegan Paul Trench Trubner & Co., 1935)

Savage, S.: *The Story of St Hilda's, Cross Green, Leeds* (author, 2003)

Scott James, B.: *Asking for Trouble* (Darton, Longman & Todd, 1962)

Scott, S. H.: *Anglo-Catholicism and Reunion* (Robert Scott, 1923)

Scott, S. H.: *Eastern Churches and the Papacy* (Sheed & Ward, 1928)

Scott, S. H.: *What Do the General Councils Say?* (Council for Promoting Catholic Union, 1933)

Scott, S. H.: *Modernism in Anglo-Catholicism* (Council for Promoting Catholic Union, 1934)

Sewell, B.: *Cancel All Our Vows: Brother Joseph Gardner and the Servants of Christ the King* (Aylesford Press, 1988)

Shaw, C. P. (ed.): *The Transactions of the 21* (Philip Allan & Co., 1930)

Simmonds, L. F.: *What Do English Divines Say?* (Council for Promoting Catholic Union, 1933)

Skilbeck, C. O.: *Illustrations of the Liturgy* (Alcuin Club, 1916)

Smith, H. M.: *Frank Bishop of Zanzibar, 1871–1926* (SPCK, 1926)

Smyth, C.: *Cyril Foster Garbett, Archbishop of York* (Hodder & Stoughton, 1959)

Stephenson, J. C.: *Walsingham Way* (Darton, Longman & Todd, 1970)

Stephenson, J. C.: *Merrily on High* (Darton, Longman & Todd, 1972)

Stewart, H. L.: *A Century of Anglo-Catholicism* (J. M. Dent & Sons, 1929)

Stockwood, M.: *Chanctonbury Ring: An Autobiography* (Hodder & Stoughton, 1982)

Symonds, H. E.: *The Council of Trent and Anglican Formularies* (Oxford University Press, 1933)

Symonds, H. E.: *The Church Universal and the See of Rome* (SPCK, 1939)

Tricker, R.: *Mr Wason . . . I Think* (Gracewing, 1994)

Vidler, A. R.: *Scenes from a Clerical Life* (Collins, 1977)

BIBLIOGRAPHY

Villain, M.: *Unity: A History and Some Reflections* (Harvill Press, 1963)

Walke, B.: *A Cornish Church* (Parish of St Hilary, 1929)

Walke, B.: *Twenty Years at St Hilary* (Methuen, 1935; Anthony Mott, 1982)

Walsingham Letters (Shrine of Our Lady of Walsingham, various dates)

Warrener, R. and Yelton, M.: *Martin Travers (1886–1948): An Appreciation* (Unicorn Press, 2003)

Wason, L. S.: *The Anathema Alphabet or Syllabus of Errors condemned by the English Bishops since 1840* (Society of SS Peter and Paul, 1915)

Wason, L. S.: *Palafox* (Cope & Fenwick, 1927)

Waugh, E.: *The Life of Ronald Knox* (Chapman & Hall, 1959)

Welsby, P.: *A History of the Church of England 1945–1980* (Oxford University Press, 1984)

Whatton, G. A. C.: *The Celebacy [sic] of the Clergy and the Church of England* (privately printed, 1942)

Whatton, G. A. C.: *The Priest and His Life of Prayer* (Knott & Son, 1946)

Whatton, G. A. C.: *The Priest's Companion* (Knott & Son, 1939, 1946, 1960)

Whiting, C. E.: *The Ordination of Women* (Coelian Press, *c.*1946)

Whitton, T.: *The Necessity for Catholic Reunion* (Williams & Norgate, 1933)

Wilcox, J. C.: *Contending for the Faith: Part I: John Kensit, Reformer and Martyr, His Life and Death* (Wickliffe Press, 1939)

Wilkinson, A.: *The Church of England and the First World War* (SPCK, 1978)

Wilkinson, A.: *The Community of the Resurrection: A Centenary History* (SCM Press, 1992)

Wilkinson, J. (ed.): *Catholic Anglicans Today* (Darton, Longman & Todd, 1968)

Williams, B.: *The Franciscan Revival in the Church of England* (Darton, Longman & Todd, 1982)

Williams, B. M.: 'Archbishop Mathew and the Old Roman Catholic Church in England together with Some Notes on Subsequent Events' (unpublished typescript in archives of British Orthodox Church, no date)

Williams, H. A.: *Some Day I'll Find You: An Autobiography* (Mitchell Beazley, 1982)

Williamson, J.: *Father Joe* (Abingdon Press, 1963)

Wilson, H. A.: *Received with Thanks* (Mowbray, 1940)

Wyatt, E. G. P.: *English or Roman Use?* (Mowbray, 1913)

Yates, N.: *Anglican Ritualism in Victorian Britain, 1830–1910* (Oxford University Press, 1999)

INDEX OF ORGANISATIONS, PERSONS AND PLACES